CONNECTIVITY AND INTEGRATION IN SOUTH ASIA

Connectivity and Integration in South Asia

Edited by

Mohanan B. Pillai
Adluri Subramanyam Raju

KALPAZ

ISBN: 978-93-5128-129-0

Price: ₹ 950

First Published, 2015

Published by

Kalpaz Publications
C-30, Satyawati Nagar,
Delhi-110052
Ph. : 9212142040
E-mail: kalpaz@hotmail.com

Printed at: G. Print Process, Delhi.

Cataloging in Publication Data—DK
Courtesy: D.K. Agencies (P) Ltd. <docinfo@dkagencies.com>

Greater Connectivity and Regional Integration in South Asia (Seminar) (2013 : Pondicherry University)
Connectivity and Integration in South Asia / Adluri Subramanyam Raju.
pages cm
Includes bibliographical references.
ISBN 9789351281290

1. South Asia—Economic integration—Congresses. 2. South Asia—Foreign relations—Congresses. 3. South Asian Cooperation—Congresses. I. Subramanyam Raju, Adluri editor. II. Pondicherry University.organizer. III. Title.

DDC 327.54 23

Dedicated to

(Late) Ambassador Dr Madanjeet Singh

Whose vision was SASIA as a South Asian Currency

Contents

PART-III: CULTURAL LINKAGES AND SOFT POWER IN REGIONAL INTEGRATION

PART-IV: BILATERAL RELATIONS

List of Contributors

Uttara Sahasrabuddhe, Professor, Department of Civics and Politics, University of Mumbai, Mumbai.

Y. Yagama Reddy (Retd.), Centre for Southeast Asian and Pacific Studies, Sri Venkateswara University, Tirupati.

Indra Nath Mukherji, former Professor of South Asian Studies, School of International Studies, Jawaharlal Nehru University and Consultant, UNESCAP.

Adluri Subramanyam Raju, Coordinator, Centre for Maritime Studies and Associate Professor, Centre for South Asian Studies, UMISARC, Pondicherry University, Pondicherry.

Som P Pudasaini, Executive Member, Nepal Council of World Affairs, Kathmandu.

C.Vinodan, Assistant Professor and Chair, Centre for Strategic and Security Studies, School of International Relations and Politics, Mahatma Gandhi University, Kottayam, Kerala.

Srikanth Kondapalli, Professor Chinese Studies and Chairman, Centre for East Asian Studies, School of International Studies, Jawaharlal Nehru University, New Delhi.

I.P. Khosla, former Secretary, Ministry of External Affair, New Delhi.

Rabindra Sen, Professor, Department of International Relations, Jadavpur University, Kolkata.

Rashmi Bhure, Associate Professor, Department of Politics, SIES College of ASC, Mumbai.

Santishree D. Pandit, Professor, Department of Politics and Public Administration, University of Pune, Pune.

Rimli Basu, Research Project Fellow, Department of Politics and Public Administration, University of Pune, Pune.

Imtiaz Ahmed, Professor of International Relations, University of Dhaka, Dhaka.

Sanjay K Jha, Associate Professor and Chairperson, Centre for Security Studies, School of International Studies, Central University of Gujarat, Gandhinagar, Gujarat.

Rajpal Budania, Associate Professor, Department of Political Science, University of Allahabad, Allahabad.

Riaz Ahmed Shaikh, Head of Social Sciences, Shaheed Zulfikar Ali Bhutto Institute of Science and Technology, Karachi.

Introduction

Mohanan B Pillai and Adluri Subramanyam Raju

South Asia represents one-fourth of world's population with low gross domestic product, low per capita and low literacy rate coupled with high birth and high death rates. It repersents the largest number of the world's hungry about 350 million people. It is afflicted by a number of problems-social, political and economic. Further, disparity between the rural and urban, poor and rich and violence (extremism, insurgency) have led to instability and insecurity in the region. No common external threat was perceived by the region. The South Asian states are plagued by inter-state conflicts over boundaries. Absence of collective identity and lack of sense of belonging do still exist in the region and thus hinder South Asia from achieving the momentum to grow at its full potential.

One of the factors that unite a group of countries is geographical proximity. However, in South Asia, except India, no country shares its border with more than two neighbours. In other words, the region was divided by a larger country. Further, there is asymmetric between India and its neighbours in terms of land, population, economy and military capability in the region. India occupies seventy two per cent of the land and represents seventy seven per cent of the population in the region. It contributes more than seventy five per cent of regional trade. Its economic and military capabilities made India a regional power in South Asia. However, India has dispute with Pakistan on Kashmir, Siachen, Sir Creek, maritime boundary in the Arabian Sea; with Bangladesh on sharing water and migration problems, whereas the dispute between India and Nepal involves Kalapani. Since, the boundaries are the manifestations of national identity in the region, the states are rigid in their stand and disputes continue to remain between India and its neighbours. The political differences and disputes have stalled the prospects of economic cooperation in the region. Since India is the larger country in the region, some of the neighbours feel that the former dominates the region and poses threat to their security.

Following factors can be viewed as obstacles for regional cooperation: trust deficiency, mistrust between India and its neighbours; rivalry between India and Pakistan; meager regional trade and the porous borders between the countries. Conflicts and disputes converted the region backward. There are hardly any pair of states in South Asia, which are not affected by trans-border spilling of ethno-nationalist, communal and militant activity. Though geographical continuity remains the greatest asset for SAARC, this potential is not harnessed. It is time for South Asia to concentrate on sustainable growth, otherwise it would be difficult to reduce violence, instability and insecurity. South Asia's rise cannot be translated into tangible benefits unless the internal problems are addressed. The region has failed to cultivate economic interdependence as a tool to counter political and military tensions. The region is the least integrated region in the world.

However, on the other hand, South Asia is seen as important region in the world and it is gaining global identity. The SAARC has enlarged its membership from seven to eight (Afghanistan was joined in 2007 as the eighth member) and nine external and major states joined as observers (Australia, China, Iran, Japan, Korea, Mauritius, US, European Union and Russia). South Asia was seen as an important region by the rest of the world. It is one of the fastest growing economic regions in the world (six per cent growth per year). Nuclear tests conducted by India and Pakistan in 1998 and the steady economic performance of the region as a whole have changed not only how the region perceives itself but the world's perception of the importance of the region. Besides, some non-state actors' activities emerge from the region was seen as a security concern for South Asian countries. Though there was no significant development towards regional cooperation, the SAARC is the only organisation where the member states can debate and discuss various issues related to the region. However, one must notice that there are some initiatives were made: the member states signed agreements -SAPTA and SAFTA, Social Charter, approved to setup South Asian Energy Grid, established South Asian University and SAARC Development Fund, agreed to strengthen transportation, transit and communications links across the region. However, some of the resolutions are yet to be implemented. South Asia is trying to integrate itself with Asia, which is expected to play a vital role in the global arena. It may be said that there is a convergence of interests among the countries in the region for regional cooperation.

At the foreign policy level, countries have been expanding their reach to form closer relations with extra-regional powers. India is seeking to build strategic, political and economic alliances at the bilateral, regional and global level. It has also been trying to enhance its capabilities and capacities to ensure its strategic autonomy which will in turn to become great power. Relationship between Pakistan and China has been cordial. Sri Lanka, Bangladesh and Nepal are moving closer to China. Pakistan is closer to the US. Such relations are also being tried by other countries to ensure a sense of independence from India's dominance in the region. Though the smaller countries in the region have concern over India's dominance, there was no coordination among them to work against the latter. The rise of India and decline of Pakistan made the region to shift from bipolarity to unipolarity in the context of a South Asian regional security complex. India realises the fact that unless it improves its relations with its neighbours, it would be difficult to transcend its role from South Asia to the rest of the world.

South Asia inherited an integrated transport system from the British, but this was fractured not only by the partition but by its political aftermath. It needs to be integrated again. Due to lack of integration of the transport system in South Asia, the logistic costs are very high and ranges between thirteen to fourteen per cent of GDP compared to eight per cent in the US. Nepal, Bhutan and northeast of India can be linked to end their land locked, which would lead to economic development and could work towards poverty reduction. Connectivity plays a significant role in combating poverty. One element of poverty is the lack of information/communication. Thanks to transformation of the communications by penetrating new technology, many poor people are being benefitted. If people are connected, they are more productive.[1] According to the World Bank, if countries in South Asia continue growing at a seven per cent rate, the incidence of poverty would be reduced from fifty per cent to twenty per cent. If transport network is improved, there may be $40 billion trade (twenty per cent of trade).[2] It is to be noted that other regional organisations have more regional trade than the SAARC. For instance, regional trade of EU is seventy per cent, North America is thirty two per cent and thirty seven per cent by ASEAN.

The twelfth summit, held in Islamabad in 2004, called for strengthening in transport, transit and communication links across South Asia. For instance, a container takes thirty-five days more for New Delhi-Dhaka, as the maritime route is via Bangladesh and Singapore/Colombo to Chittagong port and then by rail to Dhaka. It can reach within five days of direct rail connectivity was there between New Delhi and Dhaka. Similarly between Dhaka-Islamabad, it takes 7,162 km by sea instead of 2,300 km through overland across India. New Delhi and Tehran are jointly planned to develop a transport corridor between India-Iran-Afghanistan. India can access to Central Asia through Iranian port-Chabahar-Afghanistan.[3] Goods from northeast of India to China, Southeast Asia and the West take a route of 1,400 km to reach Kolkata port along the Chicken neck. There is no agreement exists for India to use the traditional route through Chittagong port which would be shorter by sixty per cent.[4] In the eighteenth summit held in Kathmandu during 26-27 November 2014 focused on three regional agreements for connectivity and integration: motor vehicles, rail and energy cooperation.[5]

Greater people to people contact, improving infrastructure facility, making soft borders, access to technology, connecting maritime, air and road ways and unrestricted trade are some of the issues to be focused by the South Asian countries. Unless these are met, it would be difficult to improve regional cooperation in the region. In the twenty–first century, South Asia has both challenges and opportunities. States need to be pro-active in their foreign policy and take pragmatic steps to achieve their national interests.

In view of the above, the UNESCO Madanjeet Singh Institute of South Asia Regional Cooperation (UMISARC) Pondicherry University, organised the international seminar entitled Greater Connectivity and Regional Integration in South Asia during 14-16 February 2013, with the financial Suport of South Asia Foundation (SAF), New Delhi. Experts-scholars, policymakers and diplomats of different parts of South Asia participated and discussed various issues related to the theme of the seminar.

Structure of the Volume

The volume is outcome of the seminar deliberation. The contributors discuss issues related to connectivity and integration in South Asia. The volume consists of fifteen papers, which are divided into four parts.

Part-I: Regionalism in South Asia

Uttara Sahasrabuddhe, in her paper entitled "Theories of Regionalism and Regionalism in South Asia", applies three international theories to understand regionalism in South Asia. The author maintains that theories could predict the future of the regional cooperation. She explains, in her paper, five levels of regionness and different regions can be seen into three categories: core, intermediate and peripheral and South Asia as a region can be considered as a peripheral region. In other words, the paper argues that it would be difficult to see regionalism in South Asia.

Y. Yagama Reddy's paper entitled "Will SAARC Ever Accomplish the Goal of Regional Integration?" maintains that regional integration enhances economic, security, political, social and cultural interactions between the countries in any region. He explains positive and negative aspects of regional cooperation in South Asia. He argues one of the apprehensions for regional cooperation is due to India's geographical size, demographic, economy and political influence in the region.

Part-II: Connectivity and Trade in South Asia

In his paper "India's Trade with South Asian Neighbours: Perceptions and Reality", Indra Nath Mukherji describes the status of trade and ways for improving trade amongst the South Asian countries. He explains various measures taken by India to reduce trade restrictions in favour of neighbouring countries such as drastic reduction in items under India's sensitive list under SAFTA, offering duty-free quota-free imports to all least developed countries and strengthening of land customs stations on its borders.

Adluri Subramanyam Raju, in his paper "Maritime Connectivity and Cooperation in South Asia: Issues and Concerns", analyses issues: resolving maritime borders and fishermen insecurity, enhancing shipping, trade and maritime connectivity and addressing maritime threats collectively by the South Asian littoral states. Further, the paper argues that through maritime connectivity, the South Asian countries would not only improve their trade but also regional cooperation.

In his paper entitled "Conflict, Transition, Connectivity and Regional Integration in South Asia", Som P Pudasaini discusses how political disputes between the countries dominate and slowdown the relations between them. The paper focuses on India-Nepal relations. Further, the paper suggests important areas i.e., connectivity of people, physical connectivity, liberalisation of trade, regional grid for energy and water, regional tourism, cultural exchange, regional educational and health networks etc., to be focused by the countries to promote greater connectivity and integration in South Asia.

C.Vinodan, in his paper entitled "Regional Connectivity and Energy Security in South Asia: Challenges and Opportunities", explains how South Asia largely depends on importing energy resources. He discusses energy scenario, energy trade and cooperation in South Asia. The paper explains importance of a common regional energy market, which would promote economic development, integration with global markets and minimise cost of supply. Further the paper discusses India's energy trade with Bhutan and Nepal and proposed pipelines such as India-Pakistan-India, Turkmenistan-Afghanistan-Pakistan-India, Oman-India and Myanmar-Bangladesh-India.

In his paper entitled "Connectivity and Infrastructure Development in South Asia: China's Perceptions", Srikanth Kondapalli describes Chinese assistance and involvement in infrastructure and connectivity projects in South Asia. The paper explains how China has been beneficial through expanding its investments, trade and connectivity with the South Asian countries. He maintains that South Asia has to concentrate on key issues: global commons, infrastructure development, trade, market and capital, environment, ecology and energy consumption.

Part-III: Cultural Linkages and Soft Power in Regional Integration

I.P. Khosla, in his paper "Cross-cultural Dialogues in South Asia", explains three basic forces which unite countries are coercive, utilitarianism and value system. He explains the US, through Marshal Plan, pressurised the European countries to unite and form the EU. However, such driving force was missing in South Asia. The author argues that culture as a commonality between South Asian countries can be challenged. However, he maintains that elements such as modernity, democracy, industrial and agricultural balance, can play a role in regional integration.

Rabindra Sen, in his paper entitled "Cultural Diplomacy and Regional Integration in South Asia: Relevance and Importance of India's Role", maintains that India has responsibility to achieve the South Asian cultural connectivity in South Asia. In recent years, there has been talk of peaceful neighbourhood, hence he argues that India should utilise cultural influence for greater understanding and mutual cooperation in the region. The author maintains though there is cultural unity but how to strengthen it is a challenge one. He concludes that greater cultural connectivity would promote each other's acceptability, mutual understanding and cooperation in the region.

In her paper "Winning Hearts and Minds: Role of Soft Power in India's Regional Strategy", Rashmi Bhure discusses about a shift from hard power to soft power in international politics. She focuses on the importance of soft power and how India can employ it as an instrumental in improving its relations with its neighbours. Soft power of a country, she maintains, can help to narrow its differences with others. She explains the roots of India's soft power in its foreign policy since its independence.

Part-IV: Bilateral Relations

In the joint paper entitled "Connectivity, Development and Regional Integration: The Case of Kaladan Project between India and Myanmar", Santishree D Pandit and Rimli Basu explain importance of Kaladan project to improve relationship between India and Myanmar. The paper discusses that both the countries would improve people to people contact, develop the northeast of India and connect India with other countries in Southeast Asia through the project.

Imtiaz Ahmed, in his paper "Bangladesh-India Relations and its Future", mentions five ways of looking at humans: homopoliticus, homo-economicus, homoculturicus, homo-technologicus and homo-psychologicus. Ahmed argues that the conflict is not only because of 'big brother', but also 'little brothers' who are creating huge problems all around the world. As long as one person feels that he/she doesn't have these inherent rights there will be problem in the society, he argues.

Sanjay K Jha's paper "Connectivity and Security Concerns: Issues on India-Nepal Border" explains how open border between the states facilitates the mobilisation of non-state actors, unofficial trade, drug trafficking, human trafficking etc. He maintains that though the open border poses a threat to India and Nepal, it contributes a greater connectivity and integration through better border management policy and integrated approach.

Rajpal Budania, in his paper "India-Pakistan Initiative for Conflict Resolution: The Challenges Ahead", focuses on various peace initiatives between the two countries. He analyses the challenges and limitations of peace process. He discusses internal developments in Pakistan, Pakistan relations with Afghanistan, Kashmir issue etc., are attributing to stall the peace process. As Pakistan, the author concludes, is strengthening as a democracy, relations between the two countries will be cordial in the near future.

In his paper "Normalisation of India-Pakistan Relations and Prospects of Economic Development in South Asia", Riaz Ahmed Shaikh discusses that India and Pakistan have common cultural heritage and long history. He argues the South Asian countries need not to give up their identity and they should carry humanism in their relations. The author maintains since cold war has ended globally, the cold war in South Asia in general and between India and Pakistan in particular must disappear.

References

1. Kishore Mahbubani, *The New Asian Hemisphere: The Irresistible Shift of Global Power to the East,* New York: Public Affairs, 2008, p. 25.
2. M. Rahmatullah, "Transport Issues and Integration in South Asia", in Sadiq Ahmed, Saman Kelegama and Egaz Ghani (eds), *Promoting Economic Cooperation in South Asia: Beyond SAFTA,* New Delhi: Sage Publication, 2010, p.175.
3. India will develop the Chabahar Port in Iran with an investment of $85.21 million and will operate the port for ten years. See *Business Line,* 19 October 2014.
4. Rahmatullah, n.2, p.178.
5. After three years gap (2011), the eighteenth summit was held. The SAARC charter maintains that the summit to be held every year. In the history of twenty nine years of SAARC existence, only eighteen summits were held. That shows the commitment and approach towards regional cooperation.

PART–I
REGIONALISM IN SOUTH ASIA

1

Theories of Regionalism and Regionalism in South Asia

Uttara Sahasrabuddhe

Introduction

The phenomenon of regionalism has evolved through two distinct phases or 'waves' - the first wave beginning in Europe in the 1950s, and the second wave, beginning since mid-1980s and shaping many regional groups, organisations and trade agreements. "It is not surprising that the experiences of the European integration project loom large in analyses of (and predictions for) regional integration elsewhere in the world."[1] Most early theories have indeed evolved around the experience of European regionalism. And while some contemporary theories of new regionalism claim to offer non-Eurocentric framework for understanding and comparing different regional experiences, their own perception of integration is, nevertheless, rooted in the European experience. The problem then is, as a Chinese scholar claims, that despite myriad forms of actually existing regionalism, "the focus remains on the potential for regionalism in the future because current regional forms do not match up to EU-centric expectations of what constitutes a region".[2] This paper applies three theories of regionalism originating from three different analytical traditions to regionalism in South Asia.

SAARC: Background and Organisational Structure

The current political map of South Asia began to evolve since the early twentieth century. Ceylon (now Sri Lanka) and Burma (now Myanmar) were separated from the British Indian administration in 1935 and 1937 respectively. At the midnight of 14-15 August 1947, British India was partitioned to create two separate independent states, viz., India and Pakistan. Ceylon became independent from the British rule in 1948. The two land-locked kingdoms of Nepal and Bhutan, though never ruled directly by the British, were under British suzerainty. With the withdrawal of the British, they became sovereign. Later in 1971, Pakistan was further divided when the geographically disconnected, Bengali-speaking eastern wing of Pakistan seceded; following a war, to form the independent state of Bangladesh. South Asia, thus, became an international system of insular newly independent states in the 1950s. The idea of regional co-operation originated in South Asia in the 1980s and SAARC was formed in 1985. Aims and objectives of the SAARC include acceleration of economic growth, social progress and cultural development in the region and promoting cooperation in these areas; strengthening 'collective self-reliance' among countries of the region; cooperating with other developing countries and with organisations having similar aims; and also cooperating with each other at the international forums on matters of common interests. Membership of the SAARC has expanded, as Afghanistan joined the organisation as a new member in April 2007. Japan and China have been attending SAARC summits as observers since 2005; South Korea and the US since 2006 and the EU and Iran since 2007.[3]

At the apex of the institutional structure of the SAARC are the summits.[4] These comprise of the Heads of States/Governments of the member states, and meet generally once in a year. The main policy-making organ is the SAARC Council of Ministers, made of the Foreign Ministers of the member states. They review the progress, explore new areas of cooperation and deliberate on the matters of interests to the regional group. There is a standing committee comprising of Foreign Secretaries of the SAARC states, which also meets twice a year. This committee monitors and coordinates the programmes. It also determines modalities of finance, sectoral priorities, and mobilises regional and external resources. In addition there are technical, programme and action committees. SAARC has a permanent Secretariat located at Kathmandu in Nepal, with a Secretary-General as its head and a Director from each state.

Concepts and Definitions

Terms that are often used in the study of regionalism need to be defined at the outset. One such set of terms is, region, regionalism and regionalisation. A region is a geographic space comprising a group of states. There is 'much more' to a region than mere geographic contiguity of the states forming it. However, there is no general agreement over what this 'more' is–the ideas of it range from shared culture and values to similar political institutions and from economic interdependence to various levels of 'complex' interdependence. There is also a disagreement over the meaning of the terms regionalism and regionalisation. While some analysts argue that regionalisation is a feature of regionalism, many others make a distinction between the two. One simple way to distinguish between the two is that to define regionalism as a political process and regionalisation as an economic process. Thus, the former takes place at the state level, it is driven mainly by government level; decisions and includes future cooperation and policy coordination among the states; and the latter takes place at the sub-state level, it is driven by economic and social forces and includes future growth of trade and investment flows.[5] The distinction may not, however, be as watertight as it appears, because the decisions about freeing or controlling cross-border flows of trade and investment continue to be made by state policies in most of the world. Another set of terms is 'old' and 'new' waves of regionalisation. The old wave refers to, mainly if not entirely, the process of European integration in the 1950s and 1960s. And its distinguishing feature is that regional integration was brought about by state policies. The new wave refers mainly to integration of regional trade in East and Southeast Asia during the late 1980s and onwards. It almost coincided with the rise of globalisation. Unlike in case of the old wave, regionalisation of trade occurred primarily due to economic forces and not due to state policy. As Mansfield and Milner observe, "rapid economic growth throughout the region contributed to a dramatic increase in intraregional trade flows", although "virtually no commercial agreement existed among East Asian countries prior to the mid 1990s".[6] However, these forces of integration of the new wave have eventually led to a proliferation of Free Trade Areas (FTAs) and Preferential Trade Agreements (PTAs) all over the world.

Although the timing of its formation coincided with the rise of new regionalism, especially in East and Southeast Asia, SAARC is not an example of new regionalism. Unlike in East and Southeast Asia, where regionalisation process was driven mainly by economic forces, and preceded the formation of multilateral trade pacts in the region; the drive behind South Asian regionalism was inter-governmental cooperation. The idea of regional cooperation in the South Asian region was first appeared around 1980. The first step towards the formation of a regional organisation was a meeting of foreign secretaries of the seven South Asian states (viz., Bangladesh, Bhutan, India, The Maldives, Nepal, Pakistan and Sri Lanka), held in Colombo in 1981.[7] This was followed by a meeting of Foreign Ministers of the seven states in New Delhi in 1983. This meeting adopted the Declaration on South Asian Regional Cooperation (SARC), and launched the Integrated Programme of Action (IPA). Heads of the South Asian states met in Dhaka in December 1985 and signed the Charter of the South Asian Association for Regional Cooperation (SAARC). Formation of the SAARC in 1985 marked the beginning of regionalisation in South Asia. In that sense, South Asian regionalism is more similar to old regionalism of the 1950s and 1960s.

Yet, unlike Europe, where regionalism had sovereignty-eroding effects on the regional states, South Asian regionalism is essentially sovereignty-based. SAARC is based on the principles of sovereign equality, territorial integrity, political independence and non-interference in the internal affairs of the other member-states.[8] Like all newly independent states, South Asian states too were zealously protective of their sovereignty and territorial integrity, as well as the "independence" to make foreign policies. Thus, despite the similarities with the formative process of European regionalism, SAARC remained sovereignty-based.

Theories of Regionalism and South Asian Regionalism

A number of international research scholars have sought to explain and analyse the phenomenon of regionalism. Theories of regional integration began to be developed since the time European integration began to evolve. Understandably, the initial theories sought to explain and analyse primarily European experience of regionalisation. As regionalism began to spread in other parts of the world, more theoretical explanations were offered. These theories claimed to avoid Eurocentric explanations of regionalisation, thereby making comparisons possible as well as meaningful. Theories of regionalism can be divided in two broad categories: those emanating from the liberal approach to international relations, and those from the realist approach. Liberal theories originate from the assumption that states are capable of overcoming their parochial orientations, that they are capable of cooperating and can form organisations to promote peace. Thus, Karl Deutsch argues that integration is linked to the sense of community among nation-states.[9] The Realist theories, on the other hand, are sceptical of the ability of nation-states to think at trans-national level and beyond their national interest. The intergovernmentalist theory argues that sovereign states pursue regional integration only when their national goals are compatible with the regional goals. This is not easy and often results in slow pace of integration. Regionalisation process involves a series of bargains among governments in the region. These bargains are difficult as states are reluctant to compromise their national interest in favour of a common regional goal or regional approach. In addition to theories rooted in the liberal and realists traditions, some contemporary theories of regionalism draw their conceptual and analytical framework from the critical theory and constructivist approach.

Functionalism/Neo-functionalism and South Asian Regionalism

David Mitrany's functionalist theory is based on two assumptions: first, states can transcend differences, seek mutual interests and evolve a web of institutions managed by technical elites; and second, states are interdependent and cannot alone solve their economic as well as social problems.[10] Another important and influential liberal theory of regionalism is the neo-functionalist theory developed by Ernst Haas.[11] Haas seeks to explain how and why states cease to be fully sovereign; how and why they voluntarily mingle with their neighbours so as to "lose factual attributes of sovereignty" while acquiring new techniques of resolving conflicts between themselves. National and regional elites, political parties, pressure groups and supranational institutions are the key actors in the process of integration. Neo-functionalism argues that it is the expectation of gain or loss of these groups that becomes the driving force of the process of integration. It speaks about possible convergence of interests and goals and the possibility of coordinated policies to seek such goals.

It is possible to argue that both these theories are rooted in the specific European experience and cannot provide adequate explanation of regionalism in South Asia. However, the SAARC has actually followed the European trajectory of developing a plethora of trans-border organisations, for economic as well as technical cooperation. It is worth taking a look at this trajectory. The SAARC Council of Ministers restructured the SAARC IPA during the twelfth Summit. Under the new Regional Integrated Programme of Action (RIPA), there are seven Technical Committees that pursue the integrated plan of action in different areas, namely, Agriculture and Rural Development; Health and Population Activities; Women, Youth and Children; Environment and Forestry; Science and Technology and Meteorology; Human Resources Development; and Transport. The revised RIPA also added a new institution to the SAARC structure. These were called Working Groups. These have been especially created to focus on five new and emerging areas: energy, tourism, information and communication technology, intellectual property rights and biotechnology.[12] The Working Group on energy has been entrusted with a mandate to study various possibilities for cooperation in the field of energy, including the concept of an Energy Ring. The Report of the first meeting of the Working Group on Energy (WORGEN) was approved by the Council of Ministers in 2004. The Working Group decided to pursue cooperation in all recommended areas: exchange of energy information, environment friendly energy, creation of a regional power-grid; and cooperation regarding renewable energy.

Promotion of intra-regional trade was one of the important aims of SAARC. With this intention, the initiative towards forming South Asian Preferential Trading Arrangement (SAPTA) was proposed in December 1991. An Agreement creating the SAPTA was signed on 11 April, 1993 during the seventh SAARC summit in Dhaka. SAPTA is a framework of rules providing for step-by-step liberalisation of intra-regional trade. It envisages periodic rounds of trade negotiations for exchange of trade concessions on tariff as well as non-tariff measures. So far, four rounds of trade negotiations have been concluded under SAPTA covering over 5000 commodities. Each round contributed to an incremental trend in the product coverage and the deepening of tariff concessions over previous rounds. SAPTA was envisaged primarily as the first step towards the transition to a South Asian Free Trade Area (SAFTA). The subsequent aim is the formation of a customs union as well as common market and economic union. In 1995, the Council of Ministers agreed on the need to strive for the realisation of SAFTA and to this end an Inter-Governmental Expert Group (IGEG) was set up in 1996 to identify the necessary steps for progressing to a free trade area. The tenth SAARC summit in 1998 decided to set up a Committee of Experts (COE) to draft a comprehensive treaty framework for creating a free trade area within the region, taking into consideration the asymmetries in development within the region and bearing in mind the need to fix realistic and achievable targets. The agreement on SAFTA drafted by the COE, was signed on 6 January, 2004 during the twelfth SAARC summit in Islamabad.[13]

Under the Trade Liberalisation Programme scheduled for completion by 2016, the customs duties on products from the region will be progressively reduced. However, India, Pakistan and Sri Lanka were to bring down their customs duties to Zero to five per cent by 1 January, 2009 for the benefit of those member-states, which are designated as the "Least Developed Countries" by the UN. The least developed member states are expected to benefit from additional measures under the special and differential treatment accorded to them under the agreement. Leaders of the SAARC states agreed in 2002 summit to accelerate cooperation in the core areas of trade, finance and investment to realise the goal of an integrated South Asian economy in a step-by-step manner. They also agreed to the vision of a phased and planned process eventually leading to a South Asian Economic Union. The 2004 SAARC summit entrusted the SAARCFINANCE with the responsibility to study and make recommendations on the early and eventual realisation of a South Asian Economic Union (SAEU) as well as to examine the concept of a South Asian Development Bank.

The above trajectory may justify applying the functionalist/neo-functionalist theory to South Asian regionalism. It may be argued that, despite over two decades of institutional development, regionalisation has failed to take off in South Asia. This is due to two reasons. First, as noted above, there was no question of losing the 'factual attributes' of sovereignty due to the formation of the regional organisation. Second, there is hardly any visible convergence of interests and goals among the regional states, thus, eliminating the possibility of co-ordination of policies. Economic cooperation does not seem to take off and SAFTA does not seem to work. Except the land-locked Nepal and Bhutan, intraregional trade of the other South Asian states is less than twenty per cent of their total world trade.[14] In addition, the trade complementarity index of SAFTA on a 0-100 scale is the lowest at 1.3 among existing free trade areas.[15] From a neo-functionalist perspective, then, regionalism in South Asia appears to be a non-starter.

Regional Security Complex Theory (RSCT) and South Asian Regionalism

The RSCT is primarily a theory of security – developed by Barry Buzan and Ole Waever that seeks to explain the nature of security-insecurity in post-Cold War world. However, it is a very useful explanatory tool for understanding the phenomenon of regionalism because it claims that geographical regions are the primary units in understanding and analysing security in international relations. As it thinks of regions from a security perspective, it draws mainly from the realist tradition of international relations. It must also be noted, however, that RSCT uses a blend of realist and constructivist approaches. The emphasis on political processes that constitute security issues is the constructivist element in the theory. "The central idea in RSCT is that, since most threats travel more easily over short distances than over long ones, security interdependence is normally patterned into regionally based clusters: security complexes."[16] The theory argues that the degree of security or insecurity is more intense inside a region and between the states of a certain region, than between the states from two different regions. Such regions are called 'regional security complexes' and are defined by durable patterns of amity and enmity taking the form of sub-global, geographically coherent patterns of security interdependence. The formation of regional security complexes derives from the interplay between, on the one hand, the anarchic structure and its balance-of-power consequences, and on the other, the pressures of local geographical proximity.[17] The impact of geographical proximity on security interaction is the strongest on military, political, societal and environmental sectors, and minimum on economic sector. Thus, the RSCT helps analyse geographical regions in terms of security interactions.

Buzan and Waever, in their book *Regions and Powers* analyse the South Asian regional security complex. One of their arguments was that South Asia was gradually transforming from a bipolar (India-Pakistan) system to a unipolar one (with Indian hegemony).[18] They had also argued that slowly South Asia was drawing closer to security interaction in the East Asian regional security complex. Buzan claims that despite many substantial events and developments in the region "few, if any, of the basic features and dynamics" of the region "have undergone sharp transformations. The main patterns are either a continuity of existing conditions or an incremental evolution of existing trends."[19] While one agrees with the four level analysis of the South Asian regional security complex by Buzan, the important question from the point of regionalism is whether SAARC has made any difference to regional security situation, or indeed, how relevant is to the security complex of South Asia? The question could be answered as follows.

The South Asian states have not been able to evolve regional approach to regional or global international issues. This is due to many factors. First, South Asian countries did not have a common perception of, or a common approach to, the Cold War and the superpower rivalry. While India opted for non-aligned foreign policy in order to keep off the superpower rivalry, Pakistan chose to become a member of US-sponsored alliances: SEATO and CENTO – created to encircle the USSR. Secondly, there was an absence of commonly perceived extra-regional threat to the regional states. Indeed, most regional states perceived India as an important threat. India's overwhelmingly large area and population and its military capability were the obvious reasons for this perception. Also responsible were the geographical and cultural realities of the region. The geography of the region is so peculiar that most of the states share a land (Pakistan, Nepal, Bhutan, and Bangladesh) or sea (Sri Lanka and Maldives) border with India; however, none of them share any border with more than two countries. In addition, the historical-cultural bonds of religion, language and ethnicity cut across the territorial borders of post-colonial states. The perception of threat from India is, thus, a result of a combination of India's soft as well as hard power. The third reason for the absence of regional approach is the India-Pakistan dispute.[20] The seemingly intractable dispute has several aspects - from river water disputes to territorial disputes; from Kashmir issue to the more contemporary issue of cross-border terrorism. The conflict between the two main powers of the region has made evolution of regional approach nearly impossible. Fourth reason for the absence of regional approach in South Asia is India's South Asian policy. Despite its rhetoric of multilateralism in global international affairs, India has always followed bilateralism in its relations with South Asian neighbours.[21] India was also anxious not to allow any leverage to outside powers in regional affairs.

South Asia as a region is very unique as far as regional conflicts are concerned. The regional states do not have a common approach to resolving inter-state disputes in the region. India emphasises bilateralism and also rejects the role of extra-regional powers in resolving regional disputes. Other regional states, on the other hand, do not reject the role of extra-regional powers. These states resent what they perceive as India's hegemony in the region and simultaneously expect India to extend helping hand. India did extend such help to Maldives in 1987, when the Indian navy helped reinstate the President following a coup against him. Similarly, the Indian Peacekeeping Force (IPKF) was sent to Sri Lanka in 1987 to fight against the separatist Liberation Tigers of Tamil Elam (LTTE) forces. The IPKF mission proved counterproductive for India, as it lost goodwill with both the Tamil rebels and the Sri Lankan people and government. In more recent incidents, India has helped Bhutan in its transition to constitutional monarchy, when the ruling monarch of the tiny Himalayan state wanted to carry out the change. New Delhi also brokered peace in Nepal when in 2006 it helped the Maoists and the parliamentarians reach an accord; on the basis of which the interim government was formed and elections to constituent assembly were held. Such efforts are, however, far short of a regional approach. Given the overwhelming presence of India in the region, development of regional approach does not seem to be easy.

The formation of SAARC has not changed the situation. It is expected that regional cooperation would complement and not substitute other forms of bilateral or multilateral cooperation.[22] Also, bilateral and contentious issues are categorically excluded from the deliberations at the SAARC. South Asia is a security complex with many pending inter-state as well as intra-state conflicts. Yet, SAARC summits or ministerial meetings do not negotiate inter-state disputes, either formally or informally. SAARC has categorically avoided any involvement at any level in any inter-state let alone inter-state – conflict in the region. There are no deliberations on major politico-security issues that affect most regional countries, such as border disputes, ethno-nationalism and separatism, and democratisation. Indeed, most issues of high politics are categorically excluded from the agenda of SAARC.

New Regionalism Theory and South Asian Regionalism

Developed by Bjorn Hettne and some other European scholars to analyse the new wave of regionalism, this theory goes beyond the liberal as well as realist approaches and uses some of the arguments of critical theory and also of social constructivist approach. The core argument of this theory is based on the concept of 'regionness'. The term "regionness" is used to indicate the different levels of integration in a geographical unit. There are five levels of regionness which are explained as follows:[23] 1. A region as a geographical unit or *regional space.* 2. Region as a social system or *regional complex.* 3. A region as transnational cooperation or *regional society.* 4. A region as civil society or *regional community.* 5. A region as acting subject or region state. It is not necessary that regions progress from the first to the fifth state of regionness. A region may recede or may even get dissolved. The theory further argues that regionalism has implications for both security and development in a region.[24] In the first case, it aims at transforming "a security complex with conflict generating inter-state and intra-state relations" into "a security community with cooperative external relations and domestic peace." In the second case, it refers to "concerted efforts from a group of countries within a geographical region to increase the complementarity and capacity of the total regional economy as well as finding the right balance between functions and territory." Based on the five levels of regionness and the success of security and development regionalism, the different regions can be classified into three categories: core regions, intermediate regions and peripheral regions.[25]

This theory is very useful in analysing the state of regional integration in South Asia. In terms of regionness, South Asia does not seem to have gone beyond the second stage. Regionalism has not made any difference to security or development of South Asia. The region continues to conflict generating inter-state as well as intra-state relations. SAARC has not transformed the security complex of South Asia into a security community as it has not been able to evolve common interests or common approach to regional security. Despite having created plethora of agreements and a FTA, South Asian regionalisation process has not led to increased complementarity of the economies of the region. While there has been economic growth of the regional countries, SAARC or SAFTA have hardly contributed to it. Thus, South Asia can be easily classified as a peripheral region.

Conclusion

The theories of regionalism help us to understand and analyse the nature of regionalism and regionalisation in South Asia in a comparative perspective. They also help us predict the future of the region. It is difficult to be optimistic about the future of South Asian regionalisation and the possibility that it may get dissolved as a political region cannot be ignored. This may be partly due to India's policies, which is slowly but definitely seeking greater engagement with the emerging larger East Asian region. It will be increasingly difficult to hold together the political region of South Asia either as a bipolar or as a unipolar system.

References

1. Shaun Breslin, "Comparative Theory, China and the Future of East Asian Regionalism(s)", p.1; http://go.warwick.ac.uk/wrap
2. Wang Shengyi of Beijing University, cited by Breslin, *ibid.*
3. Razia Sultana, "Expansion of SAARC: Implications for South Asia", *BIISS Journal,* Vol. 28, No. 2, 2007, p. 142.
4. The institutional structure is determined by the *SAARC Charter.* Full text is available on the SAARC website.
5. For a detailed discussion, see Edward Mansfield and Etel Solingen, "Regionalism", *Annual Reviews of Political Science 2010;* www.annualreviews.org on 04/10/2013.
6. Edward Mansfield and Helen Milner, "The New Wave of Regionalism", *International Organisation,* Vol. 53, No. 3, 1999, p. 598.
7. Eric Gonsalves and Nancy Jetly, *The Dynamics of South Asia: Regional Co-operation and SAARC,* New Delhi: Sage Publication, 1999.

8. See SAARC Charter, n. 4.
9. For details of the Transactionalist analysis of regionalism, see Deutsch (*et. al.,*) *Political Community and the North Atlantic Area,* Princeton NJ: Princeton University Press, 1957.
10. David Mitrany, *A Working Peace System,* Chicago: Quadrangle, 1966. It may be noted here that Mitrany was not in favour of all-encompassing international organisations.
11. Ernst Haas, *The Uniting of Europe,* Stanford: Stanford University Press, 1958.
12. *SAARC: A Profile,* Kathmandu: SAARC Secretariat, 2004. This brochure is available also on the SAARC website. For a recent analysis of SAARC, see Chaudhury, Ansua Basu Ray, *SAARC At Crossroads: The Fate of Regional Co-operation in South Asia*, New Delhi: Samskriti, 2006.
13. For the text of the Agreement on South Asia Free Trade Area, see the website of the SAARC, n.4.
14. Sharif Hossain and Ishtiaque Selim, "Regional Co-operation in South Asia: Future of SAFTA", *BIISS Journal,* Vol. 28, No. 2, April 2007, p. 172.
15. *Ibid,* p.174. The index is 56.3 for NAFTA, 53.4 for EU and 28.6 for Mercosur.
16. Barry Buzan and Ole Waever, *Regions and Powers: The Structure of International Security,* Cambridge: Cambridge University Press, 2003.
17. *Ibid.*
18. *Ibid.*
19. Barry Buzan, "The South Asian Security Complex in a Decentralising World Order: Reconsidering Regions and Powers Ten Years on", *International Studies,* Vol.48, No.1, 2011, p. 4.
20 Much has been written so far about the India-Pakistan dispute. For recent analyses of relations between the two countries, see P.M. Kamath (ed.), *India-Pakistan Relations: Courting Peace from the Corridors of War,* New Delhi: Promilla and Co., 2005; and *Prospects for Peace, Stability and Prosperity in South Asia,* Islamabad: Institute of Regional Studies, 2005.
21. The liberal-internationalist foreign policy of India's first Prime Minister Nehru broadly emphasised multilateralism in international affairs; yet, followed bilateralism in relations with South Asian neighbours. This was more clearly outlined in the Gujral Doctrine – the guiding principles of India's South Asia policy as stated by I.K. Gujral, then the Foreign Minister of India. For a detailed discussion, see Uttara Sahasrabuddhe, "Paradigm Shift in Indian Foreign Policy", *Indian Journal of Strategic Studies,* Vol. 24, October 2003.

22. See n. 4.
23. Bjorn Hettne and Soderbaum, "Theorising the Rise of Regionness" in Shaun Breslin (*et. al*), *New Regionalisms in the Global Political Economy: Theories and Cases*, London: Routledge, 2002.
24. *Ibid.*
25. Bjorn Hettne, "Globalism, Regionalism and the New Third World" in Nana Poku and Lloyd Pettiford (eds.), *Redefining the Third World*, London: Macmillan, 1998.

2

Will SAARC Ever Accomplish the Goal of Regional Integration

Y. Yagama Reddy

Regions, regionalism and regionalisation are contested and often fragile concepts. The term 'region', simply a geographical reality, denotes a cluster of states, usually a small group of contiguous states, linked together by both a geographical relationship and a degree of mutual interdependence.[1] Although regions are not naturally constituted geographical units, they cannot exist without having a physical reality. Thus, the territorial shaping of a region implies that regions require some kind of boundaries. While regions are most defined in terms of geographic proximity, it is equally possible to opt for a non-geographic definition. Even as a region predisposes to geographical contiguousness, geography does not identify which country should be included in a region. "Regional designations are no more 'real' in terms of geography than they are 'natural' in terms of culture". Thus, as products of culture and economics, history and politics, geographically defined regions change over time.

Regionalism, despite its distinction of promoting regional and international communities, has many positive as well as negative qualities and worrying aspects. As state-led initiative to foster cooperation in one or more areas, regionalism implies a policy whereby states and non-state actors cooperate and coordinate strategy within a given region. Regionalism is often analysed in terms of geographical proximity, social cohesiveness (ethnicity, race, language, religion, culture, history, consciousness of a common heritage), economic cohesiveness (trade patterns and economic complementarity), political cohesiveness (regime type, ideology), and organisational cohesiveness (existence of formal regional institutions). If regionalism is a policy or project, regionalisation, a process of cooperation led by markets, is both project and process; but both regionalism and regionalisation are clearly global phenomena.[2]

Regional Integration and Regional Cooperation

Region-building has been central to many of the debates and a salient feature of the international system and the regional organisations are thus regarded as a natural outgrowth of international cooperation. Regional integration is simply an association of states based upon location in a given geographical area, for safeguarding or promotion of the participants, rather an association whose terms are fixed by a treaty or other arrangements. Regional integration is viewed as a process that increases the interactions apropos economic, security, political, and also social and cultural issues between their components and creates new forms of organisation, co-existing with traditional forms of state-led organisation at the national level. Even as regional integration, being broader in its scope than regional cooperation, tends to subsume the latter, both are mutually reinforcing. To be explicit, regional cooperation can deepen regional integration which at the same time can prompt the institutions/ organisations to embark on collective policies and initiatives towards realising the prospects of cooperation. Regional integration, testifying to an interaction among the states in a given regional arrangement, is a process relying on regional institutions and rules in order to enhance regional cooperation through regional institutions and rules.[3]

(a) Regional Integration, a Ubiquitous Process

Regional integration arrangements (RIAs) that tend to dominate the present global economic order are now looked upon as the future of the international scene. RIAs are mainly the upshot of necessity felt by nation-states to integrate their economies for achieving rapid economic development, decreasing conflict and building mutual trusts between the integrated units. Regional integration, which has taken the form of a supranational institutional structure or an intergovernmental decision-making body, or a combination of both, portrays overlapping in its structural composition and functional characters. With scant regard to the functional efficacy of umbrella-type regional arrangements, there came into existence overarching institutions of regional integration with much avowed objective of creating a single regional market and regional community. Closer integration of neighbouring economies has often been seen by governments as a first step in creating a larger regional market for trade and investment. Regional integration agreements, which have led to major developments in international relations between and among many countries, purposely contribute to the spurt in the formation of regional trading blocs and thereby increase in international trade and investment flows. Some claim that the desire for closer integration is usually related to a larger desire for opening nation states to the outside world, or that regional economic cooperation is pursued as a means of promoting development through greater efficiency, rather than as a means of disadvantaging others. However, regional integration strategies as pursued by economic and national interests in the recent past have also been highly contested across civil society.

Past efforts at regional integration often focused on removing barriers to free trade in the region, increasing the free movement of people, labour, goods, and capital across national borders, reducing the possibility of regional armed conflict. Regional integration initiatives, according to De Lombaerde and Van Langenhove, need to accomplish at least eight important functions: (1) the strengthening of trade integration in the region, (2) the creation of an appropriate environment for private sector development, (3) the development of infrastructure programmes in support of economic growth and regional integration, (4) the development of strong public sector institutions and good governance, (5) the reduction of social exclusion and the development of an inclusive civil society, (6) the contribution to peace and security in the region, (7) the building of environment programmes at the regional level, and (8) the strengthening of the region's interaction with other regions of the world.[4]

South Asia's Basic Linkages Portraying Regional Identity

Geographical contiguity of the member countries is the cornerstone for the formation of regional blocs; consequently people in a region have a sense of nostalgia for their respective regional frameworks: EU is for Europeans, ASEAN is for Southeast Asians, African Union is for African countries; so is SAARC for South Asians. The historical geography of South Asia amply explains that the spatial dimension has always subscribed to the formal relationship between geography and history.[5] The complementary and interdependent relationship of geography and history is signified by "fundamentally inseparable" common terms such as space and time, area and era, and places and events.[6] Throughout history, South Asia has seen the movement of peoples, trade and ideas that have integrated the region both economically and culturally.[7] The flow of peoples and ideas, about the same time, shattered the South Asia's regional identity and consciousness; yet, geography had its impact on the course of events, to the extent of South Asia getting it identified as an entity within the Asian realm, typified by a set of commonalities discernible in geography, geology, climate, economy, culture and polity. Significantly, South Asia has its identity based on the geographical features that fetched a semblance of a unity sustaining the cultural, political and economic processes of integration.

Further, the network of land and riverine communications, especially between India and the smaller states (with the exception of Pakistan), and the climatic pattern in South Asia from the Himalayas to the Indian Ocean have led to the evolution of a unique eco-subsystem and a composite culture, which was a blend of Buddhism, Hinduism and Islam, providing a common basis for the norms and lifestyle of all segments of civil society.[8] Typifying as an integrated ecosystem, South Asia portrays the region's geographical cohesion which is conducive to promoting cooperation over this territory and SAARC is a logical response to the much awaited need and effort.

(a) South Asia's Potentialities for Regional Integration

The South Asian region has immeasurable and diversified potentialities, as evident from the following accounts: landforms and climatic regimes ranging from sea level to the highest mountains and deep gorges; hottest plains to snow clad mountains; wettest to driest places; dissected green valleys to coral islands; thousands of rivers with immense hydroelectric potential; mineral resources such as coal, iron and natural gas; and widespread diversity of forest resources including exclusive varieties of animals, herbs and timber. Given the trade complementarities in such areas as textile, cotton, cereals, apparels, cane sugar, plastic and chemical goods, the region is perceived as a 'geo-economic unit' becoming conducive to promoting regional cooperation and thereby regional economic integration.[9]

Historically, South Asia was one political entity with many decentralised structures, despite certain apparent intra-regional differences. Obviously, the individual countries in South Asia are closer to each other than might be suspected in the light of the political developments of recent years. That South Asia has a long and closely-interwoven history is noticeable in certain cross-border similarities in traditions, languages and customs based on culture, ethnicity and religion. Evidently, South Asians are closer to each other in their way of life, philosophy, ethics, literature, music, dance, paintings, and architecture than to countries of other regions. As a logical corollary, South Asian identity is based on their common values rooted in the historical, cultural, social, and ethnic and civilisation traditions which serve as linkages among people across national borders. Further, the shared religious faiths of Hinduism, Islam, Buddhism, Sikhism and Christianity turn South Asia into a 'single civilisational whole'. Even on the flipside, South Asia has certain distinct common features, as evident from extreme poverty, mega-urbanisation, immense disparities between rich and poor, and fundamental problems in the areas of infrastructure, energy and the environment, besides high levels of internal conflicts and political instability within the region.[10]

(b) Early Attempts at Regionalism in South Asia

Efforts for regional cooperation in South Asia can also be traced back to 1945, when Jawaharlal Nehru made a plea for 'a South Asian Federation'. He convened the 1947 Asian Relations Conference even before India's independence. This conference led to the formation of a non-governmental Asian Relations Organisation with the objective of creating a pan-Asian framework to build technical cooperation among the countries concerned. Later in January 1950, the Colombo Plan, a product of the Commonwealth Foreign Ministers' Conference, was held in Colombo for promoting technical cooperation among the South and Southeast Asian countries.[11] Subsequently, in May 1950, the Baguio Conference in the Philippines also dealt with regional cooperation in Asia. These efforts were culminated in the Afro-Asian Nations Conference at Bandung in 1955.

These attempts made by India to develop regionalism beyond and outside the bipolar framework of the Cold War were, however, turned to be discouraged. Meanwhile, the Non-Aligned Movement (NAM), which was launched at Belgrade in 1961, soon absorbed most of India's multilateral diplomatic attention.

The nonchalant attitude towards regionalism was also due to the absence of any perceived common security threat to South Asia. Lack of either a sincere, collective and grand vision, or even a strong political will among its member states pushed the idea to a state of hibernation for a considerable period. For all the overt and hidden constraints looming large, the programme of regional cooperation was expected to benefit immensely from the historical and cultural ties connecting people across national borders in South Asia. Of the various factors served as stimulants towards the end of forming a regional organisation, some of the South

Asian countries belatedly turned their attention to the need for forming a regional body in their own geographical area. Thanks to the persistent effort of smaller states of the region, especially Bangladesh, SAARC came into existence in December 1985.

SAARC's Record: Passion and Apathy Sailing Together

SAARC activity is a rather modest and more extensive record of achievement. Over the last twenty-nine years, despite extremely difficult political circumstances, SAARC has managed to create situations, institutions and forums. The establishment of the SAARC Development Fund and SAARC University in India, and the cooperation on the issues of climate change and energy crisis, and the realisation of Regional Railways Agreement and Motor Vehicles Agreement bear testimony to SAARC's progress rather achievement. SAARC Charter provisions, though led to delays and postponement of Ministerial and Summit meetings, are not necessarily viewed as "obstacles but as safeguards to protect the young organisation from entanglement in issues extraneous to regional cooperation". That the SAARC is growing significantly is vindicated by the interest and support of the observer states for the regional grouping.

Differential power potentials coupled with divergence and apathy has eventually resulted in trust deficit to the extent of inhibiting the spirit of regional cooperation in South Asia. In the context of SAARC identity or South Asian solidarity becoming, for the most part, a political rhetoric, its failure to evolve as a powerful regional body is largely attributed to national interest, rather inward looking, of each member state. Inter-state relations in South Asia are marred by mistrust, mutual threat perceptions, confrontation and hostility. Though external threat perception is lacking in South Asia, the smaller states perceive threat emanating from within the region itself and seek the help of extra-regional powers. much to the chagrin of India. These 'xenophobic considerations' render SAARC to languish. That the SAARC's journey has not been remarkably success ever since it was created in 1985 is testified by the former the Indian Prime Minister Manmohan Singh at the sixteenth summit in the Bhutan capital (28 April, 2010) that SAARC had indeed failed in meeting its aspirations. The fact that India feels responsive to the imperatives of SAARC existence is well understood from a statement of Manmohan Singh, issued on the eve of departing to Maldives for the seventeenth SAARC Summit on 10 November, 2011 that "India will work to promote greater integration as well as the development of a South Asian identity".[12]

(a) Perpetuated Irritants Inhibiting SAARC's Integration Process

Issues of political and ideological character, coupled with the issues of strategic conflict and military balance, have perpetuated the South Asia's inter-state conflicts which probably are the highest compared to any other regional blocs. South Asia is the least integrated region of the world points to big stumbling blocks and barriers inhibiting in the free movement of goods and people as well as deep rooted suspicions and differences.[13] South Asian countries hold widely divergent views on many important issues and lack a common political culture; and hence SAARC existence could not blunt the raw edges of historical irritants between members. Preoccupation with the intra-state conflicts and inter-state crises has almost restrained the South Asian states to achieve adequate degree of complementarity of interests and regional economic cooperation and thereby regional cohesion. It is also a great paradox that the overlapping of religious and linguistic groups across national boundaries becomes a trigger for internal conflicts and intra-regional political instability leading to the perpetuation of a feeling among the South Asian countries that they 'do not belong to one civilisation, nor do the peoples of South Asia have 'the feeling of belonging to one region'.[14] Despite sharing certain common civilisational links the member states cannot agree on a common future and there is no consensus on fundamental norms or values; and hence the rhetoric that South Asia was a 'region without regionalism' has its relevance even after the twenty-nine years of SAARC's existence. As the success of SAARC is contingent on unending shifts among its member-states rather than rhetorical claims, SAARC has acquired a reputation of being a non-performing entity.

The geographical contiguity of the countries, owing to common land borders among the countries of peninsular South Asia, has become of no significance for the development of transit facilities and transport network and thereby for the formation of a regional bloc. Low intra-regional trade in South Asian countries is basically attributed to high transport costs and logistic costs, which owe much to lack of transport connectivity in South Asia. The infrastructure constraints made South Asia as "one of the least connected regions in the world constituting a major structural impediment."[15] Thus, there has arisen the need for complementary improvements in trade logistics and trade facilitation and efficiency at the border crossings, if at all cross-border infrastructure is expected to realise the full potential of growth in trade. About the same time, regional infrastructure forming the bottom-line of regional integration and trade arrangements are viewed as stimulants for intra-regional FDI which, in turn, becomes conducive to economic growth and thereby poverty-reduction.

Besides the constraints of poor physical connectivity, other factors like energy crisis and trust deficit among the member states are relegating the intra-regional trade and investment flows to remain among the lowest in the world. Further, lack of trade complementarity among South Asian countries manifest in competition in their export markets in a narrow range of products-particularly in textiles and apparel and other light manufactured goods. Consequently, prospects of sub-regional integration are seriously inhibited by this trade structure. Intra-regional trade in SAARC is around five per cent only, compared to twenty six in ASEAN, fifty eight per cent in EU, and sixty two per cent in NAFTA. Improved connectivity could enhance intra-regional trade. A strong anti-export bias and high level of protectionism to the extent of limiting trade, including intra-regional trade, is rather a vestige of the strategy of import-substituting industrialisation which swayed over the South Asian economies during the post-World War II period. However, the South Asian countries which were for long indifferent to the notion of regional integration have begun getting tuned to the concept of regionalism as well as regionalisation, in response to the growing regionalism in other parts of the global economy. Yet, regionalism and regionalisation in South Asian economies have not made much headway; as a consequence, intra-regional trade and regional integration endeavours in South Asian economies continued to be very low even during the Uruguay Round, albeit they picked up markedly during the Doha Round.

(b) India-Centric Fears Inhibiting Regional Cohesion of SAARC

Negative perceptions and misapprehensions about the consequences of increased regional cooperation, as logical corollary of pride and prejudice, manifest in fears of greater domination of India, often borne out of lack of information. The basic apprehension has stemmed from India's geographical size, demographic and economic potential and political weight. India stands out for dominance in South Asian region is testified by its preponderance in population size (accounting for seventy-five per cent of the region's population), areal extent (seventy-two per cent of region's total area) and gross domestic product (seventy-eight per cent of the region's GDP). This glaring discrepancy between India and other smaller states of South Asia leads to natural concerns about the possible and potential interference of India in their affairs. Smaller states in South Asia view India as both a saviour and as part of the problem and are reluctant to work with India, fearing that such cooperation will admit Indian dominance in SAARC ; on the other hand, India has its own fears of its neighbours in terms of their possible union to oppose the country's interests.[16] Intra-regional political tensions, seldom India at the centre-stage, have resulted in uneven progress of SAARC; and hence SAARC is identified with stigma of being a non-performing entity.

SAARC is an important option, but not the only option for India gives credence to the fact that India is scarcely interested in South Asia vis-à-vis Southeast Asia. Instead, India which was disenchanted with SAARC has been pursuing trans-regional, super-regional, sub-regional, inter-regional and bilateral cooperative arrangements with so much of enthusiasm as to win the appreciation of the members of the multilateral institutions concerned. In fact, even some smaller states have in the recent times entertained fanciful notions rather insatiable thirst for joining the extra-regional institutions.

ASEAN: A Role Model or a Guide for SAARC

SAARC has not been growing at all and is still in its infancy, even as most other regional blocs are emerging as close-knit communities. ASEAN + 3, APEC and ASEM in Asia have led to improved relations between East Asian countries and to regional integration in the form of economic cooperation and political harmony. Though SAARC failed to harness the potentialities for forging cooperation on the economic and political fronts vis-à-vis ASEAN, there are many common variables between these two regional blocs so much as to draw a justifiable comparison.

The difference between SAARC and ASEAN is distinct in that the former typifies a 'system of States', as opposed to the latter's distinction of having evolved as a 'society of states'. SAARC's presence has not prevented violent conflicts, much less settled or resolved them. Regional cooperation is at a very rudimentary stage in South Asia. Conflict management of even a minimalist sort is non-existent at present .[17] It is the inability of SAARC member-states to subsume the regional peculiarities that tends to inhibit the much expected regional integration and constrain the efforts towards advanced types of regional economic cooperation. On the other hand, ASEAN member-states have precluded the contentious issues in pursuit of promoting regional cooperation and reinforcing partnerships.

Options for SAARC towards Regional Integration

Given the substantial benefits accrued by the member-states of other regional organisations, it is imperative for the policy-makers in the South Asian countries to gain a comprehensive understanding of the incentives for and progress towards greater economic integration in South Asia. If the current goals are weighed against the agenda of the organisation, SAARC is found moving slowly towards regional integration in the real sense. This integration is far ahead of a common approach to issues like poverty, telecommunication, weather, sports, culture, etc., as was envisaged in the beginning. A move towards a South Asian community can be cemented and accelerated only if a number of policy initiatives and actions, including economic, political, social and cultural initiatives, both at the governmental and non-governmental levels are taken by South Asian leaders. SAARC needs to be looked upon as a "single development unit" for accelerating the movement of people, goods and ideas as well as for sharing the capital technology and natural resources.[18] Need to bear in mind is the pertinent call made by the Indian Prime Minister Manmohan Singh at the Sixteenth summit in April 2010: "The 21st century cannot be an Asian century unless South Asia marches together. We have created institutions for regional cooperation, but we have not yet empowered them adequately to enable them to be more proactive."[19]

As the persisting regional tensions are impinging on the prospects of Regional Trade Arrangements (RTAs), a series of agreements signed over the years between India and its neighbours–could cover a range of issues that are independent of one another. The services sector is potentially a major driver of economic integration. If India's dominance in information technology is capable of triggering profitable affiliations with neighbouring countries, there are immense possibilities for joint ventures or strategic alliances in the agro-sector especially in irrigation, food processing and packaging, energy sector, technical education, textiles, tourism and health. SAARC's regional integration is linked with the need for promoting tourism, given the region's unique cultural and religious heritage that could offer enormous complementarities to bring South Asian countries closer, besides accruing social amalgamation and economic benefits.

As the heavily formal, procedural, and complex Track I initiatives hardly generated enthusiasm and interest among the people and their leaders in the region, Track II initiatives, or 'beyond the state' diplomacy has of late been recognised as a better mechanism for confidence building towards the reconstruction of South Asia as a community.[20] SAARC's failure is well-evident in addressing the subject of water rights for making best use of international river waters in South Asia.[21] Therefore, as outlined by Geoffrey Pyatt, the Career Foreign Service Officer of the US Department of State who was posted as Principal Deputy Secretary for South and Central Asian Affairs, it is high time for SAARC to embark on 'hydro-diplomacy' for promoting cooperation among the South Asian countries to find solutions on water-sharing of the Himalayan-origin rivers.[22] The rationale for increased economic cooperation among geographically contiguous countries has been a dominant feature of the global political economy and strengthened further in the 1990s by the emergence of regional trading blocs like EU and NAFTA. It is therefore imperative to restructure SAARC and revive the SAFTA to propel the South Asian economy towards greater regional economic integration. Regional integration seems to be a reality at a time when South Asian economies displayed eagerness to participate in the regional economic dynamism and be part of regional agreements in other parts of Asia and the global economy.

References

1. Joseph Nye, *International Regionalism*, Boston: Little Brown, 1968, p. vii.
2. Louise Fawcett, "Exploring regional domains: a comparative history of regionalism", *International Affairs*, Vol. 80, No. 3, 2004, pp. 429-446.
3. Asian Development Bank, *Regional Cooperation and Integration Strategy*, Manila, July 2006.
4. P. De Lombaerde and L.Van Langenhove, "Regional Integration, Poverty and Social Policy", *Global Social Policy*, Vol.7, No. 3, pp. 377-383.
5. Malcolm McInerney, "Entwining history and geography", *Spatial worlds*, 27 April 2011, http://spatialworlds.blogspot.com/2011/04/entwining-history-and-geography.html
6. Donald Meinig, *The Shaping of America: A Geographical Perspective on 500 Years of American History*, New Haven: Yale University Press, 1987 p. xv.
7. I. Mavara Inayat, "The South Asian Association for Regional Cooperation" in Alyson J. K. Bailes, John Gooneratne, Mavara Inayat, Jamshed Ayaz Khan and Swaran Singh, *Regionalism in South Asian Diplomacy*, SIPRI Policy Paper no. 15, Sweden: Stockholm International Peace Research Institute, February 2007.
8. Swaran Singh, "India and regionalism", in Alyson J. K. Bailes, John Gooneratne, Mavara Inayat, Jamshed Ayaz Khan and Swaran Singh, *ibid.*

9. IPCS Panel Discussion, "The 14th SAARC Summit: An Assessment," *South Asia Articles,* no. 2270, New Delhi: Institute of Peace and Conflict Studies, 13 April 2007.
10. Tomislav Delinic, *SAARC - 25 Years of Regional Integration in South Asia,* KAS International Reports 2|2011, SAARC_ http.www.kas.dewfdockas_21870-544-2-30.pdf110209123437.
11. M. Haas, *The Asian Way to Peace: A Story of Regional Cooperation,* New York: Praeger, 1989, pp. 275-276.
12. Manmohan Singh, "India to promote regional integration during SAARC summit", *Asia News International,* 9 November 2011.
13. Jamil Nasir, Towards Stronger SAARC, 8 November 2012, www.thenews.com.pk/Todays-News-9-141723-Towards-a-stronger-SAARC.
14. Aditi Paul, "What Impedes Regionalism in South Asia?", *Counter Currents,* 24 March 2012.
15. Secretary General, *Trade is key to SAARC's Success,* Indian Council of World Affairs, 14 September 2010, http://www.thaindian. com/ newsportal/ business/trade-is-key-to-saarcs-success-secretary-general_100428441.html.
16. Asima Noreen, "Challenges for SAARC," *Pakistan Times,* 17 February 2011.
17. Kripa Sridharan, Regional Organisations and Conflict Management: Comparing ASEAN and SAARC, *Working Paper Series,* no. 2, London: Crisis States Research Centre, Destin Development Studies Institute, March 2008.
18. Anil Kumar Mahapatra, *Small States in South Asia: A Security Perspective of the Himalayan States,* Bhubaneswar: Panchashila, 2008, p.193
19. Manmohan Singh, SAARC is *glass half empty, region needs empowerment,* Address at the 16th SAARC Summit, 28 April 2010, http:// way2online.com/?p=51137.
20. Madhavibhasin, *SAARC-III Challenges and Prospects,* 12 May 2010, http:// india. foreignpolicyblogs. com/ 2010/05/12/saarc-iii-challenges-and-prospects/ and http://india. foreignpolicyblogs. com/ tag/saarc.
21. Prabin Man Singh, "Sharing Rivers for Peace, Security and Development of South Asia", *South Asia Journal,* no.1, July 2011, pp. 32-34.
22. Geoffrey R. Pyatt, "Hydro-diplomacy for Regional cooperation over Himalayan Watersheds", *South Asia Journal, ibid,* pp. 24-27.

PART–II
CONNECTIVITY AND TRADE IN SOUTH ASIA

3

India's Trade with South Asian Neighbours: Perceptions and Reality

Indra Nath Mukherji

Introduction

All South Asian countries are in some way or the other sensitive to India's interaction with them in the region. In matters relating to trade, while India's dominant role in the region is frequently highlighted, an expectation that India needs to further open up its market to their products is also underlined. Some of the major issues for concern among India's neighbours are:

1. Adverse and deteriorating balance of trade with India.
2. A variety of restrictions on their exports to India including: (a) tariff barriers, (b) non-tariff barriers, and (c) tariff rate quotas.
3. High customs tariffs in India, particularly in textiles and clothing sector, and specific duties on them hindering the region's textile exports to India.
4. On the other hand India imposes subsidies on its agricultural exports affecting adversely the livelihood concerns of farmers in the region.

This study examines some of these concerns and addresses to what extent these are genuine and the role that India could play in further integrating with the region.

India's Trade Balance with South Asian Countries (SA-7)[1]

Figure 1 presents India's trade with the remaining seven (combined)

South Asian countries (SA-7). We notice that India's exports to the region has grown phenomenally since the 2000s, increasing from $1.7 billion in 2000 to $13 billion in 2011. While India's imports too have grown during this period, the pace is more modest, increasing from $ 0.5 billion to $ 2.5 billion during the same period. Consequently, India's export-import ratio with South Asian countries increased from 3.4 to 5.2, reflecting growing trade imbalance.

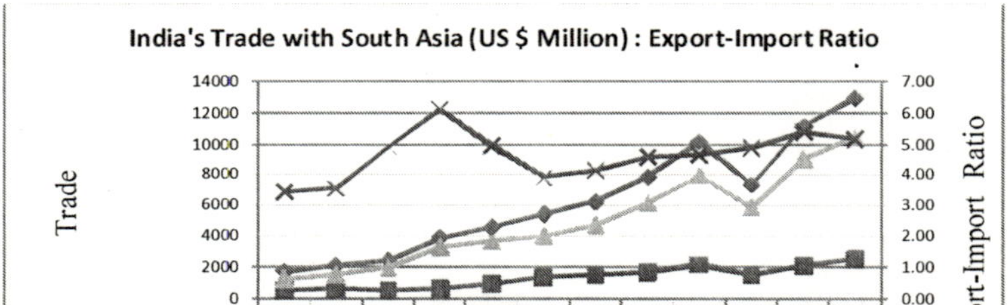

	2000	2001	2002	2003	2004	2005	2006	2007	2008	2009	2010	2011
Export	1719	2092	2415	3875	4580	5400	6233	7848	10130	7374	11114	12938
Import	501	589	492	634	926	1380	1499	1713	2180	1515	2064	2501
Trade Balance	1218	1503	1924	3241	3654	4020	4734	6135	7950	5858	9050	10436
Export-Import Ratio	3.43	3.55	4.91	6.11	4.95	3.91	4.16	4.58	4.65	4.87	5.39	5.17

Figure 1

Source: *Author's estimates from World Bank Integrated Solution (WITS) Database, April 2013.*

Figure 2 focuses on seven South Asian countries' trade with India. The figure presents South Asian seven countries' exports to India and world and also their imports from India and the world. This data enables us to examine the seven countries' trade with India in relation to the same with the world. It is observed that while India accounted for fifty-seven per cent of these countries world deficit in 2001, this country accounted for only twenty-two per cent of these countries' world deficit in 2011. Thus, while in absolute sense all seven countries have been experiencing deteriorating trade deficit with India over the 2000s, in relation to their global deficit, the Indian component has shown remarkable relative decline. In other words, the seven countries need to be more concerned with their global deficits than with their deficits with India in isolation. In fact, it can be demonstrated that seven countries growing trade deficit with India in fact, helps keep these countries' global deficit lower than what it would have been by not importing from India.

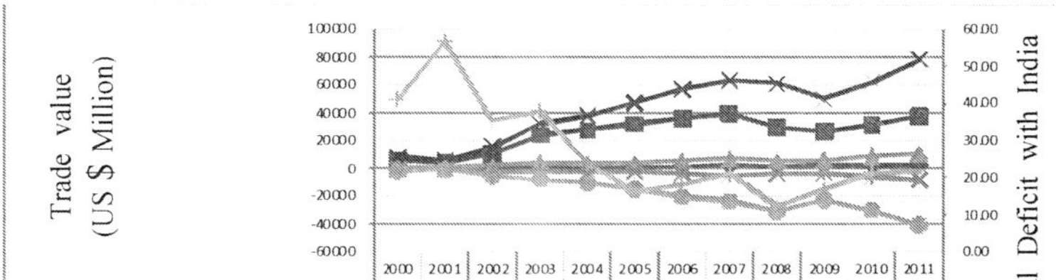

	2000	2001	2002	2003	2004	2005	2006	2007	2008	2009	2010	2011
Export to India	375	72	196	708	649	1301	1394	1883	1402	1665	1721	1824
Export to World	6122	4801	10231	23967	27283	31954	35939	39425	29644	26538	31468	37175
Import from India	1200	643	2112	3743	3154	3763	5171	6873	5179	5542	8242	10715
Import from World	8124	5806	15646	31981	37815	47166	56633	63197	60906	49602	62110	78044
Trade Balance with India	-825	-571	-1916	-3036	-2506	-2461	-3776	-4989	-3777	-3877	6520	-8891
Trade Balance with World	-2002	-1005	-5415	-8014	-10532	-15212	-20694	-23772	-31263	-23064	-30642	-40870
Trade Deficit with India as % Total Deficit	41.22	56.82	35.38	37.88	23.79	16.18	18.25	20.99	12.08	16.81	21.28	21.75

Figure 2: South Asian Countries' (Excluding India) Trade with India and World

Source: *Author's estimates from World Bank Integrated Solution (WITS) Database, April 2013.*

What needs to be considered is that when seven countries import from India at a lower cost than what they would be required to pay for similar imports from elsewhere in the world, their global trade deficit would lower to the extent of the cost difference on each unit imported from India. An illustration of this possibility is demonstrated with respect to Bangladesh's imports of top three products from India in 2011. Table 1 reveals that if Bangladesh were to import the three products from the rest of the world but not from India, while its imports from India would decline by the amount shown as being imported, it would incur additional import payments of $ 94.5 million from sourcing these imports from the rest of the world. Thus importing from a cheaper source, enable Bangladesh in keeping its global import cost and consequently global trade deficit lower.

A further dimension that needs to be factored in while observing the bilateral trade imbalances is to examine the composition of trade. It is well known that while raw materials add little value to the product, finished products add more value. Hence it may be interesting to observe how the structure of bilateral trade has undergone change, if any, in this context.

Figure 3 presents seven countries' exports to India by end-use classification. It will be observed that SA-7 countries are no longer exporters of only raw materials to India. Most of their exports to India are either intermediate or consumer goods. In 2011, raw materials accounted for only eighty per cent of their exports to India. Nevertheless looking at the trend in the increasing shares of raw materials, declining shares of consumer

Table 1: Excess Import Payments if Bangladesh were to Import from Rest of World its top Imports from India (2011)

HS Code	*Product*	*Unit of Quantity*	*Import from India (US$' 000)*	*Quantity Imported from India (Million Kg)*	*Import from rest of World (US$' 000)*	*Quantity Imported form rest of World (Millon Kg)*	*Unit Price of Import from India (US$)*	*Unit Price of Import Rest of World (US$)*	*Differ-emce in Unit Price*	*Excees Import Payment if not imported from India ('000 US$)*
1	2	3	4	5	6	7	8=4/5	9=6/7	10= 9-8	11= 4*10
520-100	Cotton, not carded or combed.	Kg	291929	95	824773	248	3.06	3.48	0.42	39900
290243	Xylenes p-Xylene	Kg	210576	132	518532	324	1.59	1.60	0.01	1520
230400	Oil-cake and other solid residues	Kg	186307	443	186703	443	0.42	0.54	0.12	53160
	Total									**94580**

Source: *Author's estimate from Export Import Data Bank, Department of Commerce, Government of India, accessed in http://commerce.nic.in/eidb/default.asp on 23 April 2013.*

goods and also the minor share of capital goods exports, one cannot notice substantial diversification of exports. Thus, much remains to be achieved in terms of diversification of the seven countries' exports to India.

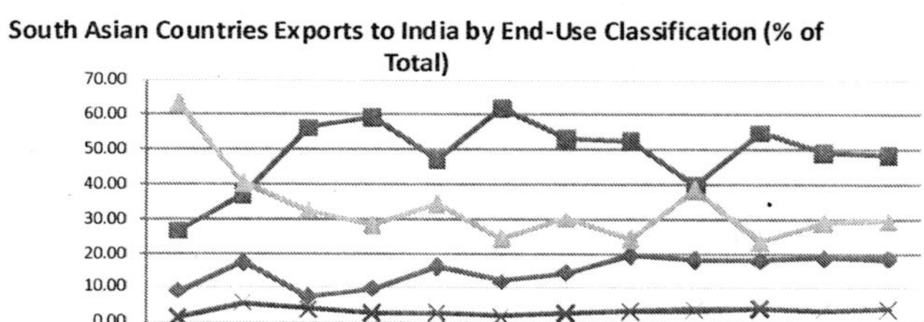

	2000	2001	2002	2003	2004	2005	2006	2007	2008	2009	2010	2011
Raw Materials	9.03	17.25	7.39	9.67	16.14	11.90	14.32	19.65	18.24	17.94	18.64	18.43
Intermediate Goods	26.57	37.04	56.21	59.17	46.96	61.85	52.87	52.47	39.85	54.81	48.96	48.29
Consumer Goods	63.15	40.13	32.56	28.45	34.23	24.45	30.03	24.42	38.29	23.33	28.84	29.42
Capital Goods	1.24	5.58	3.84	2.72	2.68	1.81	2.78	3.46	3.62	3.92	3.57	3.86

Figure 3

Source: *Author's estimates from World Bank Integrated Solution (WITS) Database, April 2013.*

The major imports of seven countries in 2011 were consumer goods and intermediate goods as may be seen in Fig. 4. The average share of intermediate goods has been the highest. Intermediate goods provide possibilities for industrialisation of these countries. Further, it should be noted that some South Asian countries (particularly, Bangladesh) have been more dependent on India for their food grains imports, an important consumer good, whose share has been rising. Bangladesh has been seeking from India to lift its export bans on grains (wheat and rice) to India to enable cheap food imports into the country that could help keep domestic food prices down and political unrest under control. Similarly, Bangladesh has been seeking assurance from India not to clamp on exports of cotton and yarn for its garment industry, the country's major foreign exchange earner.

India's growing exports of essential food grains and agricultural raw materials no doubt makes its neighbouring countries' trade balance with India more adverse, but these imports are essential to keep the seven countries' food prices down and to expand and sustain their exports to the world.

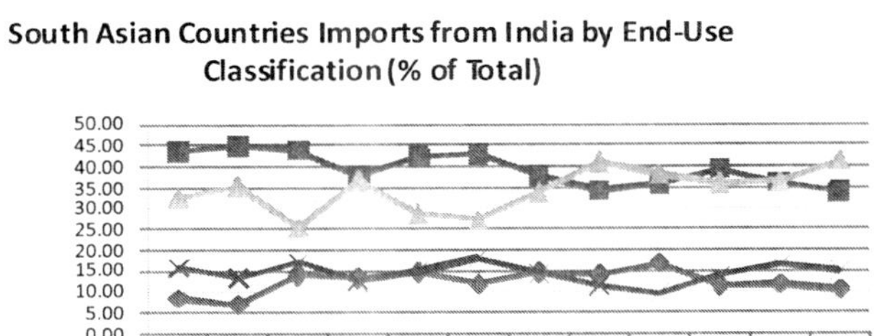

	2000	2001	2002	2003	2004	2005	2006	2007	2008	2009	2010	2011
Raw Materials	8.27	6.91	13.87	13.11	14.46	11.70	14.46	13.70	16.68	11.17	11.54	10.23
Intermediate Goods	43.42	44.82	44.00	37.82	42.08	43.11	37.64	34.25	35.70	39.38	36.11	33.69
Consumer Goods	32.72	35.26	25.28	36.67	28.63	27.21	33.70	40.90	38.15	35.83	36.23	41.25
Capital Goods	15.60	13.01	16.85	12.40	14.83	17.99	14.19	11.15	9.47	13.62	16.12	14.83

Figure 4

Source: *Author's estimates from World Bank Integrated Solution (WITS) Database, April 2013.*

Trade Restrictiveness

Various international organisations, particularly the World Bank characterises South Asia as comparatively more restrictive as compared to other regions in the world. Among South Asian countries, India's trade restrictiveness is considered to be the highest. This is also the perception of most SACs regarding India. We examine below these perceptions both in terms of tariff as well as non-tariff barriers that India imposes on its imports from the region and the world.

(a) Tariff Barriers

It is observed in Fig. 5 that the MFN rates, (particularly, weighted rates) prevailing in India does not appear to be much higher than those prevailing in the rest of South Asia. In fact, only Sri Lanka and Afghanistan appear to have these rates lower than in India. Thus, in terms of tariff restriction, the data does not support the contention that India is more restrictive than the rest of South Asia.

Besides, India has been offering duty-free imports to least developed countries since 2008, barring products in its sensitive list. In its custom notification no. 99/2011, dated 9 November, 2011, India drastically pruned its sensitive list to only twenty five products that included only non-merit goods- tobacco and alcohol.

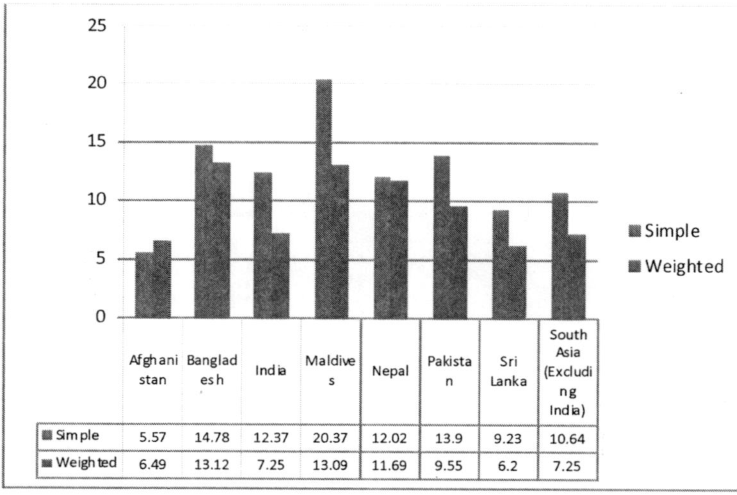

	Afghanistan	Bangladesh	India	Maldives	Nepal	Pakistan	Sri Lanka	South Asia (Excluding India)
Simple	5.57	14.78	12.37	20.37	12.02	13.9	9.23	10.64
Weighted	6.49	13.12	7.25	13.09	11.69	9.55	6.2	7.25

Figure 5: MFN Tariff Rates in South Asia (per cent)

Data for India and Pakistan is for 2009.

Source: *Author's estimate from TRAINS as obtained from World Bank World Integrated Trade Solution (WITS) Data Base, 2013.*

Regarding specific duties[2], contrary to the perception of many SACs, the incidence of specific duties on India's imports (particularly from SA-7 countries) is much lower than those prevailing in the rest of SA-7 countries. Figure 6 illustrates this. India removed specific duties on imports from SACs in December 2007.

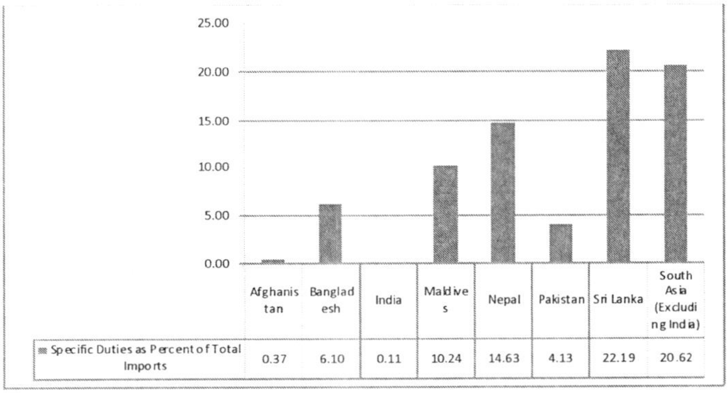

Figure 6: Specific Duties as Per cent of Total Imports

Note: *Data for Nepal, Sri Lanka and South Asia (excluding India) is for 2011.* Data for India and Pakistan is for 2009 and Data for Bangladesh is 2008.

(b) Non-Tariff Barriers (NTBs)

While a tariff is a tax imposed on foreign goods and services as they enter a country through customs points, NTBs are non tax measures that have restrictive effect on trade. Tariff barriers are easy to quantify as their incidence is measurable. NTBs are often grey and apply in various shapes and forms, the intended consequences of which may be subject to varying interpretations depending on the perceptions of the affected stakeholders. The stakeholders often express offensive or defensive interests on the same measure depending on whether they are seeking market access or offering one.

Most SACs refer to the imposition of NTBs by India on their exports to the latter. Two points to be noted in this context are: (i) all seven countries impose restrictions on their imports in larger or smaller measure and (ii) more often than not, no country imposing these restrictions would classify them as NTBs. In fact, in majority of the cases they would claim that they are legitimate non-tariff measures (NTMs). NTMs are generally designed to ensure that the products being imported are in conformity with certain standards to ensure the health and safety of humans, plants and the environment. When these measures are compatible with WTO principles and when they are applied in similar measure to domestic producers as also to third country importers, then NTMs are totally legitimate. When, however, the NTMs are applied discriminately or in a very trade restrictive manner, then they may take the shape of what we call Non-Tariff Barriers (NTBs).[3]

As noted above, NTMs are applied by all SACs in some form or the other. According to a study by Asian Development Bank (ADB) and United Nations Conference on Trade and Development (UNCTAD) (2008), the highest incidence of NTMs in South Asian region were sanitary and phytosanitary (SPS) measures and technical barriers to trade (TBT) (86 per cent), tariff quota (9.8 per cent), anti-dumping measures (7.4 per cent), license requirement (5.3 per cent), and countervailing duties (1.2 per cent).[4]

Under South Asian Free Trade Agreement (SAFTA), a Committee of Experts (COE) was formed to monitor and facilitate implementation of the agreement. A sub-group under the COE monitors NTMs as also para-tariff measures (PTMs) on goods entering territories of each contracting state. Under this committee, Pakistan, Bangladesh and Nepal notified as many as fifty such measures they faced when accessing the Indian market. The notified NTMs refer to TBT and SPS measures.[5]

An analysis of the NTMs notified against India shows that some of these NTMs did not pose any barrier to entry as they are applicable to both imports as well as domestically manufactured goods and hence in accordance with the principle of national treatment. There are also some other measures where India has already initiated corrective action but perhaps the information on such action has not been made available to other countries.[6]

Only nineteen of the notified fifty NTMs were found to impose trade barriers. In some cases the procedures to be met have been found to be too cumbersome. In others, it has been found that facilities for testing of samples are not available at the border and have to be sent to distant locations. In the meanwhile the consignment of exporters is held up for days and bears demurrage charges or may suffer loss in value. In other cases Indian authorities do not recognise pre-shipment test certificates from exporting countries which again leads to delay and additional costs.[7]

There is deep concern in Pakistan that India protects its domestic economy by a variety of non-tariff barriers. Even though India had made the necessary amendment to labeling requirement under Jute and Textiles Control Order in 2002, this was not known to the exporters. Further, when in 2002, India amended some clauses in the Indian Customs Act relating to valuation that were inconsistent with GATT Article VII , Pakistan notified this measure as a barrier to COE, indicating its lack of awareness to the amended act.[8]

At a Joint Working Group (JWG) meeting was held in August 2011, co-chaired by the Joint Secretaries of the respective Commerce Ministries, the Pakistani side furnished a specific list of NTBs, as perceived by their business community, for sectors such as textiles, leather, cement, agricultural produce and surgical instruments.

It was agreed that these would be comprehensively examined on the Indian side and interactions would be arranged between the concerned Regulators and Pakistan's business community to find solutions to all the issues raised.[9]

A comprehensive discussion, "Nuts and Bolts of Trade Facilitation" was organised in Delhi by FICCI on 29 September, 2011. The feedback received from the discussions, involving all relevant stakeholders, clarified that all standards and specifications were non-discriminatory, viz., they applied to all countries exporting goods to India.[10]

In the sixth round of India-Pakistan bilateral trade talks held in New Delhi during 14-16 November, 2011, a specific slot was allotted for discussing the non-tariff barriers perceived by Pakistan in respect of its exports to India.

The discussions explained how insistence on specific standards by importers was due to the commercial considerations and not because of any government requirement. An Annexure attached to the sixth round of India-Pakistan bilateral trade talks clarified all issues raised by the Pakistan side. On the issue of compulsory certification of cement, the Pakistani side was informed that Bureau of Industrial Standards (BIS) was mandated to give license within six months and inspection visit was to be completed within one or two months after an application is registered. Thirteen licenses were already operational and renewal licenses for two years were being given to all cement manufacturers who had applied for the same.[11]

Regarding testing of Azo dyes (a banned product, both in India and Pakistan), the Pakistani side was assured that a testing procedure is specified only if the consignments are not certified by the country of origin. A certificate by the accredited certification bodies/labs of the Pakistan National Accreditation Council is acceptable.[12]

The Pakistani side was informed that all the consignments (except those which require other mandatory procedures to be followed), would be cleared by customs within twenty-four hours. Even those consignments, which fault on some customs procedures, would be cleared immediately with the understanding that the problems will be sorted out in time.

Regarding testing and packaging requirements of food products, the Indian side agreed to send a team for educating the exporters regarding packaging and labeling requirements as and when requested by the Pakistani authorities.[13]

(c) Tariff Rate Quotas on Imports[14]

India imposes tariff rate quotas (TRQs) on a number of products imported from the region. Following a surge in imports of products such as *vanaspati* (hydrogenated vegetable oil) and copper from Sri Lanka and Nepal, India had to impose TRQs on these products to balance the interests of its domestic manufacturers with those of exporters seeking market access in India. It is important to note here that neither Sri Lanka nor Nepal manufactures the principal raw materials (crude palm oil and scrap copper required for the manufacture of *vanaspati* and copper respectively). Since the external tariff on these raw materials was low or negligible in Sri Lanka and Nepal in comparison to relatively high tariffs of the same products in India, many Indians found it lucrative to set up factories in Nepal or Sri Lanka to manufacture the finished products, taking advantage of the external tariff differential, and with minimal value addition (violating the rules of origin requirement) which they exported back to the duty-free Indian market. Following the protests made by domestic manufacturers, facing unequal competition from the imported products, the Indian government imposed quota restrictions on these imports.

When following the commodity price hike in global markets in 2007-08, India brought down its external tariffs on copper ingots and palm oil and also strengthened its enforcement of rules of origin requirement for copper and *vanaspati* imports, the advantage of manufacturing these products in Sri Lanka and Nepal was lost and exports of the same to India declined drastically. Since not even a small fraction of the quota imposed by India on copper and *vanaspati* imports are currently being met, the rationale for maintaining the quotas is lost.

Other products on which India imposes quotas on imports from Sri Lanka are tea, black pepper, bakery shortenings and margarine and garments. For imports from Nepal, India imposes quotas on acrylic yarn, and zinc oxide. Since India's neighbours have comparative advantage in these products, excluding zinc oxide, there is a case for phasing out tariff rate quotas on these products.[15]

It is notable in this context that India is already in the process of expanding the quota requirement constraint for garments in favour of Bangladesh. In 2011, India raised the quota on imports for 164 textile items from Bangladesh from eight million to ten million pieces. Bangladesh further benefited when following Indian Prime Minister's visit to that country, India totally waived quota on forty six textile items of export interest to Bangladesh.[16]

Subsidies in Indian Agriculture

The farm lobby in Pakistan is concerned about the agricultural subsidies that India applies on food, fertilisers, power and irrigation. These subsidies, in their perception, are three times of what is applied in Pakistan agriculture. On the contrary, Pakistan levies GST on all agricultural inputs at sixteen per cent. It is alleged that agricultural products do not even figure either in their negative list, or in their sensitive list. The farmers of Pakistan have not been taken on board while taking the decision to grant India MFN. Such a decision should not have been hastily taken without prior cost-benefit analysis in the two countries' respective agricultural subsidies.[17]

In reality, during 1996-97, India's domestic subsidy levels were well below the permissible de *minimis,* category both in product specific and non-product specific categories. For product specific subsidies, India's support level were negative for all the years reported by India and non-product specific categories, the support level was only 1.2 per cent of the total value of agricultural production in the last year reported by India.[18] Thus, the domestic support extended by India to agriculture and to farmers is WTO complaint. It is a different matter that India is constrained in further increasing its food security bill due to fiscal considerations. However, food security is one of the India's foremost development priorities. The objective is to procure sufficient food grains to meet the minimum dietary requirements of its vast impoverished and malnourished population and not to subsidise the country's food exports.

In reality, Pakistan has a number of options to protect its farmers. At present there are nearly eleven agricultural products in Pakistan's negative list and fifty-five are in its sensitive list. This provides an opportunity for Pakistan to protect its farm products. It retains the option to fine tune its negative and sensitive lists so as to protect its vulnerable farmers. Denying MFN status to India on this ground is not the solution.

Conclusion

While India's trade balance with SACs is becoming more adverse, in relation to global trends, it has been to the contrary. Its bilateral trade deficit with SACs is assuming a smaller proportion of their global deficit. Further to be observed is that increasing trade deficit with India by seven countries when arising from cheaper imports, will help moderate their global deficit.

Seven countries, export and import mainly intermediate and consumer goods to and from India. The figures do not show much diversification of exports. Both in case of exports and imports, intermediate goods dominate seven countries' trade with India. The intermediate goods are valuable inputs for the industrialisation of the trading partners. They also provide opportunities for developing suitable value chains for more diversified and value added trade between the trading partners in the region.

India's trade restrictiveness in terms of tariff barriers (including phasing out of specific duties) is coming down and it cannot be said that even for products like textiles, it is more protected than its South Asian neighbours. In fact, by increasing quota-free and duty-free access to least developed countries, India's trade barriers reflect significant moderation.

Besides, now that the possibility of taking advantage of external tariff arbitrage and bypassing the rules of origin requirement to manufacture in the neighbouring countries to enter the free Indian market stands greatly diminished, India may like to review its TRQ policy to do away with quotas altogether as they no longer appear to be relevant.

In terms of non-tariff barriers, no doubt some remain but again, the incidence is not as high as has been perceived by its neighbours. In most cases these have been more in the nature of measures rather than barriers. A better understanding of the regulatory requirements through more transparent information dissemination and capacity building initiatives by India in this direction can address some of the concerns. Improving trade related infrastructure at the border and beyond would also help in addressing some of the mutual concerns of India and its trading partners in the region.

Mutual recognition agreements and recognition of accredited laboratories would obviate the need for testing after the product crosses the border as pre-shipment certification would suffice.

While India has preferential trading or free trade agreements with most countries in the region, it has none with Pakistan–a non-least developed country except under SAFTA . Under SAFTA too the full trade potential is marred by Pakistan's long negative list. Hence the scope for further liberalisation with this country holds much potential.

Finally, it must be noted that this study has been aggregative, taking the seven South Asian countries in the region as a unit for analysis. There are likely to be variations across individual countries which this study is unable to capture.

References

1. India is the reporting country and its trade is with the remaining seven countries: Afghanistan, Bangladesh, Bhutan, Maldives, Nepal, Pakistan and Sri Lanka.
2. Specific duties are imposed in terms of unit of production (quantity/ volume). In this case generally higher weight/volume products carry higher duties as compared to lower weight/volume products.
3. For a comprehensive analysis of non-tariff barriers in South Asia, see Muatafizur Rahman, "Non-tariff barriers in South Asia: Nature, implication and measures to address the Challenges," in Saman Kelegama, Ratnakar Adhikary, Pusha Sharma, Paras Kharel (eds), South Asia Watch on Trade, Economic and Environment (SAWTEE), Kathmandu, pp. 55-86.
4. Asian Development Bank and UNCTAD (2008), Quantification of benefits from economic cooperation in South Asia, https:// www.gsid.nagoya-u.ac.jp/sotsubo/SouthAsian-Quantification Benefits.
5. Taneja Nisha, Sharavani Prakash, Pallavi Kalita, India's Role in facilitating Trade under SAFTA, Working Paper 263, ICRIER, January 2013, http:/ /www.icrier.org/pdf/working_paper_263.
6. *Ibid.*
7. *Ibid.*
8. *Ibid.*
9. India Pakistan Joint Working Group (JWG), 24 August 2011 www.indiapakistantrade.org/data)jointstatement/2011.
10. Joint Statement of the 6th Round of Talks on Commercial and Economic Cooperation between Commerce Secretaries of India and Pakistan in November 2011 http://commerce.nic.in/trade/Minutes14-16Nov2011.
11. *Ibid.*
12. *Ibid.*
13. *Ibid.*

14. Tariff rate quotas allow for duty-free imports to the extent of the quota and mfn rates apply on imports above the quota.
15. For details see Indra Nath Mukherji. "India's bilateral trade agreements with Bhutan, Nepal and Sri Lanka in Trade Insight, Bilateral Trade Agreements in South Asia, South Asia Watch on Trade, Economics and Environment (SAWTEE), Kathmandu, 2010, pp. 24-26.
16. Nisha, n. 4.
17. Munawar Hasan, "Farmers demand level playing field, The News, 14 December, http://www.thenews.com.pk/Todays-News-3-148188-Farmers-demand-level-playing-field. http://commerce. nic.in/trade/ Minutes14-16Nov2011.
18. For a discussion on this see Biswajit Dhar, "Agriculture and the WTO: An Indian Perspective", http://wbwto.iift.ac.in/Downloads/WSII/ WTO%20and%20Indian% 20Agriculture.pdf; Parthapratim Pal, "Current WTO Negotiations on Domestic Subsidies in Agriculture: implications for India", *Working Paper* no. 177, Indian Council for Research in International Economic Relations, New Delhi. p. 37, http:/ /www.icrier.org/pdf/wp%20177.

4

Maritime Connectivity and Cooperation in South Asia: Issues and Concerns

Adluri Subramanyam Raju

Introduction

Three-fourth of the world is covered by seawater. Sea has been focus of mankind's concern. It is important to human development. There are four attributes of the sea: as a resource, as a means of transportation, information and dominion.[1] Sea based trade leads to mutual benefit, partnership, peace, stability and security. Sea connects different people, cultures, civilisations, governments and plays a role in globalisation (borderless and trade). Ninety five per cent of the world's trade is sailed through sea.[2] Over sixty per cent of ships fly flags different from the nationality of their owners. Thus, maritime has become a dominant factor in global affairs. On the other hand, there are various threats emanate from the sea such as illegal trade, drug trafficking, terrorism, floods, tsunami, environmental degradation and rise of sea level. Since the threats through sea seem to be increasing, the littoral states need to enhance their cooperation on maritime/coastal security.

There are three land locked/linked countries (Afghanistan, Bhutan and Nepal), two island states (The Maldives and Sri Lanka) and three semi-land and maritime countries (Bangladesh, India and Pakistan). In other words, five of the South Asian countries are littoral/coastal states. Before partition in 1947, South Asia was well connected because there were no such international borders.[3] The region had integrated transport system during the British but this was fractured due to partition and its political aftermath. The paper analyses issues related to resolving the maritime borders and fishermen problems, enhancing shipping and maritime connectivity and addressing maritime threats by the littoral states collectively, which would enhance maritime connectivity in South Asia. Further, the paper examines the joint initiatives towards regional maritime security management among the South Asian maritime states.

Maritime Boundary

At the time of independence or in the immediate post-Independence era, India, Pakistan (Bangladesh was part of Pakistan) and Sri Lanka did not have maritime boundaries officially demarcated as they were ruled by one imperial power. This situation changed drastically after independence and there was a necessity of defining their maritime jurisdictions. Unfortunately, no littoral state felt the need to consult the other to determine its maritime zone.

The UNCLOS-III was ratified and came into force on 16 November, 1994.[4] It provides for a littoral state or island state to have 200 nm of exclusive economic zone (EEZ), in which the state has the exclusive right to explore and exploit the resources available.[5] India, Pakistan, Bangladesh, the Maldives and Sri Lanka are signatories of UNCLOS-III.

India has maritime border with all unlike any other country in South Asia. Sri Lanka has maritime boundary with India and the Maldives, whereas Pakistan and Bangladesh have borders with only India in South Asia. India, Sri Lanka and the Maldives delimited their maritime boundary by signing two agreements in 1976. India has come to an understanding with Pakistan and Bangladesh on some of the maritime issues. Recently India and Bangladesh had agreed to resolve their maritime boundaries. However, India and Pakistan are yet to demarcate their boundary.

(a) India and Sri Lanka and the Maldives

The Island state of Sri Lanka barely thirty kilometers away from India's southern coastal tip. The maritime boundary of India and Sri Lanka is divided at through three different points in different seas: the Bay of Bengal in the north, the Palk Straits in the middle and the Gulf of Mannar in the south. The maximum distance between these two countries in the Palk Straits is about 45 km and the minimum distance is around 16 km between Dhanushkodi on the Indian side and Thalaimannar on the Sri Lankan coast. They do not have (EEZ) in the area. They have rights over 12 to 22 km of water. Crossing that area means crossing the international boundary line rather than the EEZ. The coast of both the countries is larger in the Bay of Bengal and in the Gulf of Mannar.

India and Sri Lanka had signed bilateral agreements on the Boundary in Historic Waters in June 1974 and on the maritime boundary in the Gulf of Mannar and the Bay of Bengal in March 1976.[6] They also signed a Supplementary Agreement in November 1976 on the extension of the maritime boundary between the two countries in the Gulf of Mannar from position 13 m to the Trijunction point between India, Sri Lanka and Maldives (point T). Both the countries had settled the dispute over the Kachchativu Island by 1974 which was there between the two since the British rule.[7]

(b) India and Pakistan

The delimitation of the boundary along the Sir Creek and the demarcation of the maritime boundary in the Arabian Sea are two issues involved in the dispute between India and Pakistan. The Rann of Kutch is located between the Sind province of Pakistan and the Gujarat state of India. It is neither enough to navigate nor enough to farm. It has two distinct formations i.e., Great Rann and the Little Rann. The Great Rann has 18,000 sq.km. and lies almost within Gujarat and extends 256 kms. From west to east the width is between 40 and 100 km. The Little Rann stretches from east to west for about 110 km. and has about 500 sq.km. In the north, the Rann lies in Sind, a province of Pakistan and its south and east are the Kutch and Kathiawar regions of the Gujarat state of India. The Rann submerges in water four to five feet deep during May to October and the rest of the year it becomes a salty desert. Sir Creek is a 100 km. long estuary in the marshes of the Rann of Kutch which lies on the border between Gujarat and Sind. It is a fluctuating tidal channel and not a flowing creek. Till 1954, the border around the Sir Creek between India and Pakistan had been opened. Later it became a contentious issue between them. Pakistan insists demarcating the Creek boundary as a precondition for delimiting the maritime boundary. It demands drawing a line on the basis of the principle of equity, whereas India wants to draw a line along the middle of the Creek. Both the countries are yet to resolve the problem. It is believed that the Creek has sub-sea oil and gas deposits.[8]

(c) India and Bangladesh

After Bangladesh attained independence from Pakistan in 1971, it signed agreements with India on many issues.[9] However, both had differences on two issues i.e., demarcation of maritime boundary and sovereignty over a small Island.

Both the countries had difference over their maritime boundary over the small Island called New Moore or Purbasha in India and South Talpatty in Bangladesh, which is situated two nautical miles off the coast of India and five nautical miles off the coast of Bangladesh. This small Island emerged in 1970 after the wake of acute volcanic activity in the area. It was appeared on a satellite picture in 1975. However, recently the island was submerged.

India advocated equidistant or median line, whereas Bangladesh sought the application of the equitable principle. Both countries had taken rigid stand over the Island. India claimed the Island on the ground that the flow of the Haribhanga river is to the east of the Island and the Island lies on the natural prolongation of Indian territory. Whereas Bangladesh argued that the river flows to the west of the Island and it would be not possible to separate the natural prolongation of Indian territory and because of the concave shape of its coastlines and instability of its coast caused by periodic cyclones, soil erosion etc. Both the countries claim for the Island was due to natural resources in the Ganges-Brahmaputra delta of the Bay of Bengal. There were many meetings held between India and Bangladesh on the maritime dispute since 1974. They could not find a mutually acceptable solution despite engaging in eight rounds of bilateral negotiations between 1974 and 2009.

On 8 October 2009, Bangladesh referred the case to the International Tribunal for the Law of the Sea (ITLOS) under Article 287 and Annex VII of UNCLOS-III, 1982. The case was subsequently moved to the Hague-based Permanent Court of Arbitration (PCA) in May 2011. The Arbitration Tribunal announced its verdict on 7 July 2014. In a judgment, the PCA awarded Bangladesh an area of 19,467 square kilometers of the total area of 25,602 sq. km. disputed maritime boundary in the Bay of Bengal with India. The tribunal's award clearly delineated the course of maritime boundary line between the two countries in the territorial sea, EEZ and continental shelf within and beyond 200 nautical miles. The major issues of India-Bangladesh maritime disputes include: location of land boundary terminus; delimitation of territorial sea; delimitation of EEZ and legal continental shelf. But after the verdict, the sea areas of India shall be 117 nm from Balasore coast and that of Bangladesh shall be 169 nm from Cox's Bazar coast in the Bay of Bengal. The verdict recognised India's sovereignty over New Moore Island and received nearly 6,000 sq. km. of the contested zone including the area where once the Cap island had existed. While India's rights over extended continental shelf has been protected to a large extent, Bangladesh has acquired an outlet in the continental shelf.[10]

Fishermen (In) Security

Sixty per cent of the global population lives in coastal areas. Fish is an important source of protein for the poor in developing countries. It is one of the key sources of employment. Ninety per cent of fishermen are living below the poverty line,[11] so they go in search of fish wherever they are available. In their pursuit, they hardly respect maritime boundaries. South Asia has tremendous dependency on seaborne trade. It constitutes less than one per cent of the worldwide workforce but accounts for seven per cent of workforce mortality. Out of thirty seven million fishermen worldwide, about fifty per cent are in Bangladesh, India, Maldives, Sri Lanka and Pakistan. About 24,000 deaths occur in a year due to accidents/hazards at sea, and 7000 occur in South Asia.[12]

The South Asian fishermen have no alternative other than poaching neighbours' waters for fishing as their survival depends on fishing in neighbours waters. For instance, Indian fishermen cross the Sri Lankan and the Pakistani waters. Similarly, Sri Lankan fishermen cross their boundary and enter Indian and Maldivans waters for fishing and so as the case with Pakistani and Bangladeshi fishermen. In spite of the restrictions imposed by the respective countries' Navy, the fishermen enter the neighbours' waters for fishing. They argue that they do not have any other alternative than this as their survival depends on fishing in others waters.[13] Ocean is the workplace and survival is important and for them borders wither away.

Fishermen in South Asia are being arrested by neighbouring security forces and it is against the UNCLOS-III Article 73, which forbids the imprisonment of fishermen who are found poaching.[14] The respective Navy suspect the sailors as agents of their country. Till date the fishermen of each country are not arrested on the ground that they were carrying arms and ammunitions on board. Often the fishermen are being arrested because of security reasons. Indian and Pakistani fishermen are being arrested/ killed by authorities of the other side. Indian fishermen are suspected collaborating with Research and Analysis Wing by Pakistani security, while Pakistani fishermen are suspected to be the agents of Inter-Service Intelligence by Indian forces. The fishermen of both the countries are often arrested for crossing borders and they are becoming victims of undefined boundaries. They are being treated as prisoners of war.

There is no clear policy regarding the release of the arrested fishermen. There are incidents where the fishermen were being arrested and kept in jails for years together on both sides. Their release always depends on the state of relations between the countries. Often the fishermen are released in equal numbers on both sides. The arrested fishermen on both sides are suffering during their stay in jail. There are no proper sanitation facilities, lack of privacy and keep many of them in a crowded place.[15] The fishermen mistake is to cross over into the neighbour's waters for their livelihood. They are socially and economically poor.

Fortunately a breakthrough has been made between India and Pakistan and India and Sri Lanka to agree on a bilateral code of conduct minimising the inter-boundary cross over by the fishermen. Over the past few years, as part of the ongoing peace process the maritime dispute mechanism has been consciously incorporated into the negotiations agenda. There is evidence of the countries adopting a benign and human approach in treating the maritime trespassers. Nevertheless, positive bilateral initiatives need to be concretised into long-term plans to put an end to arrest the fishermen, who cross each other's. The nations must adopt a humanistic and sympathetic approach towards the fishermen who are crossing into each other's waters.

Shipping and Maritime Connectivity

During 1948-49, the bilateral trade between India and Pakistan was between thirty five to fifty per cent but now it has been reduced to one per cent or less due to restrictive tariff barriers and lack of transport system between them. However, in recent times, the maritime states in the region began to work towards restoration of unrestricted direct trade and shipping links. They identified maritime gateways (see Table-1) and agreed to develop their ports and enhance their trade through waters. There is a greater trade potential between them. South Asian trade would be enhanced if the region is connected. Maritime transport plays an important role in international trade.

Major trade is being conducted by the sea and hence ports play a significant role in economic development. About seventy per cent of connectivity within region is through road and rail. However, maritime transport plays a dominant role in shipping the trade to other countries.[16] The seventeenth SAARC Summit (2011) held in the Maldives declared the implementation of the Indian Ocean Cargo and Passenger Ferry Services as a priority. In a study, it was recommended ferry routings between the Maldives, Sri Lanka and India to facilitate passenger movement and trade between them.[17] The main constraint for the ports in South Asia is that adequate channel depth is not available and it fluctuates considerably with tides and over seasons (particularly in Haldia and Kolkata), cargo and ship handling equipment, and old floating craft, poor rail connectivity with the hinterland.

Table-1: Maritime Gateways

SAARC Country	*The Coastal Line Facing*	*Coastal Distance*	*Principal ports for SAARC trade*
Bangladesh	Bay of Bengal	580 kms	Chittagong, Mongla,
India	Arabian Sea on West Coast	7,517 kms	Kandla, Mumbai, Mormugao, New Mangalore, J.N.P.T, Cochin
	Bay of Bengal on East Coast	n/a	Chennai, Haldia, Kolkata, Paradip, Visakhapatnam, Tuticorin
Maldives	Indian Ocean	Comprises of Islands of 1190, corals and stretches of 470	Male
Pakistan	Arabian Sea	1,100 kms	Karachi, Port Bin Qasim, Gwadar
Sri Lanka	Indian Ocean	1,600 kms	Colombo, Trincomallee, Hambantota

Ports suffer from insufficient harbour area and channel depths to accommodate larger vessels. Non-physical barriers include poor port administration and management; no computerisation for operations in some ports. Customs procedures are complicated and time consuming at all ports. Ports need to be constructed to provide connectivity across the region and reduce transport cost.[18] In its report, Asian Development Bank discussed the status of SAARC Regional Multimodal Transport (SRMT) Corridors identified ten gateways in South Asia. The report mentions about barriers and suggest recommendations for improvement of maritime transport in South Asia.[19]

Figure 1: Liner Shipping Connectivity Index[20]

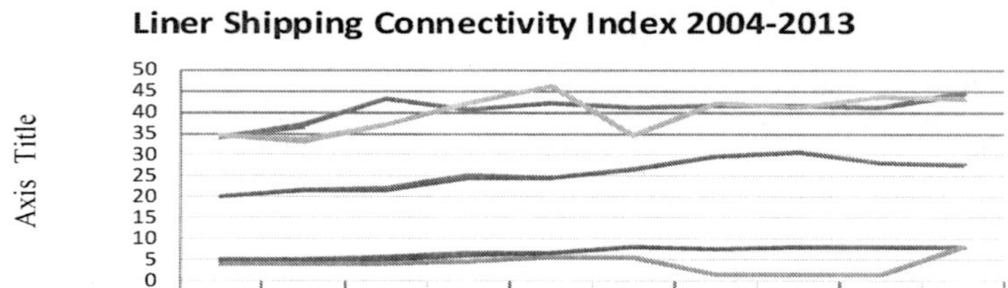

	2004	2005	2006	2007	2008	2009	2010	2011	2012	2013
India	34.14	36.88	42.9	40.47	42.18	40.97	41.4	41.52	41.29	44.35
Pakistan	20.18	21.49	21.82	24.77	24.61	26.58	29.48	30.54	28.12	27.71
Sri Lanka	34.68	33.36	37.31	42.23	46.08	34.74	42.3	41.13	43.43	43.01
Bangladesh	5.2	5.07	5.29	6.36	6.4	7.91	7.55	8.15	8.02	7.96
Maldives	4.15	4.08	3.9	4.75	5.45	5.43	1.65	1.62	1.6	8.12

Source: *UNCTAD STAT, unctadstat.unctad.org/wds/tTableViewer/tableview.aspx?ReportId = 92 Graph was drawn on the basis of the above data provided by the UNCTAD STAT.*

The trade across the world is depending on building the capacity and efficiency of major seaports, particularly container ports. No port in South Asia is among one of the world's top ten busiest container ports. Shipping connectivity is still poor in South Asia. The South Asian coastal states are connected by direct shipping services or by transshipment and transit operations through hub ports such as Colombo.[21] Three landlocked countries and one Island country (the Maldives) in South Asia depend on transshipment ports in neighbouring countries for their trade. According to the United Nations Conference on Trade and Development (UNCTAD) Liner Shipping Connectivity Index, between 2004-2013, shipping connectivity increased in South Asian littoral countries such as Sri Lanka, Pakistan and India, while for the Maldives deteriorated during 2010-12 and increased in 2013 (Figure-1). Though the Maldives is archipelago, it could not able to improve its LSCI due to weak infrastructure and port. Bangladesh LSCI in 2013 is less than other countries in South Asia. Though Sri Lanka LSCI is less than India but it seems to be that it would enhance its LSCI more than India in the near future due to Hambantota port is being in operational. Prabir De cited an ESCAP study, which argues if a country's liner connectivity index improves, the cost of shipping declines, increase competitiveness and container traffic. The countries, which have declined in liner shipping connectivity, are likely to have higher trade costs. South Asian littoral states can have more ships by investing and improving infrastructure and efficiency of land transport i.e., road and railways.[22] A regional commission in South Asia may be set-up in exchanging information on regulations and encouraging competition of shipping services. Through maritime connectivity, landlocked countries would also enhance their trade through transit ports.[23]

From the above figure, one can see that Sri Lanka has more access and the Maldives less to liner shipping network. Three out of five littoral countries of South Asia has accessibility to global trade, where major shipping takes place. For instance, twelve major ports (Chennai, Kochi, Ennore, Jawaharlal Nehru, Kolkata, including Haldia, Kandla, Mormugao, Mumbai, New Mangalore, Paradip, Tuticorin and Visakhapatnam) of India have a capacity to handle over 740 million tonns of cargo per year and account for about fifty eight per cent of external trade shipped by sea.[24]

Constraints

There was no transit MFN (Most Favoured Nation) between India and Bangladesh. Shipment of Assam tea to the West required it to be transported 1,400 km to reach Kolkata port along the Chicken Neck. There is no agreement exists for India to use the traditional route through Chittagong port which would be shorter by sixty per cent. The southern border of Tripura state is only 75 km from Chittagong port, but goods from Agartala are required to travel 1645 km to reach Kolkata port through the Chicken neck. If transport cooperation were there, goods would have travelled around 400 km across Bangladesh to reach Kolkata.[25]

One can understand how India and Pakistan are unable to promote maritime trade due to trust deficiency between them. After the Simla agreement in July 1972, India and Pakistan signed the 1974 Protocol on Resumption of Trade. Further the Protocol on Resumption of Shipping Services was signed by the two countries in January 1975. Due to the clause of 1975 protocol were so restrictive on ship registrations, volumes of cargo, equality principles, etc., resulted in a sharp decline in trade. The meeting in 1976 between the officials of both the countries discussed the transit trade to landlocked countries, carriage of passengers, shore leave of seamen and delay in freight remittance.[26] The shipping protocol stipulates, "Neither country can lift third country liner cargo originating from the ports of either country and destined for ports in third countries and vice versa."[27] The Indian ships are not allowed to carry cargo from Pakistan ports to any country other than India and Pakistani ships are not allowed to carry cargo from Indian ports to any third country. This protocol has ignored shipping concerns on both sides of the border by restricting them to lifting only bilateral cargo, which is insignificant. The reason for India not taking the issue with Pakistan may be because of the latter's denial of granting MFN status to the former. It is to be noted that India granted MFN status to Pakistan in 1996.

A flag vessel of other country, other than India and Pakistan, benefits as it falls outside the purview of the protocol. The shipping activity will not be improved unless the protocol is revised.[28] Pakistani shipping would largely benefit if allowed to join various consortiums to lift cargo to the Indian ports. Similarly Indian ship owners, having larger fleets, would benefit if they are allowed to lift the cargo at Karachi/Port Qasim Authority especially with transit cargo for Afghanistan. Currently this lucrative business goes by default to third-flag vessels. Trade is almost conducted by sea and will be continued in the future. To allow unrestricted flow of trade, it is necessary to revise the Shipping Protocol of 1975, clause five and nine of the Protocol[29] , which would help in enhancing direct trade, reducing shipping time as well as freight charges. It would also reduce smuggling and bring profits to the cargo. The two sides have discussed the issue of restoration of passenger services between Karachi and Mumbai, but a decision is yet to be taken. Transshipment between India and Pakistan is yet to be resolved. Due to absence of direct access between Indian and Pakistan vessels, maritime trade between the two countries is routed through a third country.

Connecting South Asia through Land Bridge between India-Sri Lanka

Indian and Sri Lankan governments had signed an agreement to construct a bridge between Rameswaram in Tamil Nadu and Talaimannar in Sri Lanka (see Map-1) in July 2002.[30] Through this, road, rail and bridge links would be developed, which would offer huge economic benefits to both sides of the Palk Straits.[31] Through this bridge, movement of people and cargo would be increased, which would result in increasing economic opportunities for both the countries. It would reduce travel, time and cost for the movement of goods and services.

This bridge would facilitate improving trade not only between the two countries but also among the South Asian countries (see Map-2). It was reported that the depth of water does not exceed Seven meters at any point. The study proposed a six-lane combination of bridges, causeways, and rail track.

Map-1: Sri Lankan Corridor

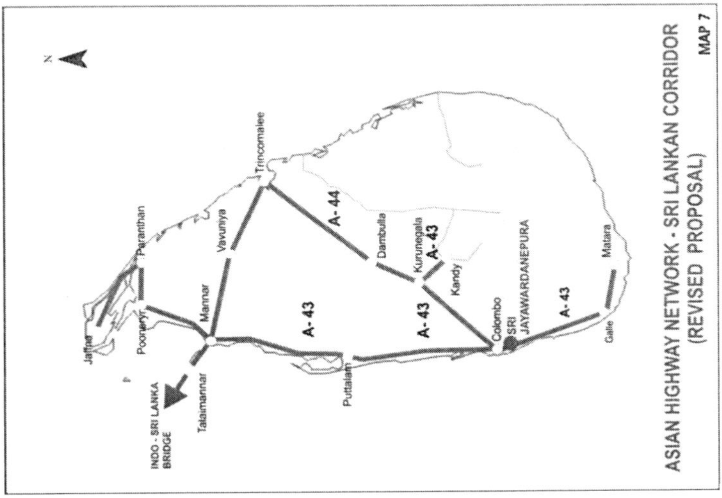

Map-2: Indian Corridor

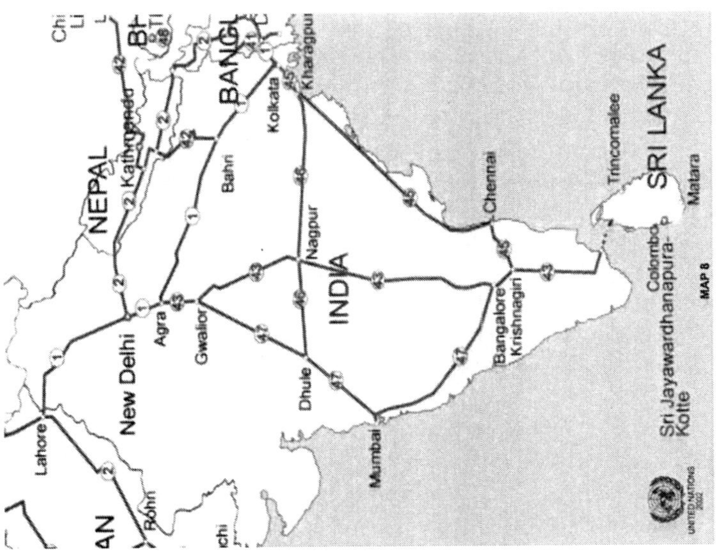

The bridge could become a connecting link between the national highways in south India and those in Sri Lanka. It would facilitate a continuous road and ferry link from Madurai to Trincomalee for cargo and passengers. Through this, Madurai and major cities of southern India can be connected through road and rail linkages.[32] The bridge would offer linkage to industries and agro-industries in South India and Sri Lanka. The link between Bangalore-Chennai-Trincomalee-Colombo would be possible and improve relations between the two countries. India must play a constructive role not only because it is emerging as one of the major economies but also geographically it shares border with South Asian countries.

Maritime Challenges

Governance at sea is to safeguarding the sea frontiers, ports, off shore; protecting marine ecosystem, lives and property; sea lanes of communication; and preventing smuggling, poaching, piracy, gun running and trafficking. Piracy has been very active in the Arabian Sea and the Indian Ocean region. According to the World Bank estimations, piracy costs the world economy about $18 billion a year.[33] Some pirates (Somalians) extend their activities upto 700 nm in the Indian Ocean region, whereas the littoral states have only 200 nm jurisdiction over the waters as EEZ. Since India and Pakistan are closer to the Gulf of Aden and the Horn of Africa, tackling piracy activity has become matter of concern.

About 400 million people live along the coastline of South Asia and the coastal communities in the region are exposed to natural hazards.[34] The discourse on climate change reveals that the entire humanity would face numerous problems such as rise of sea level, environmental hazards, cyclones, droughts, health problems, water scarcity etc., due to green house gases emissions. Though, the developing countries were no way responsible for global warming, they have to face the problem, because impact of climate change would be more on them than developed countries.

Large-scale migration from coastal zones is expected due to submergence of coast-lines after sea levels rise. This will create a large number of environmental refugees especially from low-lying regions in poor countries. Intrusion of sea-water in the ground water and changes in temperature can have impact on agricultural incomes. Climate change could represent an additional stress on ecological and socio-economic systems that are already facing tremendous pressure. Sea level rise will damage aquaculture industries, fish productivity, higher risks of increased frequency and intensity of coastal surges and cyclones. Global ocean heat content, according to the Intergovernmental Panel for Climate Change (IPCC), has increased since late 1950s. Due to the impact of climate change, it is expected that the sea level will grow up.

It is estimated that by 2050, about 250 million people may be displaced from their places due to intensifying monsoon flooding, desertification and reduced food production. Most of the developing countries, which are dependent on coastal fishery and agriculture, are likely to be affected. If a one-meter sea level rise were to take place today, it would displace seven million people in India. Many cities in the world grew in the coastal areas and in South Asia we find cities such as Chennai, Kolkata, Mumbai, Karachi, Colombo, Dhaka etc. It would be difficult to see the growth of any country if major cities are affected due to rise of sea level. Mumbai is one of the largest cities in the world and the economic capital of India. It was estimated that the cost to Mumbai of a one meter sea level rise at $71 billion, indicative of the huge economic cost of climate change faced by Asia's coastal city.[35] In the future many more may be displaced.

It was estimated that thirty-five per cent of the land in Bangladesh would be submerged by a one-meter rise. The Maldives will completely be submerged by 2100 or uninhabited due to the loss of fresh water. If 1.5 mts rise of sea level, eighty per cent of island will be submerged. Sri Lanka will have similar problem. Floods along the Ganges and Brahmaputra rivers in 2007 affected about thirteen million people in Bangladesh and economic cost was over one billion dollars. In Pakistan, in 2010 floods, twenty million people were affected and economic cost was around ten billion dollars. Land locked countries (Afghanistan, Bhutan and Nepal) will too have problems due to droughts and short of rainfalls. If rise of sea level will be inevitable, then certainly it will have negative impact on shipping connectivity as well as the ports/harbours in the region.

Conclusion

The littoral states of South Asia have been facing more or less similar problems on sea such as terrorism, piracy, illegal trade etc. Since, these problems cannot be tackled/ addressed by any single country, all the South Asian countries have to work collectively. They have to think in terms of encoding a common maritime conduct and regional maritime law.

There is a greater need to enhance mutual cooperation on maritime security. Through cooperation, they can share weather forecasting. For instance, the Indian satellites monitor the dynamics of clouds over the Indian Ocean region and the Indian Meteorological Department uses meteorological data from these satellites for operational weather forecasting.[36] The South Asian littoral states have to jointly work to develop early warning systems to avoid problems on the sea such as floods, tsunami etc. The major barriers for maritime transport are: capacity constraints, heavy siltation at navigation channels where depths fluctuate with tide, inadequate and poor maintenance of channel markings, old technology in cargo and ship handling equipment and floating crafts.[37] In view of rising merchandise trade, South Asian littoral countries have to strengthen their maritime profile for self reliance. A regional agreement to allow small sea shipping in South Asia will not only enhance ferry services across the region but also strengthen maritime profile of the countries. Through maritime cooperation/connectivity, the South Asian countries not only enhance trade but also regional cooperation in the region.

References

1. Geoffrey Till, *Sea Power*, London: Routledge, 2009, p. 23.
2. *Ibid.*, p. 26.
3. National Transport Development Policy Committee, *Promoting International Transport Connectivity between South and Southeast Asia's Region, 2013,* New Delhi: Planning commission, Government of India, p. 621.
4. UNCLOS-I was held in 1958. The conference provided guidelines for "the use of bays, islands, straits, base lines as well as 12 miles contiguous zone within which coastal states were authorised to enforce their customs, fiscal, immigration and sanitary regulations. The coastal state had territory right till 3 nautical miles from the coasts." Between 1958 and 1960, several countries claimed to extend their jurisdictions over territorial seas to 12 nm from 3 nm. But the maritime powers (the US, the former USSR, UK and France) did not agree to extend the territorial zone. See James B. Morell, *The Law of the Sea,* Jefferson, Missouri: McFarland, 1992, p. 8.
5. Stockholm International Peace Research Institute, SIPRI Year *Book 1988,* Sweden: Stockholm International Peace Research Institute, 1988, p. 26.
6. For details see A. Subramanyam Raju and S. Keethaponcalan, *Maritime Cooperation between India and Sri Lanka,* New Delhi: Manohar Publishers, 2006.
7. *Ibid.*
8. For more details see A. Subramanyam Raju, "Maritime Confidence Building Measures Between India and Pakistan", *Pakistan Journal of International Relations*, Vol.1, No.1, July 2009, pp.111-135.

9. Issues: a comprehensive new boundary agreement, 1974; the Indo-Bangladesh Land Boundary Agreement, 1974 (but it is yet to be ratified); the Indo-Bangladesh Water Sharing Treaty, 1996; India lifts non-tariff barriers, 1998; a Joint Indo-Bangladesh Chamber of Commerce has been established.
10. Rupak Bhattacharjee, "Maritime ruling lifts Delhi-Dhaka prospects", *Asia Times,* 18 August, 2014, http://www.atimes.com/atimes/South_Asia/SOU-01-180814.html
11. National Fishworkers Forum, *Charter of Demands 2002,* Thiruvananthapuram: National Fishworkers Forum, 2002, p. 23.
12. Rear Admiral Daya Dharmapriya, "Countering Maritime Piracy: A South Asian Perspective", http://oceansbeyondpiracy.org/sites/default/files/dharmapriyas_paper_formatted.pdf
13. In his field study, the author met the affected fishermen's families in Tuticorin and Rameswaram districts. They said that their whole family was dependent on fishing activities. They don't have any other source of income. Since women can't fish in the waters, they have to depend on their husbands only.
14. UNCLOS-III Part-V, Article73, under Enforcement of laws and regulations of the coastal State, "Arrested vessels and their crews shall be promptly released upon the posting of reasonable bond or other security."
15. For the fishermen experience in jail, see Charu Gupta and Mukul Sharma, "Blurred Borders: Coastal Conflicts between India and Pakistan", *Economic and Political Weekly*, Vol. 39, No. 27, 3 July 2004, pp. 3010-3013.
16. National Transport Development Policy Committee, "Promoting International Transport Connectivity between India and the South and South East Asian Regions", Chapter-13, p. 642, http://planningcommission.nic.in/sectors/NTDPC/voume2_p2/promoting_v2_p2.pdf
17. *Ibid,* p. 643
18. *Ibid.*
19. Asian Development Bank, Working Paper, *SAARC Regional Multi Modal Transport Corridors,* Prepared by Partha S. Banerjee in consultations with Government Officials from South Asian countries and SAARC Secretariat, Manila, 2012, cited in National Transport Development Policy Committee, "Promoting International Transport Connectivity between India and the South and South East Asian Regions", Chapter-13, pp. 664-671, http://planningcommission.nic.in/sectors/NTDPC/voume2_p2/promoting_v2_p2.pdf
20. LSCI is to capture a country's level of integration into existing liner shipping networks by measuring liner shipping connectivity.
21. Prabir De, *Connectivity, Trade Facilitation and Regional Cooperation in South Asia,* April 2013, p. 4.

http://ris.org.in/images/RIS_images/pdf/Southper cent20Asiaper cent 20meetingper cent202-3per cent20mayper cent2020013per cent20PPT/ Prabirper cent20De.pdf

22. *Ibid.*, p. 5.
23. *Ibid.*, p. 6.
24. UNCTAD, *Review of Maritime Transport 2013*, New York: UN, 2013, p. 97, http://unctad.org/en/publicationslibrary/rmt2013_en .pdf
25. M. Rahmatullah, "Transport Issues and Integration in South Asia", in Sadiq Ahmed, Saman Kelegama and Egaz Ghani (eds), *Promoting Economic Cooperation in South Asia: Beyond SAFTA*, New Delhi: Sage Publication, 2010, p. 178.
26. See Raju, n.8, p. 126.
27. Hasan Ansari and Ravi Vohra, *Confidence Building Measures at Sea: Opportunities for India and Pakistan,* New Mexico: Sandia National Laboratories, December, 2003, p. 23.
28. De, n.21, p. 34.
29. Nirupama Subramanian, "India-Pakistan trade stuck on SAFTA", *The Hindu,* 31 July 2006.
30. The bridge would carry transmission lines to hook up Sri Lanka to India's Southern Region Electricity Grid with the Kudankulam nuclear power plant serving as a base load station. Both countries can cooperate in the area of power if an electric grid stretching from Nepal to Sri Lanka is established. It is reported that a firm (NEXANT) carried out a study on the feasibility of a 30-km submerged High-Voltage Direct Current (HVDC) link through the Palk Straits between the two countries for export of 500 MW power to Sri Lanka.
31. Ranil Wickemesinghe, "Making Our People Rich", *The Hindu*, 25 August 2004, p. 10.
32. Arjuna Mahendram and Rajive Casie Chitty, "Hanuman's Bridge: Facilitating Trade and Investment between Sri Lanka and Southern India", *South Asian Survey,* Vol.7, No.1, January-June 2000, p. 31.
33. Salman Khurshid, Julie Bishop and Marty Natalegawa, "Putting out to Sea a new Vision", *The Hindu,* 2 November 2013, p. 9.
34. Sriyanie Miththapala, Vishwas Sawarkar, Pramod Krishnan and Madhavi Malalgoda Ariyabandu, *A Toolkit for Integrating Disaster Risk Reduction and Climate Change Adaptation into Ecosystem Management of Coastal and Marine areas in South Asia,* South Asian Consulatative Workshop, New Delhi, 6-7 March 2012, http://www.undp.org/content/dam/undp/ library/Environmentper cent20andper cent20Energy/biodiversity/ UNISDR-UNDP-Ecosystem-Management-of-Coastal-and-Marine-Areas-in-South-Asia.pdf
35. TERI (Tata Energy Research Institute), "The Economic Impact of a One-Metre Sea Level Rise on the Indian Coastline: Method and Case Studies" (report submitted to the Ford Foundation, 2006),

cited in Roland J. Fuchs, "Cities at Risk: Asia's Coastal Cities in an Age of Climate Change", *Asia Pacific,* no. 96, July 2010, p. 4, http://www.eastwestcenter.org/fileadmin/stored/pdfs/api096.pdf .

36. Gaurav Rajen, *Cooperative Environmental Monitoring in the Coastal Regions of India and Pakistan,* http://www.cmc.sandia. gov/links/cmc-papers/sand-98-0505-11/sand-98-0505-11.html

37. See De, n. 21, p. 34.

5

Conflict, Transition, Connectivity and Regional Integration in South Asia

Som P Pudasaini

Harmonious relations, disputes resolution and adequate connectivity are critical for enhancing regional integration and prosperity in South Asia. However, inter-state and intra-state conflicts are widely prevalent in South Asia. Also, intra-state and inter-state connectivity is far from satisfactory. Consequently, connectivity is a major problem in the region. Increased focus on conflict resolution, infrastructural development, better transport and communication networks and greater intra-regional trade must be at the heart of the South Asian agenda. Recent SAARC summits have been increasingly committed to strengthening connectivity and regional integration. Efforts are also underway to tackle bilateral and regional conflicts. Progress towards achieving these goals has, however, been sluggish. The foremost need now is to build neighbourly diplomacy among SAARC nations. Only with better intra-region relations will it be possible to tackle the difficult work of poverty reduction, conflict resolution, greater connectivity, regional integration, enhanced security, greater energy development, enhanced intra-regional trade and addressing illegal activities at international borders demand prioritisation and commitment. While SAARC has only a limited progress, it is hoped that leaders are ready to "truly commit to the South Asian regionalism". But the question is "Can the SAARC leaders now rise above petty national interests and ego to commit to the South Asian regionalism to build a prosperous region through shared wisdom and resources based on equality, friendship, understanding and comparative advantages?"[1]

This paper explores above themes in three sections. The first section briefly sketches the state of broad political relations and disputes between the different South Asian nations. Key conflicts and disputes, which have come to dominate and hamper bilateral and regional harmony, are particularly highlighted. The second section tackles the state of the connectivity agenda within SAARC. Across both this sections, there will be in-depth focus on Nepal, particularly the Indo-Nepal relationship in the South Asian regional context. The advantages and barriers evident in this relationship also demonstrate common problems faced across the region, in other bilateral relationships. The third section concludes by presenting possible pathways to improve regional integration and connectivity.

The State of Diplomacy and Disputes Within SAARC

Many key factors shape the state of diplomacy and nature of disputes within SAARC. Political mistrust, perceived or real interference in internal affairs and territorial or border disputes are, however, three overarching factors in the regional mindset. As the largest and most powerful state, India plays a big role in these arenas. First, it is the only country that borders with all the other seven SAARC nation-states. Second, because it sees the region as its backyard, it plays a major or minor role in the internal affairs of the other nation-states regularly or on an adhoc basis depending on its top political leadership in New Delhi and the power as well as perceptions of its foreign affairs, military and security apparatus. This exertion of influence is often a source of resentment for the smaller nation-states and its citizens even though some politicians in these countries may themselves be occasionally culprits in inviting some interference to meet their short-term political and economic interests. Of all the SAARC relationships, India and Pakistan continue to be most insecure about their relationships. The tension and disputes between India and Pakistan, which happens to be the second most powerful SAARC member, has been a major constraint to better connectivity and integration of the region.

In addition, China, a nation with an observer status in SAARC currently, has been strengthening its political, economic, security and trade relations with almost all the SAARC member states. The rising influence of China in the region also adds to India's sense of insecurity and periodically colours its relationship with the other member-states even though China is already a big trading partner of India itself.

While tensions between Pakistan and India are the biggest bottleneck for the promotion of SAARC regionalism and neighbourly diplomacy, there was some hope that the peace initiative, which faltered after the 2008 attacks on Mumbai, would be reinitiated after Pakistani prime minister

Nawaz Sharif and Indian former minister Manmohan Singh committed to dialogue. However, the nostalgia of potential talks evaporated quickly after killing of five Indian soldiers in Kashmir on 6 August, 2013, according to India by Pakistani Special Forces. Pakistan denied the accusation. The 'New Beginning' expected to start with Nawaz Sharif's participation at Narendra Modi's inauguration as India's prime minister on 26 May, 2014 also has not made any constructive difference in continuing tense Indo-Pak relations. In fact, Nawaz Sharif's address at the United Nations General Assembly on 26 September strongly raising the issue of Kashmir and non-implementation of 1948 UN Resolution. The following day, Narendra Modi addressed the assembly stressing that the UN is not the right forum to raise bilateral issue. He further stressed that dialogue with Pakistan would only be possible in peaceful environment 'without the shadow of terrorism'. Neither of these statements suggests an immediate move towards the possibility of a new beginning. In fact, shootouts took place between border security forces of the two nations in Kashmir further souring the goodwill badly. According to the *Himalayan Times* "the death toll from this week's cross-border violence rose to 17" and "thousands of civilians living on both sides of the border" were fleeing their homes.[2]

India also feels insecure as China's influence over its neighbourhood increases. This is especially true of the increasing China-Pakistan camaraderie. China's interest in the region and its alliance with Pakistan is well-established and is being continually strengthened. For instance, "The operation of the Gwadar port, located near the Strait of Hormuz, was handed to the China Overseas Port Holding Co. last year, a success in China's plan to secure maritime hubs around the Indian Ocean. Regional rivals such as India are suspicious that the Gwadar port deal may strengthen military ties between Islamabad and Beijing."[3] Alongside ports in Pakistan and Sri Lanka, Beijing and Islamabad are currently negotiating the construction of a New Economic Corridor from Kashgar (in Xinjiang) to Gwadar. China has also made some moves to improve road links and modernise harbours across South Asia. The Corridor would consist of a series of special economic zones, a rail link, and a pipeline. The project would give China greater access to the Indian Ocean, further enhancing New Delhi's suspicion.

India's tension with China results from border issues as well as competition for strategic leadership in South Asia and beyond. The border issue dates back to 1914 when Britain signed an agreement with Tibet making the McMahon Line the de-facto border which the People's Republic of China does not accept. However, its trade with China has reached almost US $ 70 billion by 2014 and likely to reach $100 billion soon. But its trade deficit with China has also surged to more than $ 40bn from $1bn in 2001-2002. During the Chinese President Xi Jinping's India visit, during 17-19 September, 2014, Indian prime minister Narendra Modi and Xi agreed to 'revitalise' the India-China relationship and pledged to work towards peace at the disputed border. In addition, India and China signed twelve agreements, including the one in which China agreed to invest $20bn in India's infrastructure over five years. Modi and Xi seems to have developed good dynamics. How much this dynamics bodes well for SAARC and India's relations with its neighbour only time will tell. In addition Xi has also been promoting the 'New Silk Road' and the "New Maritime Silk Road" concept. He has been requesting India and many other South Asian nations to participate in the efforts. How India responds to the call will also have ramifications for SAARC cooperation.

Important as India is, its size and power alone cannot be considered everything affecting South Asian dynamics. The situations of the other state in the region are also crucial. Unfortunately, all the South Asian states are in some state of turmoil. Afghanistan, for instance, continues to be unstable. Its security situation is likely to be no less volatile after the withdrawal of over 100,000 international combat troops by the end of 2014. The new deal with President Ashraf Ghani Ahmad Sai which may allow about 10,000 American troops to stay in the country after December 31 to support Afghan forces is unlikely to make a significant impact. The continuing Indo-Pak rivalry as it is played out in Afghanistan will also negatively impact the embattled country. As William Dalrymple says, "The continuation of clashes between India and Pakistan in-and over-Afghanistan after the U.S. withdrawal is dangerous for all countries in the region and for the world".[4] Meanwhile, Pakistan and Afghanistan themselves have bilateral problems which are far from being resolved. After the acrimonious six-month election deadlock Ghani was declared the president of Afghanistan in September 2014. Ghani and his rival Abdullah Abdullah ratified a power-sharing agreement in which the later will assume the role of the chief executive considered to be a role equivalent to that of prime minister. Ghani, an ethnic Pashtun, and Abdullah with support from the second largest Tajik ethnic group confront an uphill task of ensuring unity in the face of troubled personal dynamics, security gaps, economic impact of reduced foreign aid, massive corruption, serious Taliban threat, as well as prevalent ethnic and tribal rivalries.

The Maldives was also in turmoil after the forced removal of a democratically elected president. The new election has alleviated political and socio-economic issues confronting the country to an extent. Meanwhile, in Sri Lanka, stability has improved after the end of overt conflict. But the grievances of the Tamil population, especially with regard to rights and autonomy, are yet to be addressed satisfactorily. This will continue to be a key source of tension for years to come. Bangladesh too continues to face a plethora of socio-economic and political problems. The tussle between two rival political parties frequently lead to hartals, disturbances and shifts in internal and external political dynamics. Internally, the country is plagued by fundamentalist violence and ethnic tensions. Dhaka also has security, border, and water resources issues with India.

Bhutan held elections in July 2013. The results were rather surprising, with Tshering Tobgay from the opposition People's Democratic Party (PDP) elected prime minister. Overall, Bhutan's process of democratisation is moving slowly in terms of qualitative transfer of power from the king to the elected prime minster. Only in recent past did Thimpu openly articulate its desire to open up its relationship with states other than its close ally India. The previous government of Jigmi Y Thinley of the Druk Phuensum Tshogpa (DPT) or Peace and Prosperity Party had established relations with thirty two countries in the five years since it came to power in 2008. Its move to establish relations with China is believed to have annoyed India. Right before the elections, India cut off its subsidy on cooking gas and other essèntials imported into Bhutan. This was seen as New Delhi's attempt to influence the electoral outcome in favour of the opposition party lead by Tobgay.

On the other side, Bhutan and Nepal also have an ongoing dispute over the fate of over 100,000 people mostly forcefully expelled from the former over a decade ago. People of Nepali origin claiming Bhutanese citizenship have been living as refugees in camps across Nepal for over a decade. According to UNHCR and the International Organisation for Migration (IOM), 80,000 refugees have recently been settled in third countries. The majority of the refugees (66,134) were resettled in the US by April 2013. Among the over 38,000 remaining refugees in Nepal, some 29,000 have thus far expressed interest in resettlement. In this context, Bhutan will have to take back only 10-20 thousands of the remaining refuges who are unwilling to be resettled elsewhere. Some of the remaining refugees are also likely to be assimilated into Nepali society. With the resolution of the refugee issue, the otherwise friendly Nepal-Bhutan relation will take a definite turn for the better. Nepal's grievances concerning Indian non-cooperation on the refugee issue will also be resolved.

Even with these issues resolved, Nepal is passing through a difficult political transition. The decade-long conflict ended in 2007 after the Maoists joined mainstream politics. The Constituent Assembly (CA), elected in May 2008, was dissolved in May 2012 without completing its task of drafting a new constitution. A new constitution has become indispensable for doing away with a long political transition and attaining political stability. The second CA election took place as scheduled on 19 November, 2013 in spite of a call for an electoral boycott by a number of political parties, including a breakaway Maoist party, CPN (M). At 78.3 per cent, voter turn-out was impressive. The UCPN (M), which was the largest party after the first CA election, dropped to third position after the second elections. The Nepali Congress (NC) and the United Marxist Leninist (UML) parties became the first and the second largest party respectively. A coalition government of NC and UML with an absolute majority in the Legislature-Parliament was formed on 10 February, 2014 under the leadership of NC President Sushil Koirala. The government has promised to deliver a new constitution by 22 January, 2015. The contentious issues related to federalism, electoral system, judiciary, and form of government, which led to the death of the first CA, are far from resolved even 10 months after the second CA elections. However, in view of public pressure and desire to cover naked inability of political leaders of major political parties, there is hope that an inclusive constitution will emerge during the four-year term of the second CA if not within a year as promised by key political parties.

However, the promulgation of new constitution has been presented by political leaders as a panacea for all social, economic and political ills confronting the country so far. Whether the internally factionalised and short sighted political leaders can deliver economic prosperity and social justice to the poor common folks through coalition governments after the constitution comes out is a matter of concern. "People can't eat or live on a good constitution even resulting from CA. New constitution and political leadership should be able to guide everyone to deliver food, education, jobs, health services and opportunities to catch up with the fast moving neighbours and the rest of the world".[5] Also, single ethnic-based federalism proposed by UCPN (M) with over 100 linguistic groups in existence in Nepal, single Madhesh region-based Pradesh expected by Madhesi leaders and multiple identities-based federalism stressed by NC and UML has led to polarisation that will require a great tact to deal with complicated situation arising before and after the promulgation of the new constitution.

Nepal, in particular, has a long open border with India. The two countries are bound by close cultural, economic, political, diplomatic, military and trade ties since time immemorial. Thus, Indo-Nepal relations are complex and sensitive. In spite of major ups and downs at various moments of history, the relationship has remained fairly stable on the whole. India's perception of its security interest in Nepal and its view of Sino-Nepal relations are probably the two most important barometer of its relation from the Indian perspectives.

Real and imagined, as well as invited and uninvited, Indian interference in Nepal's internal and external affairs constitutes the key irritants in Indo-Nepal relations from Nepal's perspective. As an example, Prashanta Jha writes "India invested enormous political and financial capital in preventing the Madhesi parties from supporting the Maoist party in the contest (for prime ministerial position after Madhav Nepal's resignation in June 2010). RAW was understood to have offered much money to the Madhesi parties to lure them away from the incentives Prachanda was offering. Two Madhesi leaders who received the cash confirmed the exchange. The stick came along with the carrot and, when cash didn't work they threatened the MPs who were planning to cross the floor."[6] He adds, "The fundamental fact of India's leverage over Nepal, and its ability and inclination to shape local politics, had not changed (over 50 years). Only the actors have."[7] Thomas Bell's observation concerning Indian interference is that "the RAW works on infiltrating and manipulating Nepali political parties, and many other institutions......It does political interventions".[8]

Similarly, Sudhir Sharma states that India is inspired to practice a kind of "Controlled Instability" in Nepal; it does not let any single Nepali political force become strong. In this way, New Delhi can guide its dependent - due to an open border, economically, large number of Nepali workers in India, and Nepali leaders' tendency to seek political patronage - neighbour as per its style.[9] Concerning India's over emphasis on security concern Jha quotes a discussion between Brajesh Mishra, Indian prime minister Atal Bihari Vajpaee's security advisor, and Hari Sharma, Nepali prime minister GP Koiral's Principal secretary, when the former visited Nepal in 2000 in the aftermath of 1999 IC 814 hijack from Kathmandu in which Sharma "posed a question to Mishra when India's security interest was being questioned, how many bodies came to your village after the Kargil war? Mishra kept silent, and Sharma added, four came to my village. and six came to Foreign Minister Chakra Banstola's village. Nepali's have paid with their blood for India's security. Please don't question us."[10] In addition, developing and sharing water resources, Nepal's perceived unfairness of the 1950 Treaty of Peace and Friendship, trade and transit arrangements, massive trade deficit and border issues, particularly Susta and Kalapani, are key tension points. Conflict transition, enhanced connectivity and better integration of landlocked Nepal with SAARC and beyond depends on constructive support from India. However, Nepali political leaders have also failed in most occasions to come up with a clear vision and consensual stand on its political, developmental and foreign affairs agenda.

It is widely believed that Nepal's relations are largely left to Indian technocrats, bureaucrats, and the security apparatus, particularly RAW. This leaves the relationship vulnerable to misunderstanding. For instance, almost every Nepali prime minister in the last decade or before, except J N Khanal who did not receive an invitation from India, has officially visited India. But no Indian prime minister had reciprocated for almost two decades since the last official visit by I.K. Gujral in June 1997. Except Narendra Modi visit in August 2014, Atal Bihari Vajpayee did visit in 2002, but he was a participant at the eleventh SAARC summit held in Kathmandu. More frequent exchange of visits by the top political leaders, including Indian prime ministers, would be helpful to further Indo-Nepal relations. Naturally, an adequate interaction between bureaucrats and technocrats at all levels would have to be built in to prepare the ground for the high-level meetings and implementation of the agreements.

In the context, the series of exchanges, where prime minister Man Mohan Singh invited senior Nepali leaders – Sher Bahadur Deuba and Sushil Koirala of Nepali Congress, Pushpa Kamal Dahal "Prachanda" of UCPN (M), Madhav Kumart Nepal of UML to Delhi between April-August 2013 was seen positively by a section of Nepali politicians and intellectuals. However, a wide suspicion also prevails on the utility and continuity of such visits as the Nepali leaders went and came back without any significant agreements on key issues confronting Indo-Nepal relations. Nor their visit led to timely implementation of past agreements such as Pancheswar multipurpose project at Mahakali river signed in 1996. As per media the only focus during such visits was that the Indian leaders stressed the need to hold CA elections on 19 November, 2013 and Nepali leaders assured them that polls would take place. A CA election is certainly important. Nonetheless, it is equally important to have the highest level actions on other pressing matters.

The situation, however, has changed towards positive direction after recently elected prime minister of India Narendra Modi visited Nepal on three-four August, 2014. The tone of his address to the Nepali parliament, the content of the joint communiqué at the end of his visit, and some follow-up activities has enhanced hope for better relations and reduced trust deficit. In September, a twenty-five year long Power Trade Agreement (PTA) was signed for trading power at market rate, building cross-border transmission lines and increasing grid connectivity. A Project Development Agreement (PDA) was also finalised with India's GMR Company for the development of the 900 MW Upper Karanali Hydro Power project. In addition, a border task force was authorised to initiate steps to repair border pillars and evacuate illegal occupants from Dusgaza, no-man's land. On 23 September Nepal and India endorsed the statute for the Pancheshwar Development Authority to guide early implementation. The Pancheshwar project on the Mahakali River on the Nepal-India border is expected to generate over 5000 megawatt hydropower and irrigate 93,000 hectares of land in Nepal and 1.6 million hectares on the Indian side.

SAARC Connectivity and Regionalism

Adequate connectivity and a commitment to regionalism must be central objectives of any regional organisations. SAARC has aimed to achieve shared prosperity with enhanced connectivity and regionalism since its inception in 1985. However, it took quite a long time to clearly stress the ways in which connectivity could be achieved. During the fourteenth SAARC summit concluded in Delhi on 4 April, 2007, prime minister Singh stressed the need for SAARC to foster "connectivity - physical, economic and of mind" to fully utilise regional resources and "flourish" through connection to "itself and the rest of the world". Singh also offered "duty free access" to the least developed SAARC member states and opened India's vast market "without insisting on reciprocity" from them.[11] In addition to the earlier commitments, the latest seventeenth SAARC summit held in the Maldives themed "Building Bridges" concluded with agreements aimed at improving intra-SAARC connectivity.[12] The areas covered during the summit were comprehensive: enhanced transport (road, rail, and air), trade, education and cultural exchanges, tourism and travel, diplomacy and friendly relations, as well as better climate change and counterterrorism initiatives. These goals are indeed noteworthy and important. But, to date, SAARC has had greater success in declaring its commitment to connectivity rather than operationalising it.

A large part of Nepal, a country with high mountains, has very poor road and other infrastructure. Most districts of Nepal are hardly accessible from Kathmandu, its capital. Mule tracks, small air planes, and helicopters crisscross the country meeting minimum emergency and essential transport needs. There is talk of railways and additional airports. But many tracks roads, some Hulaki roads in Terai-Madhesh as well as a Mid-Hill Highway are already under construction. In the years to come, these are likely to increase internal connectivity gradually. Nepal's connectivity to SAARC is no better than its internal state. Nepal's air link to SAARC nations is limited to India, Bangladesh and Pakistan. As a landlocked country its access to other SAARC nations through roads, train, and sea ports is possible only through India.

Even in a more advanced SAARC nation such as India, connectivity to different states and regions, particularly the northeast, remains far from adequate. A large chunk of Bhutani, Pakistani, Bangladeshi and Afghanistani territories, particularly the hinterland and mountainous areas, have limited road and other infrastructural connectivity. The island nation of Maldives faces a great difficulty in connecting with atolls and hundreds of small inhibited and uninhabited far flung islands. Sri Lanka is probably internally more connected than other SAARC nations but its total infrastructural development needs are also yet to be met. As with intra-country connectivity, inter-SAARC connectivity among most countries is miniscule and inadequate.

SAARC inter-regional trade is also miniscule constituting only five to six per cent of the total global trade. "The countries of South Asia have a long history of inward-looking trade policies. Until the early 1990s, with the lone exception of Sri Lanka, few recognised that trade could serve as an engine of growth and poverty reduction" and "missed the historic opportunity for rapid export and general economic growth that other developing countries-especially in East and South East Asia-seized during the 1960s, 1970s and 1980s".[13] Interestingly, South Asia's approach to intra-regional trade was even more restrictive than against the rest of the world and the intra-regional trade declined to 4.1 per cent of the total South Asian trade in 1974 from 19 per cent in 1948. It picking up somewhat (4.9 per cent, 1998) only after trade liberalisation started in the countries of India's periphery.

There is a widespread skepticism about whether intra-regional trade can or will expand adequately. Imtiaz Ahmed, highlights the predicament with a statement that, "After almost three decades of economic activities, with the intra-regional trade within SAARC moving from 3.2 per cent in the 1980s to just 5.8 per cent in 2009, it can safely said that the outcome is far from promising".[14] The challenges confronting intra-regional trade expansion are definitely enormous and the efforts and achievements so far are rather disheartening. However, SAARC's intra-regional trade potential is much larger than the current level of trade. Also, informal trade between countries of SAARC are quite significant even though the level and modality of such trade may vary between any two countries depending on their size, price differential, scarcity of items and boarder situations.[15]

Nepal and Bhutan's trade with India and that of the Maldives with Sri Lanka have been relatively less restrictive than intra-regional trade among other SAARC nations. But Bhutan, the Maldives and Nepal are smaller nations within SAARC accounting for only a small proportion of total intra-regional trade. India and Pakistan, for instance, are far from reaching their full trading potential. As is the case in many other regions, efforts are underway in SAARC towards promotion of regional trade integration on the one hand and the signing of bilateral free trade agreements on the other.

SAARC, born in 1985, with economic growth through regional cooperation as an objective of its charter, moved closer to explicit commitment to economic cooperation in 1987. A framework and institutional basis for trade liberalisation and economic cooperation emerged only in 1993 when the South Asian Preferential Trade Agreement (SAPTA) was signed by the original seven-member countries in Dhaka during the seventh SAARC summit. The agreement provided a basis for exchanges of concession on tariffs, para-tariff and non-tariff barriers through four approaches of exchange: product by product, across the board, sectoral and trade measures. The key objective was to promote regional trade by enlarging the scope of tariff concessions.

SAPTA had no significant impact on intra-regional trade. There were a number of key problems. First, tradable and traded commodities covered by regional tariff concessions were low. The imposition of rule of origin (ROO) condition limited trade. Second, there was reluctance among important member countries to make any meaningful concessions. For instance, Pakistan had a ban on imports from India except from its 'positive list'. India's import licensing system was similarly cumbersome. Improvement in intra-SAARC trade during that period was largely due to trade liberalisation by individual countries.

In view of the minimal impact of SAPTA, the SAARC council of ministers decided in 1995 to recommend the formation of the South Asian Free Trade Area (SAFTA). SAFTA was to be formed within 2001-2005. The principle objective of SAFTA was to go beyond the exchange of trade preference to the abolition of intra-regional trade restrictions. However,

SAFTA came to be operational only in January 2006 after the twelfth SAARC summit held in Islamabad on six January 2004. SAFTA was a significant improvement over SAPTA as it was aimed to provide impetus to dealing with infrastructural deficiencies, institutional shortcomings, strengthening SAARC's bargaining positions in multilateral negotiations, as well as building stronger economic and trade relations.

SAFTA does, however, have its own set of constraints. First, it focuses on reducing custom duty and tariffs missing a mechanism to deal with para-tariffs. Second, it has no specific provisions concerning agricultural tariffs even though agriculture constitutes a major sector in most SAARC countries. Third, it provides only for the trade of goods not services. The latter are, however, equally if not more important. In addition, a significant uncertainty was built in the 'sensitive list' to be drawn by member countries. Further, the usual problems of lack of adequate trust, political instability, inadequate generosity on the part of bigger nations, and continuing Indo-Pak tensions have plagued SAFTA. However, desire to strengthen intra-regional trade continues among SAARC members, each with its own level of commitment.

In view of the sluggish pace of intra-regional trade integration, key countries of SAARC are also pursuing bilateral free trade initiatives with individual countries while still engaged in SAFTA and intra-SAARC trade promotion. This is a point noted by other scholars:

> While trade liberalisation in South Asia under a regional trade agreement (RTA) – the Agreement on South Asian Free Trade Area (SAFTA) – moves at a sluggish pace, there are already five effectively operational bilateral trade agreements (BTAs) between South Asian countries involving at least some exchange of preferences, with several more in the pipeline. Political, economic and geographical factors drive these agreements.[16]

India has so far four BTAs, one each with Afghanistan, Bhutan, Nepal and Sri Lanka. Pakistan has one with Sri Lanka. Negotiations are ongoing between Bangladesh and Nepal, Bangladesh and India. And there are precedents to these agreements. Far before SAARC came into being, more than six decades ago, bilateral agreements were signed between India and Nepal, and India and Bhutan. The Indo-Bhutan Treaty of 1949 and the 1950 Indo-Nepal Treaty of Peace and Friendship are still valid. BTAs have also gone beyond SAFTA in a number of respects. However, BTAs also continue to be hampered by many restrictions and barriers.

In terms of Indo-Nepal bilateral trade relationship, subsequent to the treaty of 1950, the two countries formally entered into a Treaty of Trade and Transit in 1960. The Treaty was split into two separate treaties of Trade and Transit in 1978. The treaty guides the relationship of the two nations even today. The latest Treaty of Trade between India and Nepal was signed in 2009. Valid for seven years, this treaty is a revision of the one signed in 1996. The 1996 revision was in some ways a landmark as it "contained provisions that reflected the stage of development of Nepal, the weaker partner" resulting in an impressive increase in bilateral trade.[17] The provisions included duty-free access of most primary products (except those in small negative lists) to each other's markets. Nepal granted preferential access to Indian industrial products in view of the duty free access to Nepali industrial products granted by India.

India imposed restrictive provisions in the Treaty revised in 2002 that resulted in a significant reduction in the value of exports from Nepal to India. Restrictive measures included: ROO requiring thirty per cent value addition to Nepali exports, submission of the criteria applied to ROO on an annual basis, imposition of tariff-rate-quotas (TRQs) on four important Nepali exports- vegetable ghee, acrylic yarn, copper and zinc oxide and change in tariff heading (CTH) at a four-digit level of the Harmonised System (HS) to be eligible for preferential market access. The quantitative restrictions hit the export of a dominant Nepali export - vegetable ghee-hard. The reduction of tariffs on palm oil, a raw material for the ghee production, by India subsequently Nepal's vegetable ghee export to India has fallen to almost zero in 2009/10.

Imposition of para-tariffs and non-tariff barriers (NTBs) on Nepali exports and quarantine certificate requirements on forest, food and agricultural commodities export by India has been problematic. Additionally, "sanitary and phytosanitary (SPS) quarantine inspection and food testing facilities are available only at six of the twenty six border crossings. Moreover, there is no predictability in the way quarantine-related rules are applied."[18] An imposition of para-tariffs such as an agricultural development fee has been practiced by Nepal. But NTBs on Indian exports to Nepal are unheard of. Nepal, as a member of the World Trade Organisation, has started to reduce and remove such "other duties and charges." While Nepal's imposition of para-tariff is largely due to economic reasons, India's are either for political-economic reasons or purely political reasons.[19] The 2009 revision of Indo-Nepal Trade Treaty includes some provisions for addressing Nepal's concerns. However, these provisions only find a place under 'best-endeavour clauses.'

While Nepal has over thirty key trading partner countries, India is the most prominent trading partner. India accounted for 65.5 per cent of the total Nepali exports (NRs 60.95 billion, IRs 1 is fixed at NRs 1.60) in 2009/10. Nepal's imports from India constituted fifty seven per cent of its total imports (NRs 375.61 billion) in the same year. Nepal's trade deficit with India has been sharply rising. For instance, the trade deficit jumped by almost NRs 70 billion in just two years between 2007/08 (NRs 103.82 billion) and 2009/10 (NRs 174.34 billion). SAARC countries accounted for 73.9 per cent of Nepal's total exports and 57.4 per cent of its total imports in 2009/10. Country-wise breakdown demonstrates that 88.6 per cent of Nepal's export to SAARC was to India in 2009/10, while Bangladesh and Bhutan accounted for 7.5 and 3.5 respectively.

In terms of total imports from SAARC to Nepal, India accounted for almost the total amount (99.4 per cent). On the whole, Nepal's exports' share in the total trade has been significantly declining (31.7 per cent in 2000/01 to 14.0 per cent in 2009/10). Meanwhile, the proportion of imports has been sharply rising with an alarming spike in the trade deficit. According to the latest data available, in the last five years the merchandise trade deficit doubled (NRs 631 billion from NRs 314 billion) and imports rose by twenty per cent per year and "export earnings amounted to one-eighth of imports in the last fiscal year".[20] The import of not only modern goods-machinery, automobiles, electronics, construction materials, petroleum products- but also agro-based products is increasing. It is troubling to note that in agriculture-based economy like Nepal the imports of agro-based products— rice, soybean oil, vegetables, maize etc– constituted eighteen per cent of total imports in 2013/14 and has increased by almost three per cent between the past two years. The remittances (NRs 543 billion) send by workers mostly in the Middle East and Malaysia has been the biggest source of financing the imports and any security problems (as is happening in Iraq and Syria) or labour policy shifts in these areas are likely to introduce severe economic vulnerability and ability to pay for imports.

Nepal's Trade Integration Strategy (NTIS) 2010 focuses on twelve goods for exports. Of these, seven are agricultural products: large cardamom, honey, lentils, tea, instant noodles, medicinal herbs and essential oil. Services include tourism, labour service (remittances), information technology and business process outsourcing, health services, education services, engineering services and hydro-electricity. The top ten markets identified for the seventeen goods and services are mostly outside SAARC. Within South Asia, India naturally ranks high and existing Indian market access barriers are matters of concerns for Nepal.

Given the early stage of development, landlocked location, infrastructural and institutional bottlenecks, Nepal's manufacturing sector is unlikely to have comparative advantage. Agro-based products, cottage and small industries, water resources (estimated 84000 megawatts potential) offer greater hope. In addition, tourism is already a money-maker and have much greater potential given Nepal's rich cultural heritage and beautiful landscape, including the highest peak the Mt. Everest. This includes Janakpurdham, Sita's birthplace, Gautam Buddha's birthplace Lumbini and Lord Shiva's famous abode Pashupatinath Temple. Further, Nepal also has lofty mountains, including the highest peak in the world, Mt. Everest. Service sector carries equally impressive potential, particularly in education, health, and especially skilled and unskilled manpower supply. NTIS 2010 now recognises these potentials. It must be implemented with commitment to enhance trade with India, SAARC and abroad.

Indian agriculture is subsidised through seeds, equipment, power and tube-wells. Nepal's farmers do not get such protection and subsidies except in fertiliser. It also has the comparative advantage of scale for Nepali products to compete effectively. India may help Nepal's agro-based trade by enhancing market access to these products. Since Nepal's exports are largely agro-based products, it also must pay adequate attention to alleviate supply side constraints in the sector resulting from low productivity, poor access to energy, inadequate roads, labour problems etc. Necessary incentives to farm product exports may have to be considered.

Hydro-power development, power purchase and exchange offer another mutually beneficial sector for SAARC region. Nepal's hydro-power sector is only marginally tapped and India's energy needs are huge and rising. Nepal's capacity to develop large hydro-projects and utilise large quantities is constrained. Power/ electricity exchanges between India and Nepal now are miniscule but can be substantially increased by upgrading and adding new transmission lines. Nepal usually faces power shortages in dry winter season while India faces greater shortages in the hot wet season, when Nepal incurs over supply. Bangladesh, Bhutan, Nepal and India can also work together in the field of energy development and sharing.

Being a landlocked country, Nepal's needs better transit facilities. Access to ports is critical to diversify trade to countries of SAARC region and to international markets. The Kolkata and Haldia facilities provided by India have been found to be inadequate. Nepal has been requesting India for the use of alternative ports such as Jawaharlal Nehru Port in Mumbai, which according to one study, would be forty per cent cheaper and twenty days faster for overseas trade to US and Europe. Similarly, transit to Bangladesh ports via Phulbari and Banglabandha in India is constrained as no Indian custom office exists in the area. It has been found also that Rohanpur-Singhbad transit point would be more suitable for Nepal to access Bangladesh ports. While preparing for the seven-year renewal of Transit Treaty effective from January 2013, Nepal had requested India to provide access to five more trade and transit routes between Visakhapatnam sea port and four major customs, rail route between Birgunj dry port and Vishakapatnam, and Rohanpur-Singhabad-Jogbani and Phulbari-Banglabandha.

During negotiations, the Nepali team had also sought an optional port for trade facilitation. India had agreed to the changes in principle. But New Delhi renewed the treaty without the requested changes as its proposal of imposing additional lock on containers ferrying third country consignments was turned down by Nepal. Kathmandu claimed this to be against international norms and to undermine its transit rights. India extended Nepal's direct transit routes to Bangladesh for bilateral and third country traffic under the treaty for road route through Kakarbitta-Panitanki-Phulbari-Banglabandha corridor and rail route through Radhikapur-Birol interchange point on India-Bangladesh border. Also, Nepal's transit trade was agreed to be routed through twenty two designated routes from India-Nepal border to the port of Kolkata/Haldia as in the past treaty.

Given the booming economies of China and India and their fast expanding trade and commerce, it is believed that Nepal can be used as a cost-effective transit point, particularly for trade with Tibet region and North India. This proposal, rather premature in the present politico-economic milieu, may be further explored to assess its benefits, validity and acceptability to all the three party concerned. There has been an initial proposal to develop and implement Trilateral Agreement between India, China and Nepal to promote the "transit point" concept. India is yet to warm-up to this idea. China's railway has reached Sigatse in Tibet and is likely to reach Kerung in Sino-Nepal border in few years. Given the possibility of it reaching Kathmandu and existence of six profitable potential roads connecting Tibet with Northern India through Nepal the transit point proposal may deserve due attention from India.

On the Nepali front, it also needs to produce more exportable items of high quality. Those goods must be sold at competitive prices in SAARC and beyond to reduce Nepal's burgeoning trade deficit. In addition, Nepal must upgrade the skills of its manpower that is and will be working in foreign nations, including India, to ensure better earnings to them and the nation. Their welfare and rights in the countries must be enhanced. The remittances, which currently account for about 23 per cent of GDP, have been important source for foreign exchange, maintaining positive balance of payments and an economic life line in a sluggish (3.5 per cent growth in 2012) economy. The remittances must be utilised better, including by encouraging investment, rather than be simply used for current consumption. Petroleum product imports constitute the biggest item of imports in Nepal and it may be substituted to a large extent by generation of cheap hydro-power. Instead, Nepal faces a load shedding of over twelve hours in winter when the run-off the river hydro-power generation goes down significantly. Hotels, business and factories use petroleum products to meet their power needs or curtail their production or services with severe negative impact to economy and raise trade deficit.

The Future of SAARC Connectivity

Two dominant views have emerged on whether SAARC regional integration and connectivity can be enhanced in the near future. The first view is that the chances for effective connectivity and integration in South Asia are bleak in the foreseeable future. According to this view, India, the largest and the most powerful member of the South Asia, is already seriously looking towards East and South-East Asia and beyond under its "Look East" initiatives. This is part of New Delhi's attempt to ensure an international role and respect for itself which reflects the country's dynamic economy and growing military strength. Others also argue that India has limited economic incentive to push for closer ties in the region. Considering the minimal scope of resources and opportunities within the region, a country of India's size has little to gain economically. This group believes that the current situation is unlikely to alter significantly in the near future in view of the prevalent inter- and intra-country conflicts and the consequent trust deficit in the region. Also, New Delhi feels its South Asian neighbours' are offering it inadequate space and trust. New Delhi further feels that its neighbours are giving undeservedly growing space to its rival China. In the context, one important point to note is that "in the eighteenth century China and India (undivided) were the first and the second largest economies of the world respectively."[21] Thus, we may be witnessing "not just a rise but a re-rise of the region provided of course both China and India are able to mend all the fissures both within and outside their respective boarders, with India having an added challenge of mending a divisive South Asia.[22] Also, this group argues that most SAARC member states unduly whip "Nationalistic Rhetoric" rather than promoting regionalism.

The second group is more optimistic, arguing that cultural and people-to-people contacts driven by geographic proximity are strong in South Asia. Further, most countries in the region are achieving notable economic growth and are capable of doing much better with collective efforts. In view of its long-term interests, India gains from being engaged in the region. Indeed, it needs to tackle issues in its own backyard before it is taken seriously further afield. What India and other members require, argue this group, is a clearer vision for South Asia. This must then be complemented by sustained efforts around regional cooperation and connectivity. The younger generation will, of course, be crucial to seeing this task through. They must be educated on the collective benefit of regional connectivity and integration.

All SAARC nations have the right to seek connections with other Asian nations and beyond. But this must not be pursued at the cost of collective interests within the neighbourhood. Within the region, there is a strong connectivity between people due to socio-cultural commonality and proximity. States must further foster these ties by minimising the barriers created by undue concerns based on national security and nationalism. At the same time, genuine concerns for sovereignty of all nations, small and big, must be respected. Also, any significant contribution of larger nations for the promotion of South Asian development, connectivity and regionalism must be recognised by all.

SAARC could be the ideal institution to foster greater connectivity, integration and progress in South Asia. But the regional body has made wobbly progress in the course of eighteen summits over the twenty-nine years since its establishment in 1985. The major weaknesses within SAARC are undue trust deficit, inadequate commitment and an inability to implement its own directives. While many of its declarations, policies, and programmes are often sensible, they are not adequately turned into practical action. To be effective, SAARC must evolve its current largely declarative mode towards improvements in implementation. Its charter that requires consensus in decision-making and prevents discussion of bilateral issues may need review as their initial relevance may have been finished, as a group argues. Nevertheless, only greater commitment, a clearer vision and more concerted effort will enable SAARC to attain its goals related to enhanced connectivity, regionalism, harmony and shared prosperity.

Clearly, attaining adequate connectivity and strong South Asian regionalism is a tough venture. However, as plagued as SAARC is by many woes, it is unlikely to become completely irrelevant in the near future. Indeed, it has also has some success in implementing declarations. The SAARC Development Fund, SAARC University, SAARC Secretariat, SAARC Regional Centers are some of the important actions. Also, greater connectivity and strengthened regionalism is beneficial to all the nations and the peoples of South Asia in the short as well as in the long run. Imtiaz Ahmed stresses, "If we are serious in transforming the region and making it socially, economically and intellectually prosperous, then I am afraid there is no option other than taking lessons from the universality of regionalism in South Asia. The hope now lies in our personal yet collective creative effort."[23]

I.P. Khosla states there are three necessary preconditions for regional cooperation to succeed: absence of intra-regional coercion, which tend to negate all cooperative efforts, "states accept each other's sovereignty and legitimacy" and existence of "a mutual dispute settlement system that is seen as impartial enough to inspire trust among the participating states."[24] If any of the three necessary preconditions is absent, "regional cooperation may go forward in hesitating steps, but has little chance of sustained success" and "note that all of them are absent in South Asia."[25] Further, "utilitarian self-interest and shared norms and values", which bring states together constitute sufficient conditions. However, extra-regional coercion may also play a role as a sufficient condition."[26] "In sum, the unifying force of common norms and values has been sufficient to prevent SAARC from breaking....there is a strong hope that this unifying force will generate sufficient utilitarian self-interest to take regionalisation forward. However, the self-interest was not an origination force and still has an uncertain future, so the regional cooperation will be weak, unstable, and dependent on the leaders and their interaction" but given the frequent meetings "learning effects which are constructive" are likely.[27]

Conclusion

In conclusion, a more concerted and committed effort with focus on ten key areas to foster greater connectivity and regionalism may be worth pursuing by all the nations of SAARC. First, strong connectivity of people and of mind are crucial. Second, improved and expanded physical infrastructure consisting of roads, railways, air services, ports, and custom facilities within each country and across the region is essential. Third, enhanced and more liberalised inter-regional trade must be promoted by going beyond the SAFTA provisions. Fourth, energy and water resources development and building of regional grid deserve greater commitment. Fifth, regional tourism and travel must be promoted adequately. Sixth, greater cultural exchanges and better communications must be ensured. Seventh, the quality and quantity of regional educational and health networks must be strengthened. Eighth, adequate people-to-people contact must be promoted. Ninth, greater efforts must be made to ensure good neighbourly diplomacy and friendly relations, including by promoting Track II and III contacts. Tenth, better mechanisms must be developed and higher commitment must be made to tackle terrorism and illegal activities at international borders.

SAARC with over 22 per cent (about 1.5 billion) of the global population and less than five per cent of the physical area is one of the most densely populated regions of the world. Much of this population consists of a huge mass of poor, illiterate and deprived peoples. But it is also a fast growing region with huge potential for development. In view of this potential, many powerful nations including the US, Japan and China have increased their presence in the region. They have also obtained observer status of SAARC. Consequently, there is an opportunity and challenge for SAARC to deal with the increasing international interest by demonstrating the best political and developmental strategies. In this context, one interesting but contentious suggestion by Imtiaz Ahmed, particularly from the Indian perspective, is to offer full membership of SAARC to China as it is already "the largest trading partner of almost all the South Asian countries, including India" and the "largest development partner" of many countries, including Pakistan. Beijing's inclusion as a full member would only "rejuvenate SAARC as an economic region" in addition to helping it "overcome its current limitations resulting from the irreconcilable differences between Pakistan and India."[28]

With so many internal, bi- and multi-lateral conflicts, the high level of trust deficit within SAARC is hardly surprising. The constant task of managing conflicts has drained the region of its energies, limiting its aspirations. As the largest and most powerful member, India has the most number of conflicts with its neighbours. Consequently, it also has the greatest role in conflict transition, enhancing connectivity and promoting regional integration. Narendra Modi's stress on enhancing relations with neighbours that started with his invitation to all the SAARC head of the governments during his inauguration as prime minister and his utterances during his visits, including to Nepal, has raised hope for India's larger contribution to strengthening regionalism. The second most critical role would be wisdom of Indian and Pakistani leaders to resolve their conflicts. It goes without saying, of course, that all the remaining six members will have to play their part constructively to attain the goals too. The SAARC summit provides opportunity for the leaders to seriously review the past performance and redirect with concrete, time-bound and implementable initiatives to promote South Asian regional integration through better connectivity and conflict management based on the lesson learned, peoples expectation and contemporary realities in the region and beyond.

References

1. Som P Pudasaini, "Peace, Neighbourly Diplomacy and Poverty Reduction for Building a New South Asia", in T. Nirmala Devi and Adluri Subramanyam Raju (eds), *Envisioning A New South Asia,* New Delhi: Shipra Publications, 2009, p.120.
2. "India Warns Pakistan over Strikes", *The Himalayan Times,* Kathmandu, 10 October 2014.
3. "Xinjiang-Gwadar port economic corridor tops Pakistani leader's China agenda", *South China Morning Post,* 8 August 2013.
4. William Dalrymple, "A Deadly Triangle: Afghanistan, Pakistan and India", *The Brookings Essays,* Washington, D.C: Brooking Institute, 28 June 2013.
5. Som P Pudasaini, "Negotiated Resolution of Conflicts in South Asia: Efforts in Mainstreaming the Nepalese Maoists", *South Asian Affairs,* Vol.1. No. 1, January-June 2008, p. 96
6. Prashant Jha, *Battles of the New Republic: A Contemporary History of Nepal,* New Delhi: Aleph Book Company, 2014, p.140
7. *Ibid,* p. 85.
8. Thomas Bell, *Kathmandu,* Gurgaon, Haryana: Random House India, 2014, p. 360.
9. Sudhir Sharma, *Prayogshala* (in Nepali), Kathmandu, Bhadau: Fine Print Books, 2070 (2013), pp. 389-390.
10. Jha, n.6, p. 91.
11. *Frontline,* Vol. 24, No.7, 7-20 April 2007, www.frontline.in/static/html/fl2407/stories/20070420003202700.htm
12. SAARC Secretariat, Kathmandu, 2011, www.saarc-sec.org/2011/11/14/news/ADDU-DECLARATION/79/
13. World Bank, *Trade Policies in South Asia: An Overview,* Report no. 29949, September 2004, Washington D.C:World Bank, 2004.
14. Imtiaz Ahmed, "Regionalism in South Asia: A Conceptual Analysis",

International Journal of South Asian Studies, Vol. 5, No.1, January-June 2012, p. 6.

15. Som P Pudasaini, "Regional Integration and Bilateral Free Trade Agreements: In the SAARC and Indo-Nepal Contexts", paper presented at an international seminar entitled *Promoting Interregional Trade in South Asia: Role of SAARC,* organised by SAARC Law Centre, NALSAR University, Hyderabad, India, on 26-27 March 2011.
16. Ratnakar Adhikari and Kharel Paras, "Bilateral Trade Agreements in South Asia", *Trade Insight,* Vol. 6, No. 2, 2010.
17. *Ibid.*
18. *Ibid.*
19. Michael L. Faye, John W. Mcarthur, Jeffry D. Sachs and Thomas Snow, "The Challenges Facing Land Locked Developing Countries", *Journal of Human Development,* Vol. 5, No. 1, March 2004.
20. "Krishijaya Aayat 18 Pratishat", *Kantipur (in Nepali),* Kathmandu, 23 Asauj 2071 (9 October 2014).
21. Martin, 2009 and Chung, 2010 as cited in Ahmed, n.14, p.7.
22. Ahmed, n.14, p. 7.
23. *Ibid,* p. 8.
24. I.P. Khosla, *How Neighbours Converge The Politics and Economics of Regionalism,* New Delhi: Konark Publishers, 2014, pp. 84-86.
25. *Ibid.,* p. 87 .
26. *Ibid.*
27. *Ibid.,* p. 96.
28. Ahmed, n.14, p. 8.

6

Regional Connectivity and Energy Security in South Asia: Challenges and Opportunities

C. Vinodan

Energy security has moved into the forefront of the academic and policy discourse in South Asia in recent times due to the impressive growth performance as well as the continued socio-economic backwardness of the region. In South Asia, poverty alleviation is an issue of high economic development priority. The supply of reliable, sustainable energy, particularly electricity to the rural poor households is critical to address this issue. Energy is a key ingredient of the socio-economic development of any region. Economic growth and burgeoning populations have put South Asia's energy security in a perilous state. Already energy and power shortages are stunting development in some of the region's least developed locations spurring political insurgences and social dislocation. A large portion of the population lacks access to modern sources of energy and depends on traditional sources that are not only inefficient but also have severe health and environmental problems associated with them. Increasing oil import dependency and huge investment needs for energy market development pose a further challenge. Delay's in decision- making to ensure stronger and mutually beneficial cooperation efforts is associated with high costs not only to the energy sector but also for the entire development agenda of the region. The availability of energy, that advances or at least is compatible with long term human well being and ecological balance, is a key to the sustainable development of the region. South Asia's mushrooming energy demand is driving growing dependence on energy imports that is likely to accelerate over the next two decades. The result is a deepening sense of energy insecurity that promises to have important long-term geo-political implications for the region. South Asian states are responding more often with "energy nationalism" than with energy cooperation as they reach out to secure future supplies. In this context, the paper argues that increased regional cooperation and connectivity are important factors determining the future of South Asia in the emerging world order. There are substantial gains from the potential regional energy trade in South Asia. All countries in South Asian states have an inadequate supply, current or potential, of some energy form or other, while some of the countries have certain forms of energy far in excess of their demand in the foreseeable future. They are eager to have common or collaborative plans to meet the shortages and also to deal with the surplus energy. This will certainly enhance sustainable development by means of developing and sharing critical resources as a region and minimising the risk of resource nationalism. The paper also surveys the present and future energy scenario in the region where there is a vast potential in renewable energy sources such as hydropower, wind power, and solar power. Such cooperation and connectivity in the energy sector will help countries to strengthen national energy security, reduce the costs of energy supplies, and minimise adverse impacts from energy price volatility. This will involve a wide range of actions including establishing cross-border infrastructure and promoting regional forums for sharing knowledge and experience widely available within the region.

South Asia is in the midst of a historic transformations which consists of eight states and more than one-fifth of humanity, has emerged as a vital region to the emerging global order due to its geostrategic significance, growing economic dynamism, fragile state structures and crisis in governance. For the first time in the last 350 years, the international system is undergoing a shift in its centre of gravity from the continents of Europe and North America to the rising Asia. It is argued that if South Asian countries develop an integrated economy, then South Asia could become the second largest economy in the world after China. Given the geographic proximity and economic complementarities between South Asia and China, this region could become the greatest economic powerhouse in human history. The rising menace of transnational terrorism and nuclear proliferation further invited global attention to the region. For many years conflict and violence have been endemic to South Asia, leading to experts terming the region as 'the most dangerous place on Earth'. Threats to security in South Asia stem from five main sources: the unresolved nature of the Kashmir dispute and growing Indo-Pakistani hostility in the wake of the Mumbai terrorist attacks of November 2008; the strengthening of the Taliban insurgency in Afghanistan, with serious spill-over effects in Pakistan and to a lesser extent in India; internal divisions and schisms in South Asian states leading to various types of violent intra-state 'identity conflicts'; the enormous spread of transnational terror networks in the region and the failure of the South Asian Association of Regional Cooperation (SAARC) to promote regional integration, cooperation and peace.

Regional Energy Profile of South Asia

Over the past few years, energy security has moved up the global agenda. There are three major reasons for this: first, the impact of high and often volatile energy prices; second, rising Asian powers and the growing demand for energy in India and China; and third, concerns over environmental sustainability and particularly about the global climate change. All these issues are critically important for South Asia in which impressive economic growth has boosted the demand for energy and put corresponding strains on the environment. South Asia is not only one of the fastest growing regions in the world; it is also one of the poorest, which thus puts energy at the very heart of the development process in the region. While the per capita energy consumption is one of the lowest in the world, energy intensity continues to be very high.[1] The aspect of sustainable energy supply is critical in the context of South Asian region, as it is poised for higher growth.

The growth of economy, along with the population growth in South Asia, has resulted in rapid increase in energy consumption, which is well above the world average of Organisation for Economic Cooperation and Development (OECD) rates. Thus, the South Asian region faces the sustainable development challenge of meeting the rapidly increasing energy demand as well as conserving the natural resources and protecting the environment. With both Indian and Pakistani annual GDP growth rates now in the six to eight per cent range and an increasingly young and urbanised population throughout the region, already approaching 1.5 billion people, the South Asian states face instability unless they can quickly find external sources of energy. A future where these states will largely depend on petroleum imports, particularly given the increasingly competitive world market, means that energy security is a primary concern in their foreign policy. The risks of terrorist attacks on vital energy infrastructure are rising, fueling fears of supply disruptions and political instability. South Asia accounts for about 5.9 per cent of the world's commercial energy consumption. This does not include the non-commercial energy sources such as wood, animal waste and other biomass that account for more than half of the region's total energy consumption. Despite rapid rise in demand, South Asia continues to average among the lowest per capita energy consumption of 443 kilogram of oil equivalent (KgoE), which amounts to 26.2 per cent of the world average of 1692 KgoE. However, energy consumption per dollar of GDP is amongst the highest in the world, which indicates the inefficient utilisation of energy. Improved energy security is vital to South Asia's economic growth and stability, given that demand for energy in the region is expected to double over the next fifteen years. South Asian nations rely heavily on imported energy, yet the region has large amounts of untapped energy resources. The lack of regional energy cooperation and trade compounds the problem. Energy cooperation has the potential to be mutually beneficial for all regional players, with some countries acting as net suppliers, some as net consumers, and some as net distributors of energy. Paucity or lack of capacity, awareness, development of regional energy resources, and sustained regional dialogue is a barrier to increased regional energy cooperation and, therefore, economic growth and could lead to instability. It is one of the fastest growing regions in the world with an average growth rate of above six per cent over the past eight years and has demonstrated its potential for emerging as a significant economic entity in the world economic space.[2] South Asia's prospects changed in the 1980s as it adopted pro-growth policies. It opened up markets to international competition, replaced the public sector with the private sector as the engine of growth, and improved macroeconomic management.[3] It is now the second-fastest-growing region in the world, after East Asia.

Despite its recent achievements, South Asia continues to be home for more than forty per cent of the world's poor. Large sections of the South Asian people do not have access to education, health, nutrition, and basic amenities like safe drinking water, sanitation and electricity. Hence the region is facing acute developmental challenges. Two major negative developments have emerged: (a) growing income inequality in South Asia and (b) growing imbalance among regions within countries and among the countries themselves. With fairly large and open borders, the growing imbalances in incomes and opportunities among South Asian countries present similar social and economic problems to the prosperous neighbours as the imbalances within these countries. The recent trends in economic growth shows the demand for energy in South Asia is going to increase steadily and substantially for the foreseeable future. According to the International Energy Agency forecast for the region this demand will probably more than double over the next thirty years–Indian requirements alone are projected to increase more than 140 per cent–compared with an increase of only fifty-five per cent for the world as a whole.[4] This rapid rise in energy needs is, of course, a necessary corollary of continued economic growth. It is well known that although countries may differ in their ratios of energy consumption to economic output, or energy intensity, there is a clear and unavoidable correlation between the two.[5] Moreover, this energy intensity tends to increase in any given economy as the focus of production shifts from the agricultural to the manufacturing and service sectors[6] exactly what economists say has to happen in countries such as Pakistan and India if recent growth rates are to be sustained.[7] Even without such a shift, two other factors suggest that energy intensity in South Asia will have to increase nevertheless. One is that, according to the World Bank, unreliable supplies of energy, particularly electricity, are already the most important factor in the high cost of doing business in South Asia compared to other regions. Reducing such costs is one of the essentials of sustained growth.[8] The other is that whether or not economic activity shifts away from the agricultural sector, the pressing need to improve standards of living in the backward regions will require a range of specific measures such as rural electrification, improving transportation of crops to markets, better medical care, clean drinking water, and access to cleaner cooking and heating fuels, all of which will further drive up energy requirements.

Another major reason for the energy crisis in South Asia is the volatile situation in the energy pricing especially in the international crude oil prices. Energy economists say that we are never going to see the days of cheap energy again.[9] Strategists in the developed countries have generally accepted such an upward trend and started diversifying their energy security policy. The reality is that no South Asian country is going to be able to meet its energy needs entirely from within its own domestic resources. Most of the countries in the region have energy endowments of one kind or another: India has significant coal deposits, Bangladesh has natural gas, and the countries across which the Himalayas and Hindu Kush lie have substantial hydroelectric potential. But development of the transportation sector in these countries is going to depend on oil, which no South Asian country has yet discovered in any substantial quantities. In other words, none of the South Asian countries possesses the entire range of energy resources to meet its development objectives. The obvious conclusion is that energy trade must be part of the solution to South Asia's continued development. A large share of that trade must clearly come from outside the region. After all, the South Asian countries collectively are now able to meet less than thirty per cent of their combined oil needs from within the region; if increasing demand is to be met at all, most of the new supplies will have to come from the Persian Gulf or beyond.[10] However, in addition to external sources of supply, international energy experts increasingly believe that greater cooperation within South Asia and with adjoining regions would be one of the most effective ways–perhaps an indispensable way–to deal with the regional energy deficit.[11] This emphasis on regional cooperation has caught the attention not only of academic economists but of the official development community as well. The rationale to look for regional cooperation as the key to meeting South Asia's burgeoning energy needs is laid out in a recent World Bank study that describes such an approach as providing a "logical and rational public policy choice . . . a win-win situation to all the participants."[12] The study points out that the fundamental economic conditions for trade exist: some countries in and near South Asia (specifically Bhutan, Burma, Iran, Kyrgyzstan, Nepal, Tajikistan and Turkmenistan) have more fossil or hydropower resources than they can use, while others (Afghanistan, Bangladesh, India, Pakistan and Sri Lanka) face a widening gap between demand and supply.

In 2000, energy cooperation was brought directly under the purview of the SAARC Integrated Programme of Action. Under the programme of Action the subject was being dealt with by the Technical Committee on Science and Technology. In view of the increasing importance of cooperation in this sector SAARC established a Technical Committee on Energy in 2000. Recognising that this vital area needed intensive attention, the twelfth SAARC summit held in Islamabad in 2004 to set up a specialised Working Group on Energy to undertake a focused study on various possibilities for cooperation in the field of energy including the concept of an Energy Ring that would include transnational energy lines for trade in electricity, gas and oil.

The subsequent induction of Afghanistan in SAARC introduced an added dimension to the issue as that country, connecting Central Asia with South Asia, can play an important role in energy sector. Special attention was given to the development of environment friendly energy to promote non conventional and renewable sources of energy for economic development and poverty reduction and to give special focus on energy availability in rural areas. It has formulated the terms of reference for study on energy trade in the region.[13] At the SAARC energy minister's conference in Islamabad in September-October 2005, it was agreed to establish a SAARC Energy Center (SEC) in Islamabad. The primary objective for the establishment of SEC is to have a regional institution of excellence for the initiation, coordination and facilitation of SAARC programmes in energy.

The promotion of private sector investment and participation in energy activities of the region assumed topmost priority. This is to convert the saving potentials into investments in energy projects (electricity, liquefied natural gas) through both the public as well as the private sectors, as integrated favourable investment policy should be formulated that can attract region's private investors to invest in energy projects. The SAARC countries current dependence on outside sources for their growing energy requirements can be removed by better management efficiency and stronger cooperation amongst themselves.[14] The sixteenth SAARC summit also focused on issues of energy security and regional energy cooperation, under the sprightly banner of 'A Green and Happy South Asia.'

Regional Connectivity and Energy Security in South Asia

Regional economic integration depends critically on the development of infrastructure that will strengthen connectivity both within and between countries, freeing up the flows of goods and services, investment, people and ideas. There are clearly wide disparities in the breadth and quality of infrastructure between countries of the region. From the perspective of regional connectivity, the gap between the few wealthier countries and the middle and lower-income countries is hindering the full participation of countries in the region's economic development. The region has vast potential to utilise its energy resources more efficiently through the interconnection of producers and consumers of energy by oil and gas pipelines and electricity grids. Such interconnection could be cost-effective and offer opportunities in reducing the cost of energy, which is a critical input for development. More than 400 million people in India continue to live without electricity. With a growing population and strengthening economies, energy cooperation among SAARC countries is gaining recognition. The SAARC energy ring is aimed to reduce supply disruptions and delivery constraints in a sustainable manner.[15] Energy resources are distributed unevenly around the region. The overall energy need for South Asia is predicted to become more intense in the coming years (see Table 1) and it will probably be more than double in next twenty to thirty years.

Table 1: Long Term Forecast of Commercial Energy Demand by 2020

Item	*Unit*	*Afgha-nistan*	*Bangla-desh*	*Bhutan*	*India*	*Maldives*	*Nepal*	*Pakistan*	*Sri Lanka*
Electricity Demand Forecast (2020)	MkWh	3,877	72,791	6,876	1,755,685	1,571	8,076	251,039	23,867
Oil Demand Forecast (2020)	mtoe	3,483	11.6	0.62	246.9	1.661	1.61	30.94	7.82
Gas Demand Forecast (2020)	mtoe	0.92	44.03	0.0	101.88	0.0	0.0	72.75	0.0
Coal Demand Forecast (2020)	mtoe	0.0	0.9	0.11	447.6	0.0	0.78	13.9	7.0

Source: *Regional Report, South Asian Initiative for Energy,* pdf.usaid.gov/pdf_docs/PNADS866.pdf, p.19.

Note: mtoe: Million Tonnes of Oil Equivalent, MkWh = Million Kilowatt Hours.

Power and energy trade in the region were identified as one of the solutions for a crunching energy deficit because the region is unevenly endowed with natural resources and production capabilities. Reliable energy supply is needed to alleviate poverty and achieve sustainable economic growth. The key aspects, however, obstructing progress are domestic politics and international politics vis-a-vis the countries' neighbours, as well as institutional incapacities. The lack of separation of economic and political interests has defined electricity as a strategic commodity which has fallen prey to political instability and politics. There have been several international good practices of energy cooperation, particularly in establishing regional power grids.

Energy Trade and Cooperation in South Asia

There are substantial gains from the potential regional energy trade in South Asia. All countries of the South Asian region have an inadequate supply, current or potential, of some energy form or other, while some of the countries have certain forms of energy far in excess of their demand in the foreseeable future. They are eager to have common or collaborative plans to meet the shortages and also to deal with the surplus energy. The energy security plans of these countries indicate that all countries are eager to develop and increase the energy trade within the region. The policy makers and strategic planners in South Asia are well acknowledged the vast energy potential of the region. Afghanistan and Nepal are sitting on water resources that could potentially generate some 24,000 megawatts of electricity from Afghanistan and an estimated 83,000 megawatts from Nepal. These countries together account for forty per cent of South Asia's presently installed capacity. Bangladesh, India and Pakistan are power-deficit countries, especially India. The growing electricity constraint is threatening the ability to sustain rapid growth. Yet, less than one per cent of the region's electricity-generating potential has been used so far. The reason for this energy constraint is the lack of cooperation and absence of energy trade among South Asian countries. Indeed, if one were to imagine South Asia without borders, perhaps the highest priority investment would have gone to develop the hydropower resources. While all countries would benefit from the development of South Asia's hydropower resources, Afghanistan and Nepal, the two poorest South Asian countries, would benefit most.

After decades of insignificant cross-country electricity trade and the absence of any trade in natural gas through pipelines, regional political leaders and business people recently have evinced a great deal of interest and enthusiasm in cross-border electricity and gas trade, not only within South Asia but also with its neighbours in the West (Central Asia and Iran) and in the East (Myanmar).[16] South Asia has two regional energy clusters. The eastern market includes India, Bangladesh, Bhutan, Nepal and Sri Lanka, extending to Myanmar; the western market includes Afghanistan, India and Pakistan, extending to Central Asia and Iran. India bridges these two clusters. Some activities are under way, including a successful hydropower trade between Bhutan and India in the eastern market and an ongoing project in the western market that will bring electricity from Tajikistan and Kyrgyzstan to Afghanistan and Pakistan.[17] The current regional security environment is not favourable to exploit the full potential of the region. It will mainly rely on the will of the policy-makers and administrators to take concrete and decisive actions in the energy front. It is argued that the governments of the region need to continue reducing political and security tensions; consider energy trade as an enhancement of energy security and political and economic cooperation; continue energy sector reforms; improve commercial performance of the utilities; improve the credibility, competence, and accountability of regulation; adopt sustainable (cost-reflective) tariffs and a social protection framework; promote commercial approach to energy trade; encourage private sector participation in the form of public-private partnership (PPP) structures in cross-border investments; help the transit countries (especially Afghanistan) integrate; reach water-sharing agreements; seek accession to international agreements (such as the Energy Charter Treaty); strengthen regional institutions at both political and technical levels; and identify priority trade-oriented investment projects and pursue their implementation. The success of India-Bhutan electricity trade offers useful lessons to other countries in the region. Restrictions in transport border crossings are a major constraint to global and intraregional trade in South Asia. Removing these restrictions would boost trade within South Asia as well as lower costs for international trade in general, as many land-locked countries and regions would benefit from access to the closest ports. Currently, efforts to improve trade facilitation and transport networks are being pursued in a fragmented manner, and where cross-border issues are involved, little cooperation exists. Establishing corridor-based approaches for improving the trade, such as a transport arrangement for intra-regional trade, would be essential to improve the efficiency of regional transport and to reduce trade costs.

Some of the larger countries are also proposing joint action to explore and procure energy resources, especially hydrocarbon resources, from areas outside the region. There is also the possibility of jointly procuring some fuels, which could result in economies of scale in transaction and transportation costs.[18] In this respect, given complementary energy resource endowments, unlocking the vast untapped energy trading potentials through regionally integrated energy cooperation assumes significance, as it would not only enhance the region's perennial energy security but also work as a hook for broad-based regional economic integration.[19] Regional trade in energy is practically non-existent in South Asia, with the exception of small pockets of bilateral power exchanges between Nepal, Bhutan and India. Long standing disputes, political exigencies and mistrust between the countries of the region have effectively blocked even modest efforts to encourage regional energy trade.[20] In view of the ever increasing global demand for energy and steep rise in price, the South Asian countries are finding it difficult to adequately meet the demand of an expanding economy on one hand and the rising aspirations of its people on the other. To enhance energy security and to achieve sustained economic growth in South Asia it will be essential to maintain energy supply in an efficient and reliable manner. This will call for the long-term vision to develop an integrated energy market in the region.[21]

With the geography of energy supply options not confined to political boundaries, South Asian countries would need to depend upon each other for the cheapest and cleanest energy sources. Cross-border energy supply would not only provide diversified energy supply, which is a key component of energy security but also foster regional cooperation. Therefore the importance of regional integrated energy cooperation is vital to South Asia's development and prosperity. A common regional energy market would provide, among others, (i) tremendous scope for regional economic development through increasing access to reliable and affordable energy sources, (ii) enormous financial gains through freer energy trade, (iii) mainstreaming energy trade as a fundamental aspect of regional resource management to foster broader regional integration, (iv) more attractive markets for private investment, (v) better use of global investment flows and technology transfers, (vi) easier integration with global markets and (vii) reduced cost of supply for all participants. The South Asia countries have huge potential for energy trade by developing integrated energy infrastructures such as power grids and pipelines. The general consensus is that deeper regional energy cooperation would mitigate the localised shortfalls in energy production through regional transfers of bulk energy from areas of surplus or potential surplus to the deficit regions in South Asia.[22] The two generally accepted power trading mechanisms are: bilateral power trade and pool-based power trade. Cross border power trade on a bilateral basis already takes place widely between India and Bhutan and to a certain extent between India and Nepal. Currently the power trading is in its infancy in the region. Whatever trade takes place as of today are basically bilateral exchanges or apportioning of power from surplus areas to temporarily needy regions. In most cases, the tariff has been fixed mostly on the basis of negotiations and to a large extent determined by political consideration, diplomatic goodwill and convenience. Such an adhoc arrangement based on negotiations and goodwill could work in the past mainly because the quantum of power purchase was limited. However, in years to come the size of power purchase would be substantial. Power trading will be on bulk supply and have to have a more detailed framework of contracts and operating procedures. The proposed Iran-Pakistan-India pipeline, Turkmenistan-Afghanistan-Pakistan-India pipeline, Oman-India subsea pipeline and the Myanmar-Bangladesh-India pipeline projects offer promises for energy security; however, each has been plagued with political, economic or security obstacles that have prevented tangible progress.

In South Asia, stark institutional barriers hinder regional cooperation in energy. Besides the SAARC, there is no institutional and legal framework for the promotion of regional energy trade. Though SAARC has one of its objectives of strengthening and expanding electricity grid in the region, no progress has been made so far in inter-regional power trade. At the moment there is no institution outside of SAARC framework to play the coordination and energy trade enhancement role. Although there is huge need and possibility for regional trade in energy, the existing regulatory and pricing policies do not address the eventuality of regional trade. Regulatory barriers and distorted energy pricing and subsidy regimes in countries of the region precludes trading of energy at the commercial terms, as these entities, which are selling energy at subsidised rates, will have to bear the energy at cost, with the consequence of being impacted negatively on the financial health of the purchasing entity.

Conclusion

South Asia is in the process of rapid transformation in the social, economic and political spheres due to global and regional changes. The issue of energy and resource security has moved into the forefront of the development discourse in South Asia due to the impressive growth performance as well as the continued socio-economic backwardness of the region. Poverty alleviation is an issue of high economic development priority in the region. South Asia needs an inclusive energy governance framework for managing energy poverty in the region. The supply of reliable, sustainable energy, particularly electricity to the rural poor households is critical to addressing this issue. With less than twenty-five per cent of the population having access to electricity in rural South Asia, the task ahead is gigantic. Rising economies and burgeoning populations have put South Asia's energy security in a perilous state. Already energy and power shortages are stunting development in some of the region's least developed locations spurring political insurgences and social dislocation. Satisfying the region's growing demands will require a heightened degree of energy interdependence among historically antagonistic states. Consequently, like it or not, the states in the region will face a tradeoff between traditional desires for energy self-sufficiency and the ambitious development targets that they have set for themselves. Achieving such growth, therefore, requires that India, Pakistan and the other countries of South Asia first address the persistent border disputes that hamper cross-border energy trade, establish effective control over presently ungoverned areas, reorient the missions of military forces to some extent and develop a better understanding of the effects that energy interdependence will have on broader relations with neighbours. With the precarious energy situation in the region and unprecedented increases in international oil prices seen in recent times, it is high time for policy makers, financing institutions, NGOs and the civil society to push for a greater integration of the energy sector. To pursue energy security, the countries of the region needs to ensure that energy supplies are available, sufficient, affordable and sustainable. This will mean taking a broad range of measures: conserving and raising energy efficiency; rationalising pricing and taxation systems; improving energy sector governance; and diversifying energy supplies, in particular making greater use of alternative and renewable resources. The huge rural population and the economics of South Asia constitute two main challenges facing access to electricity in rural areas. Successful models of rural energy practices are available, which can be considered for replication in other countries of the region. Greater regional connectivity can be an ideal framework for such cooperation. Greater energy trade and cooperation within South Asia and with adjoining regions would be one of the most effective ways to deal with the regional energy deficit.

References

1. Charles K. Ebinger, *Energy and Security in South Asia: Cooperation or Conflict?*, Washington, D.C.: Brookings Institution Press, 2010.
2. Sadiq Ahmed, Saman Kelegama and Ejaz Ghani, *Promoting Economic Cooperation in South Asia: Beyond SAFTA*, New Delhi, Sage Publication, 2010; Also see Sumita Kumar. *Stability and Growth in South Asia*, New Delhi: Pentagon Press, 2014.
3. Amitendu Palit and Gloria Spittel, *South Asia in the New Decade: Challenges and Prospects*, Singapore: World Scientific Press, 2012.
4. *International Energy Agency Report*, 2009.
5. J. P. Singh and Vinay Pannu, "Geopolitics of Energy Cooperation in South Asia", www.visionriviewpoint.com
6. David Newberry, "Power Sector Reform, Private Investment, and Regional Cooperation," in Sadiq Ahmed and Ejez Ghani (eds.) *South Asia: Growth and Regional Integration*, Washington, DC: International Bank for Reconstruction and Development/World Bank, 2007.
7. Ahmed and Ghani, *ibid.*
8. *Ibid.*
9. Daniel Moran and James A. Russel, "The Militarisation of Energy Security," *Strategic Insights* 7, no. 1, February 2008, www.ccc.nps.navy.mil/si/2008/ Feb/moranFeb08.pdf.
10. See Ebinger, n.1.

11. See Newberry, n. 6.
12. Venkataraman Krishnaswamy, *Potential and Prospects for Regional* Energy *Trade in the South Asia Region,* Washington, DC: World Bank, 2007.
13. C. M. Shafi Sami, "Connectivity through Energy and Harmonisation of Resources", in Deepankar Banerjee and N. Manoharan (eds), *SAARC: Towards Greater Connectivity,* New Delhi: KAS Publication Series, 2008.
14. Nitya Nanda, "Energy Cooperation and Connectivity in South Asia", in Banerjee and Manoharan (eds.), *ibid.*
15. Gunatilake Herath and P. N. Fernando, *Energy Trade in South Asia: Opportunities and Challenges,* Phillippines: Asian Development Bank, 2012.
16. See Nanda, n.14.
17. *Ibid.*
18. Anasua B. R. Chaudhury, "The Energy Crisis and the South Asian Security: An Indian Perspective", *India Quarterly,* Vol. 65, No. 2, 2009.
19. Research and Information System for Developing Countries, *South Asia Development and Cooperation Report,* New Delhi: Oxford University Press, 2008.
20. SARI, Regional Energy Security for South Asia, 2009, www.sari-energy.org
21. See Sami, n.13, p.150.
22. See n.18.

7

Connectivity and Infrastructure Development in South Asia: China's Perceptions

Srikanth Kondapalli

Introduction

China had been viewing with interest in the recent period the initiatives of several South Asian states in expanding their infrastructure projects such as roads, railways, air-fields, riverine traffic and harbours. Chinese officials, scholars and others think that their country has significant stakes in such projects in connecting to the South Asian region bordering China, enhancing and diversifying overland and maritime trade, avenues for mutually beneficial investments, create inter-dependent stakes with the region and possibly provide for strategic leverages for China in the coming decades. Such perceptions in China are closely linked to the internal developments with the leadership formulating the "Go Out" policy of investments and western development campaign of refurbishing infrastructure projects in the sixteen interior and backward provinces of the country in the last decade of tenth and eleventh Five Year Plans. In 2012 a new policy of "Go West" was suggested in China that called for renewed focus on enhancing connectivity with the South Asian states. It is argued in this paper that such connectivity between China and South Asia or within South Asia with Chinese-aided projects provides for expanding avenues for investment and mutually beneficial outcomes, specifically in the context of lack of capital availability in the backdrop of the Euro Zone crisis, although China's objectives in this regard could position itself as a contestant in the short to medium term perspective and as a dominant player in the region.

One of the most visible aspects of China's rise is the country's infrastructure development projects that had expanded connectivity in various domains, further contributing to the economic development. Indeed, during the Asian financial crisis of 1997 and 2007-08 global financial crisis, successive leaderships of China sought to overcome economic problems by expanding investments in the infrastructure projects across the country. After the reform programme was announced in the late 1970s, China attracted over $1 trillion in foreign direct investments from different countries, specifically Taiwan, Japan, South Korea and others. A majority of these investments went into the improvements in the infrastructure of the country, such as super highways, railways and hi-speed railways, airport construction, shipyards expansion and telecommunications. While earlier investment was mainly in the coastal regions, from the tenth Five Year Plan onwards China started emphasising on the Western development campaign of infrastructure development in the sixteen backward interior provinces. Also, the sixteenth party congress of the communist party in 2002 launched a "Go out Policy" of diversifying investments abroad. However, due to restrictions in the western countries on sovereign wealth funds and the like, China did not achieve major successes till recently in the mergers and acquisitions. Hence, China expanded investments in the resources acquisition and infrastructure projects in other countries. Recently, in the back drop of the Euro Zone crisis, China had launched "Go West Policy" in 2012 of expanding connectivity with its western areas - mostly bordering Central Asia and South Asia.

Western Development Campaign by the Chinese leadership as a corrective measure to expand economic growth from eastern regions to the backward western areas of the country.[1] Current efforts are in terms of developing infrastructure projects in the western regions which are relatively inaccessible. Mention should be made of the tenth Five Year Plan (2001-2005) focus on the 1,118 kilometre long Tibetan railway from Golmud to Lhasa, expanding the road, airfield and fibre optic network, apart from the East-West energy pipelines from Xinjiang to Shanghai. As a part of this project, China has proposed a sub-regional economic cooperation of its Yunnan and Sichuan provinces with Myanmar, Bangladesh and northeast region of India through its Kunming Initiative proposal. In this context, enhancing relations with South Asian countries is crucial for the progress of this campaign.[2]

China also has plans for expansion of Karakoram highway with Pakistan through Northern Areas, Lhasa-Shigaxe-Kathmandu, Lhasa-Nathu La- Kolkata, etc. In 1954-57, China built a road connecting Xinjiang with Tibet passing through Aksai Chin. The western highway through Karakoram ranges proved to be quite useful for the Chinese military supplies and deployments in the western areas. Other projects followed, including a railway line that was laid out to connect Kashgar with Urumqi by mid 1980s and subsequently the July 2006 railway line in Tibet. In 2007, Pakistan announced plans to connect Havellian with the Karakoram highway with a railway line. Yet, despite these projects in the vicinity, there appears to be no major plans between China and Afghanistan to physically connect each other in effective manner. This is probably a reflection of the cautious approach of China given the flow of militants and drugs through this region that could be detrimental to China's interests.

As an important transhipment corridor in the world, the Indian Ocean Region (IOR) is of considerable significance for China. The IOR links Asia with Africa and Oceania. Some Chinese reports indicated that nearly one-sixth of the global cargo and about one-tenth of global cargo turnover is through the IOR.[3] More importantly, the two main routes of Persian Gulf to the West (to Europe and the Americas through the Cape of Good Hope/ Suez Canal) and the east (through the Straits of Hormuz, Malacca and Lumbok) are considered to be the hub of these transfers. These geo-strategic routes are considered to be "very important" [feichang zhongyao] from the Chinese point of view. Several transportation corridors are being worked out by China to connect it to the IOR. Yunnan provincial leaders also have been pushing through these ideas in the recent past.[4] Yunnan intends to connect to the Bay of Bengal and then to the IOR through a series of networks connecting with Salween, Mekong and Irrawaddy rivers.[5] While China has been an active participant in the revival of the Asian highway and railway concepts and has made efforts to open up the country for expanding transportation corridors linking it with Southeast Asia, Central Asia and South Asia, China has been selective in expanding the sea routes. It is here that the recent enunciation of the "string of pearls" becomes evident.

Adjoining provinces in China connecting to South Asia have taken keen interest in attracting and inviting the chambers of commerce and industries from the South Asian states. This is useful to exert pressure on governments in South Asia for more liberalisation of trade structures and investments from China in these states. Every year, Xinjiang conducts cross-border trade and investments fairs with the Central Asian states in the format of China-Eurasia Expo in Urumqi. Also, Sichuan and Yunnan provinces have been organising similar trade fairs in the recent period. For instance, the Sichuan province conducted three such interactions with the South Asian chambers of commerce and industry by June 2012.[6] Yunnan organises every year industrial and agricultural fairs with the adjoining states in South and Southeast Asia.

This is the context for China's interest in the on-going infrastructure developments in the South Asian region. China's objectives in this regard are several. Chinese officials, scholars and others think that their country has significant stakes in such projects in connecting to the·South Asian region bordering China, enhancing and diversifying overland and maritime trade, avenues for mutually beneficial investments, create inter-dependent stakes with the region and possibly provide for strategic leverages for China in the coming decades.

India

India is a major country where infrastructure developments provide for huge opportunities for India. Prime Minister Manmohan Singh had announced in 2012 a requirement for over $1 trillion in investments in this sector. Also, Indian commerce minister suggested to the plan for expanding the manufacturing sector's share from the current fourteen per cent to twenty nine per cent in the GDP. All these require China's active participation as China is sitting on $1.8 trillion in foreign exchange reserves and has gained expertise in the manufacturing sector. China's companies have expanded considerably in India, including Huawei, ZTE, Shanghai Electric Power, Harbin Electric, etc. It is estimated that over one-tenth of electricity in India is produced by the Chinese supplied electricity generators and over thirty per cent of the telecommunications equipment originates from China. China's Development Bank had extended nearly $10 billion in loans to several private power sectors of India. China's companies also started bidding for dredging projects – sometimes in the security sensitive regions of Mumbai and others.

Adjoining India, China had expanded its infrastructure rapidly. China built a highway through Aksai Chin in 1954-57. Four such highways exist today in Tibet including Qinghai-Tibet road of 2,122 km (with a capacity to handle 500,000 tonnes of goods a year), Chengdu-Lhasa road of 2,413 km, Tibet-Xinjiang road of 1,179 km, Yunnan-Tibet road of 315 km and Nepal-Tibet Kodari road of 736 km. Once the Nathu La route is opened,

Kalimpong to Lhasa route would be nearer by one-third the Kodari road. The importance of these roads, prior to the arrival of railway is seen from the fact that these highways handled eighty per cent of the cargo transport in Tibet.

Tibetan railway construction, completed in October 2002 and put to trials from Beijing and other places on 1 July 2006, is considered as a "strategically important project" by the Chinese leadership. An estimated three million tonnes of cargo and a million 'visitors' were expected to be carried by the Tibetan railway by 2010. China also has plans to construct railroads from Lhasa to other provinces such as up to Chengdu, Lanzhou and Dali till 2038. Some of these railways, such as the Lhasa to Dali route would be a few kilometres from the line of actual control in Arunachal Pradesh and Nyingqi prefecture borders.

China spent an estimated $3.16 billion for construction, although this Tibetan railway expenditure surpasses that of the $3 billion GDP of entire Tibet (as in 2005). The railway construction costs could be reclaimed by several means, including by tourists and exploitation of natural resources in less than a decade. For instance, about 8,00,000 visitors are expected to visit Tibet by the railway alone a year with their figures expected to gallop to about 5.28 million by 2010, according to the estimates of Tibet Autonomous Regional Academy of Social Sciences and Industrial Economics Studies Institute of the Chinese Academy of Social Sciences. This in itself is expected to fetch more than $725 million. In contrast, those 1.8 million visitors who arrived in Tibet by means other than railway in 2005 contributed an income of only about $250 million.

In addition, Bomda, Damshune and Gongkar airports are opened for civilian aerial traffic connecting to major Chinese cities and Kathmandu with plans to open another airport thirty kilometres from Shiquanhe. This town is a few kilometres from Demchok in south-eastern Ladakh. While China reportedly objected to the re-building of dilapidated Fukche airfield in Ladakh, China is going full steam with construction activities in the region. In the Nagari prefecture, bordering Ladakh, China is planning to construct a nuclear power plant.

The 1970s built 1,080-km pipeline from Golmud to Lhasa that carries over eighty per cent of petroleum transported in the region is considered to be the lifeline of Tibet. This pipeline, with its capacity to carry about 250,000 tonnes, annually carried between 1,00,000 to 1,50,000 tonnes of oil.

China had laid down fibre optic lines connecting Beijing and other parts of the country with Lhasa, Xigaze and other regions of Tibet. With this China could expect a quantum jump in its communications with Tibet. A Chinese company based at Wuhan also contributed to the completion of an optical fibre-based transmission for Thimphu, Paro and Phuentsholing in Bhutan–although both countries do not have diplomatic relations so far. For enhancing mobile phone capacity, China has introduced eighty five channels in Tibet that currently boast of more than 60,000 subscribers. Programme-controlled telephones and satellite communications ground stations were also set up in Tibet.

China's plans to construct railway networks, asphalt roads in all counties, electricity availability in all townships and radio communications in all villages in Tibet are expected to enhance Chinese integration with even remote parts of Tibet. These are expected to enhance Tibetan border trade from the current figures of about $90 million in 2005. Although estimates of trade volume through Nathu La – opened for border trade in July 2006, may be minimal in the bilateral trade (of about $20 billion), it still forms a significant portion (of an estimate of about $20 million in 2007 and $2 billion in 2015) in the Tibetan trade.

Pakistan

China has established a number of infrastructural projects in Pakistan and provided aid to these ventures in basic engineering plants at Taxila, textiles, electrical products, nuclear, coal and hydro-energy projects, highways, and the like. China plans to expand the infrastructure projects in Pakistan from Kashgar (where a special economic zone was established) by railways and roadways connecting it to Gwadar.[7] Also, China is showing interest in the Iran-Pakistan pipeline as with the Turkmenistan-Afghanistan- Pakistan-India pipeline.

China's investments in 122 projects in Pakistan have reached more than $25 billion by August 2011, which is a minor figure in the overall Chinese investments abroad (of about $200 billion).[8] Yet, Pakistan provides for a special place in the Chinese calculus as seen from the fact that Islamabad became one of the nine countries in the world with which Beijing concluded a FTA. Also, China's investments in the construction, transport and other related areas in Pakistan have been stepped up and form an important component in Beijing strategic calculus in this region. According to some observers, furthering such economic ties is necessary for China to displace the US influence in the region.[9]

To enhance trade and economic cooperation with Pakistan, China signed a number of agreements starting with the trade agreement of

January 1963, a few months after the Sino-Indian clash on the border areas. In the last decade there has been a qualitative increase in the trade ties between the two. These are visible in the stepped up activity in the number of trade agreements signed between the two. These include, six agreements and a MoU on 12 May 2001; November 2003 Joint Declaration on Direction of Bilateral Relations; seven agreements in December 2004; twenty-one agreements in April 2005 during visit of premier Wen Jiabao; eighteen agreements in November 2006 visit of President Hu Jintao; and Thirteen agreements during president Zardari's visit in 2007.[10] China had also agreed to float a joint infrastructure development fund in Pakistan. The depth of Chinese involvement in Pakistan can be seen from the fact that by early 2010, there are about 10,000 Chinese engineers working in Pakistan on 122 different projects. Following the October 2008 agreement between the two on cooperation in mining, the geological survey establishments of both countries have initiated a programme for systematic surveys and mineral exploitation in Pakistan. The defence ministry of Pakistan had given clearance to such activities.[11] Pakistan also had mooted the idea of setting up a megacity Zulfiqarabad in Sindh mainly to attract Chinese investment. President Zardari on a visit to Beijing appeared to have convinced the Chinese leadership to finance $1.25 billion in the Pakistan portion of the proposed Iran-Pakistan line with the prospect of the line extended to China.[12]

Among these, free trade zone is a major instrument in economic integration. In November 2003, both signed a preferential trade agreement, which became operational from January 2004. After the visit of the Chinese premier Wen Jiabao to Islamabad in 2005, both sides agreed to implement Early Harvest Programme (which became operational from January 2006). By this, China agreed to reduce tariffs on 767 items to zero. By 2008, the FTA was to be implemented covering nearly ninety per cent of commodities.[13] In all about 2,500 tariff lines are allowed under this FTA. However, to the chagrin of the Pakistani Directorate-General of Intelligence and Investigation, Federal Board of Revenue, massive misuse of this facility had been reported, including sudden jump in the mobile phone sets imports, wrong "certificates of origin", false declaration of imports (from Hong Kong), resulting in loss of revenue for Pakistan.[14]

China's provincial level economic cooperation with Pakistani counterparts had also increased in the recent period. For instance, Guangdong and Zhejiang provinces have substantial (more than $3 billion) in trade with Pakistani provinces, although the Peshawar-Xinjiang cooperation had not really taken off.[15] This explains to partly to the recent efforts to enhance links with the neighbouring regions of Xinjiang with Pakistan and the infrastructure plans.

For further integration between the two, China had started ambitious projects to interlink with Pakistan and farther towards West Asia. China is assisting Pakistan in 122 projects in several fields, essentially in the infrastructure.[16] In September 2009, both signed an agreement to construct twelve dams in Pakistan worth $1 billion. The Chinese import-export bank is to provide $700 million for these projects.[17] Besides, the Pakistani side also had requested for the Chinese investments in up-gradation of the 1300-km Karakoram highway,[18] establishment of transportation linkages between Pakistan and Afghanistan, up-gradation of rail link between Pakistan and Turkey and Chinese participation in Iran-Pakistan (IP) and Turkmenistan-Afghanistan-Pakistan (TAP) gas pipelines.[19] In February 2007, Pakistan has awarded contracts for feasibility studies worth about $1.2 million for the laying down of about 750 km railway line between Havellian and the 4,730-meter-high Khunjerab crossing over Mansehra district and the Karakoram highway.[20] China is building a road passing through the northern areas. Pakistan's transfers of Sakshgam valley in 1963 comes in handy here for connecting its western highway into Pakistan. In April 2010, addressing a Pakistani planning commission delegation, the Chairman of China's National Development Reform Council stated that both countries would further explore possibilities for cooperation in the oil and gas explorations and water resources.[21]

One of the major projects is the Gwadar port. Indeed, collaboration between China and Pakistan on the Gwadar port is termed as a landmark in the bilateral relations similar to the Karakoram highway project officially opened in 1978. Gwadar naval port in the western Makran coast of Pakistan was built with Chinese assistance by the China Harbour Engineering Company, a subsidiary of China Communications Construction. The first phase of the project, conceived in 1964 but started in 2002, was completed with China spending $198 million as against Pakistani share of about $50 million in a project estimated at over $1 billion and completed by 2006. China harbour was given the contract for the first phase of Gwadar port construction. The same company is also involved in the construction of Quay Wall and Break Water (Marine Protection Works) to develop Deep Water Container Terminal at Karachi.[22] Of the nearly 3,000 Chinese in Pakistan, about 450 engineers worked for the Gwadar project. Gwadar overlooks the Strait of Hormuz, through which an estimated forty seven per cent of West Asian oil passes. China has agreed to increase the deep-sea port from fourteen meters to nineteen meters. The plan included construction of a total of about twelve berths. In general, larger displacement vessels (such as aircraft carriers, etc.) would require about eleven meters depth ports for berthing. Increasing the depth of this port further indicates to a long-term plan of China in the naval sphere. China has promised to sell Pakistan four F-22P frigates and jointly produce JF-17 multi-role aircraft. A signals outpost was reportedly in place at Gwadar to monitor maritime traffic in the region.

In 2011, the then Pakistan's defence minister, Chaudhry Ahmed Mukhtar, suggested that China should build a naval base at Gwadar. Subsequently, in August 2012, Pakistan planned to transfer the operational control of the deep water port from Singapore's PSA (Port of Singapore Authority) International (which was running the port on a contract for forty years to that of a Chinese state owned company.[23] This was finally realised in January 2013 when Pakistan transferred the port to Chinese Overseas Port Holdings Limited.[24] According to Andrey Volodin, these infrastructure projects, along with the proposed idea of a PRC military base in Pakistan, all point to Beijing's three strategic objectives, viz., "putting military and political pressure on India, limiting Washington's influence in Pakistan and Afghanistan, and monitoring directly the activity of "Uygur separatists" in the NWFP".[25]

Nevertheless, despite these initiatives and developments, China's efforts at expanding connectivity and infrastructure projects in Pakistan are constrained by security problems for its personnel and investments. For instance, China's coal mining company Kingho Group withdrew in 2011 from the $19 billion venture in coal mining and power and chemical sector in Tharparkar district of Sindh province citing the series of bomb blasts and security concerns of its personnel.[26] Sindh and Baluchistan, which witnessed an upswing in the Chinese investments in infrastructure, also reported opposition to the Chinese activities. Some commentators in Pakistan argued that China is colonising Pakistan. Some Sindh nationalists have also called for the boycott of Chinese goods.[27] Scores of Chinese workers were targeted and even killed. Political opposition to China also grew putting to risk the investments.[28]

Afghanistan

China has been participating in the reconstruction work of war-torn Afghanistan, which shares over 90-km border with China. After the 9/11 events, China had shut down its borders with Afghanistan citing possible influx of militants into Xinjiang. Recently, however, it had been concerned about the US-led forces withdrawal from Afghanistan by 2014. Also,

China eyes on the resources on which Afghanistan is sitting - specifically iron ore, copper and others. For successful extraction of resources, China estimates that it should be able to build infrastructure - specifically roads, railways, etc., in Afghanistan.

China is a late entrant in the Afghan reconstruction as its contribution is less as compared to other donors, referred to in official discourse as "render[ing] assistance to this process within its capacity."[29] China cites this aspect as indicating its serious intent to help Afghanistan. While China announced an economic aid package of about $3.6 million to Afghanistan (and then increased this amount by $ One million more), seeing the multinational efforts at reconstruction of Afghanistan, China thought it prudent to enhance this amount further. In 2002, China announced assistance to Afghanistan in several projects worth about $ 150 million, including in financing of Republic Hospital of Kabul and Parwan water and irrigation project.

In September 2003, both countries signed an agreement on trade, transit and investments, while in October a trade fair was held in Kabul.[30] In March 2004, foreign minister Li Zhaoxing, attending the Berlin conference, announced $15 million in gratis aid to Afghanistan and $1 million for the electoral machinery, etc.[31] China is in negotiations with the concerned institutions in Afghanistan for a long-term contract and rights to explore and exploit mineral resources in this country, specifically copper at the Ainak mines. As the insatiable hunger for resources increased in China due to the economic growth rates, China has been scouring through almost every other region of the world for such resources.

The Chinese working in Afghanistan are also being targeted by some Afghan groups. On 10 May, 2004, for instance, eleven Chinese workers were killed and five injured in terrorist strikes in Jalowgir area thirty six km near Kunduz in northern Afghanistan. A new terror group, reported to be closer to the Taliban, was suspected to have carried this mission.[32] These workers belonged to a Chinese railway company Shisiju group and involved in construction work. On this occasion, Afghan finance minister agreed to pay compensation of $5,000 per a victim.[33] In May 2006, in another incident, a riot took place in Kabul, injuring some Chinese. The Chinese foreign ministry spokesman, on this occasion, requested the "relevant" Afghan bodies to ensure the safety of the Chinese.[34]

Bangladesh

While China does not border with Bangladesh, it sees huge prospects in entering into the infrastructure development projects in this country so as to extract huge resources and for productive investments.[35] China's overall trade and economic cooperation with Bangladesh, however, are miniscule, in comparison to other partners. As both countries celebrated a "Year of Friendship" in their thirtieth anniversary of establishment of diplomatic relations in 2005, Bangladesh saw China replacing India as its largest trading partner, thanks to China's surge in its exports of textile fabrics, capital machinery and dyeing chemicals.

However, what this meant was not to be of a beneficial outcome—for Bangladesh at least. Overall bilateral trade was minimal - $1.2 billion in 2002; $4 billion in 2008, about $5 billion in 2010 and $6.3 billion in 2011. However, China's exports to Bangladesh overwhelm that of Bangladeshi exports to China. In 2005, of a bilateral trade of $2 billion, Bangladesh exported goods valued at about a mere $45 million to China. In 2011, Bangladesh exported only $320 million worth of goods while importing nearly $6 billion, while in 2012. Bangladesh imported from China $6.4 billion worth of goods and exported $401 million. In other words, every year China had surplus balance of trade position over Bangladesh and this has become a bone of contention between the two countries.

In the economic field, with repeated protests from Dhaka, Beijing made amends to bridge the burgeoning trade deficit. China offered concessional facilities for imports from Dhaka, in addition to giving fiscal incentives to Chinese entrepreneurs for investing in Bangladesh in three selected sectors, viz., home appliances, light engineering and agro-based industries. China has assisted in projects such as fertiliser plant, textile factory, six friendship bridges and the Bangladesh-China Friendship Conference Centre at Dhaka. Here again, as some Bangladeshi experts commented, as China wishes to transit into hi-tech products in the recent reform and opening up drive, it is dumping environment-unfriendly low technology products on to Bangladesh.

China also sent purchasing missions, provided government subsidies in trading with Bangladesh. At the January 2005 Bangkok meeting, the Bangladeshi team has proposed a list of 245 products for duty-free access to the Chinese market. But the Chinese government has allowed only eighty three items in this list from 2006. These include leather products, jute, textile products and garments, fish, soap, automobile parts, bicycles and pharmaceuticals. Nevertheless, competition in the textile field threatens to put millions of Bangladeshis out of job in the next few years. However, to offset trade imbalance, by the recent period, nearly 7,000 items from Bangladesh have been declared by China as duty-free.

China eyes a large portion of the potential sixty trillion cubic feet of natural gas that Bangladesh reportedly possessing. Indeed, the Bangladeshi government has granted exploration rights to China and Begum Zia has invited China, during her visit to Beijing in August 2005, to develop gas fields. China is currently exploring gas explorations and possible construction of gas pipelines.

Construction of 1,250-kilometer pipeline from gas fields in Myanmar to its Yunnan province is being considered. This may be connected with Bangladesh in future. Reports indicate to the Chinese interest in acquiring container port facility at Chittagong – an offer made by Bangladesh prime minister during her visit to Beijing in March 2010 – and other military facilities in Bangladesh.[36] Also, the Kunming-Chittagong road through Myanmar is under negotiation with the concerned parties.

Besides, China is exploring the first coal mine and constructing the coal-based power plant in Barapukuria and in November 2005 the first 125×2 MW power plant was put into production. China built the Bangladesh-China Commercial Town with 500 Chinese shops at Kanchpur built at a cost of about $6 million from April 2005. This would further give a boost to the entry of Chinese goods into Bangladesh.

Other projects where Chinese investments were sought include expansion of the Pagla Water Treatment Plant in Narayanganj (at a cost of $ 226 million), Mukhterpur Bridge over the river Dhaleswari (completed in 2008), construction of multi-lane tunnel under the river Karnaphuli, Sonadia deep-sea port and Dohazari-Cox Bazar railway link, $800 million loan to construct Shahjalal Fertiliser Factory and others.[37] In June 2011, Bangladesh signed a loan agreement with EXIM Bank of China worth about $200 million for upgrading the telecom network of the country.[38]

With the neighbouring Myanmar, China had signed an agreement in 2004 for constructing a 1,250-kilometer pipeline connecting the deepwater port of Sittwe on the Bay of Bengal coast to Kunming, the capital of Yunnan province. China has executed dredging projects across the Irrawaddy river and has made efforts to enter the Bay of Bengal. It has listening posts in Great Coco Islands and has developed other ports like Hyangyi, Kyaukpyu and Mergui to berth larger displacement vessels. In addition, China expanded Mandalay and Pegu airfields to receive heavy transports. The Kunming Initiative launched in 1999 as a sub-regional cooperative effort between Bangladesh-China-India-Myanmar which was later in 2013 in the form BCIM is meant for expanding infrastructure projects so that interior land-locked provinces like Yunnan and Sichuan could have maritime outlets through Myanmar.

Nepal

Bordering the sensitive region of Tibet makes Nepal a valuable neighbour for China. In order to stabilise its borders and possibly make a dent in the 1950 Nepal-India treaty, China had in the recent period initiated several plans for expanding infrastructure projects in Nepal. These include construction of another Kodari road, an extension of Tibet railway into Nepal, telecommunications and others.

China has extended cooperation to Nepal in terms of aid in constructing several highways including the Kathmandu-Lhasa route, leather factories, textiles, paper mills, sugar factories and other such projects.[39] The total trade volume between China and Nepal is miniscule, although within this China enjoys a favourable balance of trade position.[40] It was $67 million in 1997, $220 million in 1999 to $1.2 billion in 2012.[41] Most of Nepal's trade with China is through Tibet or Hong Kong, with the overland trade passing through six border points with Tibet, viz., Kodari-Nyalam, Rasua-Kerung, Yari (Humla)-Purang, Olangchunggola-RIYO, Kimathanka-Riwo and Nechung (Mustang)-Legze.[42] In March 2006, visiting state councillor Tang Jiaxuan agreed to bridge the unfavourable trade by agreeing to provide duty-free treatment to about 1,550 Nepalese goods exports to China. This limit was raised later to 7,787 products of Nepal in 2012.[43] About twenty Chinese joint venture companies with investment of about $100 million in Nepal exist mainly in food processing industries - in comparison to the presence of about 399 foreign-funded projects overall in Nepal.[44] During premier Wen Jiabao's visit to Nepal in January 2012, $750 million in assistance was announced for the next three years. More controversial was the August 2011 announcement of China that it had secured rights to develop Lumbini at an investment of $3 billion.[45] Also, the $43 million project of ZTE, China's telecommunications giant for setting up four data centres in Biratnagar, Kathmandu, Hetauda and Pokhara, have led to concerns.[46]

China has emphasised on extending cooperation with Nepal in infrastructure development programmes connecting Tibet and Nepal. Araniko highway of 104 km was built in 1967 connecting the two countries. The 174 km Prithvi highway was built with Chinese assistance, as with thirty-six km Narayanghat-Mugling road and sixty-five km Pokhara-Baglung Road.[47] Other projects include plans to extend the Golmud-Lhasa railway line to Kathmandu. If implemented, these could enhance further the logistics facilities of the PLA in the region. Apart from the economic benefits that such projects entail, especially for Tibet, the strategic and logistics importance of overcoming Himalayan barriers may not be out of place.[48] In February 2012, Nepal signed a contract with Three Gorges International Corp for building a 750-megawatt West Seti dam in the northwest Nepal with investment of $1.6 billion by 2019.[49] Another hydro-electricity project includes Trishuli project in central Nepal.

China and Nepal had agreed in 1994 to start transport service along the 873 km highway, linking Kathmandu and Lhasa. It took nearly a decade for this proposal to materialise. The Nepalese government-run transport organisation Sajha Yatayat announced that in September 2004 such trips will be made.[50] However, this was delayed further till 1 May, 2005 when in March 2005 both sides signed an agreement to start a two-way bus ride.[51] Other projects include upgrading the twenty-seven kilometers Kathmandu ring-road and in May 2012 a dry port at Nepal-China border of Larcha.[52] In addition, in September 2011, Nepal signed a contract with a Chinese company CAMC Engineering Co. to construct an airport at Pokhara.[53]

Maldives

China had opened its embassy in the Maldives in 2011. However, interactions between the two countries continued since the 1972 diplomatic relations was established. Although trade between the two is minimal ($ 2 million in 2002 increased to $64 million by 2010), tourism from China to the island had picked up with over 120,000 visiting in 2010.[54] China's investments in the island are mostly in the Ihavandhoo, Marao and Maarandhoo.[55] Specific construction projects include that of the ministry of foreign affairs building as well as the national museum, the 1000 housing units project, renewable energy, hotels, telecommunications, etc.[56]

Premier Zhu Rongji visited in May 2001 in which it was reported that China had signed an agreement with the Maldivian government to construct a naval base for the Chinese Navy at Marao, forty kilometers from the capital Male.[57] The visit by Wu Bangguo, the second ranking politburo standing committee member of the communist party of China in May 2011 was also significant for further expanding cooperation between the two countries.

Sri Lanka

China's involvement in Sri Lankan infrastructure development projects is widespread and include construction of Hambantota port (to cost $1.5 billion), Norochcholai power plant that is to generate 900 MW of thermal power ($1.3 billion), Palai-Kankasanthurai railway link, Colombo-

Katunayake Expressway, Jaffna Housing complex for the army personnel, a Special Economic Zone at Mirigama (being developed by China's Huichen Investment with $28 million investment), developing 1,000 acre Tapioca farm and others.[58] For executing these projects, already 30,000 Chinese workers have been sent to different parts of the country. In November 2012, China also launched a communications satellite for Sri Lanka as part of a contract between SupremeSAT (Pvt) Ltd. and the China Great Wall Industry Corp. In all, according to the Sri Lankan deputy minister for economic development, Lakshman Yapa Abeywardene, China had committed $3 billion in these projects by 2010, while by 2004 China's investments amounted to about $250 million.[59] Other estimates indicate to over $12 billion in investments by the next decade.[60]

China Harbour Engineering Company and the Sino Hydro Corporation are involved in the Hambantota project. Originally offered to India, one phase of this port was opened - after cost escalation (with an estimated $40 million in additional costs out of a total $400 million for this phase) and time overruns (by one year) - for international shipping in June 2012.[61] China also offered to construct another port at Colombo with reports of possible investments from China amounting to $50 billion.[62] In January 2007, Sri Lanka signed an agreement with China for building Hambantota port facility. In 2010, China also agreed to construct an airfield at this port with $209 million.[63] Besides, the Chinese have long expressed interest in the building of the Trincomali port – the fifth largest natural harbour in the world.[64]

The Joint Trade Committee, established between the two countries in 1982, formed the nodal organisation to pursue economic cooperation in several fields. In the early 1990s this organisation was amalgamated with another to form the Joint Commission to look after trade and economic issues. From 1957 to 2000 China had provided Sri Lanka with economic aid to the tune of about Yuan 702 million to carry out various infrastructural and joint ventures in piggery and poultry, toy-making projects, deep sea-fishing, chaff-processing and pencil-making and the like. Bilateral trade between the two countries, in addition to the traditional items like rice and rubber, included Chinese imports of red tea, precious stones coconut oil and main exports to Sri Lanka include rice, light textile products, medicine equipment, metal fittings, machinery, tobacco, sugar and so on. The bilateral trade increased gradually over a period of time to about $458 million in 2000, with $445 million in export and $12.85 million in import on the Chinese side.[65] In 2011, these figures increased to $3.14 billion – still the balance of payments position in favour of China. Clearly the trade figures showed a heavy imbalance at the cost of Sri Lanka.[66] It is in this backdrop and Sri Lankan displeasure at the negative balance of payments, that the PRC was compelled to invest in joint venture projects. Nearly 300 contracts were signed between the two countries worth about $400 million for cooperation in textile, electric power, water conservancy, highways, communication, fishing industry and agricultural sectors of Sri Lanka.[67]

Conclusion

China's assistance to connectivity and infrastructure projects in South Asia have been largely beneficial to China in many ways - as profitable investment destinations in tax-free exclusive industrial zones, garnering assured resources to its domestic industry, opening windows into the South Asian market for its goods on a long-term basis, favourable balance of payments position, etc. For many a South Asian country as well, these projects provided scope for expansion of economic development. Such connectivity between China and South Asia or within South Asia with Chinese-aided projects provides for expanding avenues for investment and mutually beneficial outcomes, specifically in the context of lack of capital availability in the backdrop of the Euro Zone crisis, although China's objectives in this regard could position itself as a contestant in the short to medium-term perspective and as a dominant player in the region.

While the overall investments of China in such projects is minimal and in fact seen by many South Asian countries as reply to offset trade imbalances heavily in favour of Beijing, several reservations were expressed on China's involvement. For instance, in countries like Pakistan, Bangladesh and Nepal, even as connectivity improved with China's assistance, several reports indicated to the flooding of the local markets with the cheaper Chinese goods, often to the detriment of indigenous cotton textile, jute or leather industries.

Also, most Chinese investments in infrastructure projects are by state-owned enterprises and several times the host country had waived the global tendering process to favour the Chinese companies. This had resulted in monopolies and political pressures from Beijing. Again, most of such transactions are not transparent – indicating to the rampant corruption or bribery by Chinese companies to the local political elites.

More problematic is that today China is insisting on protection for its companies in trouble-torn areas of Pakistan, Nepal, Bangladesh and other South Asian states. This is expected to increase the costs for the host countries in the future.

China's forays in South Asian telecommunications and IT sector could have security implications. Huawei and ZTE companies of China are operating extensively in India, Pakistan, Sri Lanka, Nepal, the Maldives and other countries. India had insisted that these companies desist from using embedded software for possible information-gathering, no such restrictions are in place in other countries.

References

1. Yang Jirui and Sun Jin (eds). *Zhongguo Xibu da kai fa yu Nanya: Xianzhuang yu qianjing [China's Western Development and South Asia: Current Situation and Prospects]*. Chengdu: Sichuan Publication Group, 2004.
2. Han Hua, "China and South Asia", in K Santhanam and Srikanth Kondapalli (eds.), *Asian Security and China 2000-2010*, New Delhi: Shipra Publications and IDSA, 2004, pp. 290-300.
3. See *"Zhongguo ying da tabu dizou jin Yinduyang"*, 15 February 2007, http://military.china.com/zh_cn/critical3/27/20070215/139439 14.html; *"Yinduyang"* [*Indian Ocean*], http ://baike.baidu.com/view/29284 .htm
4. For the Yunnan to Chittagong railway proposal see Xiao Anfu, *"Da Xinan duiwai jiaotong jianshe de sikao yu shexiang - Zhongguo-Yinduyang (Chengdu-Jidaguang) tielu"* [A reflection and consideration of traffic construction in Southwest China- China-Indian Ocean (Chengdu-Chittagong) Railway] Tianfu Xinlun Vol. 6, 2001. See also for Dehong in Yunnan as the strategic petroleum reserves base Ma Ce, *"Yunnan zai Zhongguo Yinduyang haiquan zhanlue zhongde zhongyao diwei" [The important position of Yunnan in China's Indian Ocean maritime* power strategy] Dehong Shifan gaodeng zhuan kexuexiao xuebao [Journal of Dehong Normal College] January 2007.
5. "Yunnan Working To Link Southern Water Outlets" Xinhua, 23 June 1998, *FBIS-CHI-98-174*, 24 June 1998.
6. "China asked to invest in Pakistan power projects", 9 June 2012, http://www.pakistantoday.com.pk/2012/06/09/news/national/china-asked-to-invest-in-pakistan-power-projects/
7. These include raising the height of the Mangla dam, Kohala dam, Neelum Jhelum dam, the Nandipur and Chichokimalian Thermal power projects. See "Pakistan envisions $ 11 billion Chinese investment in energy sector", http://pakistanchinafriendship. wordpress.com/20 11/10/20/ pakistan-envisions-ll -bln-chinese-investment-in-energy-sector/.
8. The February 1989 bilateral investment treaty between the two guides the investments flows. On the August 2011 figure, see "Chinese investment in Pakistan crosses $25 billion mark", AFP, 6 August 2011, http://dawn.com/ 2011/08/06/chinese-investment-in-pakistan-crosses-25-billion-mark/. See for the limitations of China's investments in Pakistan, Lisa Curtis and

Derek Scissors, "The Limits of the Pakistan-China Alliance", 19 January 2012, http://www.heritage.org/research/reports/2012/01/the-limits-of-the-pakistan-china-alliance. Curtis and Scissors argue that between 2005 and 2010, China invested only $1.2 billionin Pakistan.

9. Andrey Volodin, "Soft displacement plus a military-economic link", *Voyenno-Promyshlennyy Kuryer website,* 20 April 2010, NewsEdge Document Number: 201004201477.1_46d203eaca31c102 *World News Connection* File Number 985, accession Number 297701801
10. This is based on Samina Shabir and Reema Kazmi, "Economic Effects of the Recently Signed Pak-China Free Trade Agreement", *The Lahore Journal of Economics,* September 2007, pp. 173-202
11. Mushtaq Ghumman, "Government will allow Chinese Geological Survey" , *Business Recorder Online,* 11 March 2010, NewsEdge Document Number: 201003111477.1_cc8f005da297a9c0 World News Connection File Number 985, accession Number 295700320
12. Tom Wright and Jeremy Page, "China Pullout Deals Blow to Pakistan", http://online.wsj.com/article/SB10001424052970203405504576600671644602028.html; "Chinese investment in Pakistan continues to grow", http://www.worldfinance.com/inward-investment/asia-and-australasia/chinese-investment-in-pakistan-continues-to-grow
13. Shabir and Kazmi, n.10.
14. Sohail Sarfraz, "Massive misuse of Pak-China FTA detected", *Business Recorder Online (Karachi) 15 April 2010,* NewsEdge Document Number: 201004151477.1_21340163442cf 073, World News Connection File Number 985 Accession Number 297450439
15. "Zardari's visit to China" *The News,* 23 October 2009, http://pk.chineseembassy.org/eng/zbgx/t622031.htm. However, according to Andrey Volodin, the agreement between Xinjiang and North Western Frontier Province provides a foothold for Beijing in the long-term perspective.
16. See for the statement of Xu Zuyuan, Vice Minister of Transport of China, "Pakistan to welcome Chinese involvement in Gwadar projects: Gilani", 30 March 2010, http://pk.chineseembassy.org/eng/zbgx/t676106.htm
17. "Pakistan, China Sign $1b Dams Project", *The News,* 23 September 2009, http://pk.chineseembassy.org/eng/zbgx/t603981.htm
18. This is funded now by the Chinese state banks to the tune of $400 million. See Hasnain Kazirn, "The Karakoram Highway: China's Asphalt Powerplay in Pakistan", 17 July 20 12, http://www.spiegel. de/intemational/world/china-expands-karakoram-highway-to-pakistan-a-844282.html; "Dirt road to mega-highway: China invests in Pakistan", 17 July 2012, http://www.globalposl.com/dispatch/news/business/120717/dirt-road-mega-highway-chinas-latest-investmentpakistan.
19. This was stated by Pakistan premier Gilani in early 2010. See "Pakistan to welcome Chinese involvement in Gwadar projects: Gilani", 30 March

2010, http://pk.chineseembassy.org/eng/zbgx/t676106.htm. The Iranian side as well had suggested that a Chinese oil firm and Russian Gazprom are interested in the laying down of the IP line, with the Chinese firm showing interest in the Pakistani portion after the March 2009 proposal was approved by Islamabad. See "China, Russia Keen To Invest In Iran-Pakistan Gas Pipeline Project", *Fars News Agency,* 17 April 2010, NewsEdge Document Number: 201004171477.1_f0a40062966ab27d File Number 985 Accession Number 297550337

20. Syed Fazl-e-Haider, "China-Pakistan rail link on horizon", *Asia Times,* 24 February 2007, http://www.atimes.com/atimes/South_Asia/IB24Df02.html
21. "China promises to help Pakistan in development of energy sector", 5 April 2010, http://pk.chineseembassy.org/eng/zbgx/t677522.htm
22. The latter project was inaugurated by Xu Zuyuan, Vice Minister of Transport of China in early 2010. See "Pakistan to welcome Chinese involvement in Gwadar projects: Gilani", 30 March 2010, http://pk.chineseembassy.org/eng/zbgx/t676106.htm
23. Farhan Bokhari and Kathrin Hille, "Pakistan in talks to hand port to China" , *Financial Times,* 30 August 2012, http://www.ft.com/cms/s/0/5c58608c-f2a6-11e1-ac41-00144feabdc0. html
24. "Pakistan approves Gwadar port transfer to China", *AFP,* 30 January 2013, http://dawn.com/2013/01/30/pakistan-approves-gwadar-port-transfer-to-china/ and Hao Zhou, "China to run Pakistani port", *The Global Times,* 1 February 2013, http://www. globaltimes.cn/content/759538. shtml
25. Volodin, n. 9.
26. "Chinese investment in Pakistan continues to grow", http://www.worldfinance.com/inward-investment/asia-and-australasia/chinese-investment-in-pakistan-continues-to-grow
27. Alok Bansal, "Why Pakistan's rebels are attacking Chinese projects", 17 July 2012, http://www.rediff.com/news/column/why-pakistans-rebels-are-attacking-chinese-projects/20120717.htm. Bansal also cited the cases of bomb blast at the Karachi Consul office of China on 18 July 2012 in addition to three Chinese engineers killed at Gwadar in May 2004; February 2006 killing of Chinese engineers of a cement factory at Hub; attack on a Chinese workers convoy in Khuzder in July 2007; attack on Chinese engineers at Dera Bugti on 22 November 2011; 2004 kidnapping and killing of a Chinese at Gomal Zam Dam in South Waziristan Agency; July 2008 kidnap of three Chinese women at Lal Masjid; May 2011 attack on PNS Mehran naval base; 28 February 2012 killing of a Chinese woman at Peshawar, etc. See also, Ananth Krishnan, "Fearing instability, Chinese companies rethink Pakistan investments", *The Hindu,* 13 January 2012, http://www.thehindu.com/news/international/article2799122.ece .

28. Lauren Frayer, "China's Increased Investment Upsets Some Pakistanis", 21 August 2012, http://www.npr.org/2012/08/21/159531740/chinas-increased-investment-upsets-some-pakistanis
29. *China's Foreign Affairs 2006,* Beijing: Ministry of Foreign Affairs, 2007, p. 74.
30. *China's Foreign Affairs 2004,* Beijing: Ministry of Foreign Affairs, 2005, p. 77.
31. *China's Foreign Affairs 2005,* Beijing: Ministry of Foreign Affairs, 2006, p. 74.
32. Guo Nei, "New terror network attacked Chinese workers" , *China Daily,* 14 June 2004, http://www.chinadaily.com.cn/english/doc/2004-06/14/content_339131.htm
33. "Afghan government to compensate Chinese terror victims", *Xinhua,* 20 June 2004, http://www.chinadaily.com.cn/english/doc/2004-06/20/content_340943.htm
34. "China urges Afghanistan to ensure safety for Chinese citizens", *Xinhua,* 30 May 2006, http://news.xinhuanet.com/english/2006-05/30/content_4622296.htm
35. For an overall perspective, see M. Shahidul Islam, "China-Bangladesh relations: Contemporary convergence", 25 January 2012, http://www.thedailystar.net/newDesign/news-details. php? nid = 219707.
36. "China's help sought for deep-sea port, road link", 20 March 2010, http://www.thedailystar.net/new Design/news-details.php?nid= 130836.
37. These details are from "China offers to invest more", 22 October 2012, http://www.thedailystar.net/newDesign/news-details.php? nid=254797 and "$300m Chinese loan to build 3-D IT village" , http://www1.bssnews.net/newsDetails. php?cat=0&id=221439& date=2012-01-17.
38. Sergei DeSilva-Ranasinghe, "China's investment spurs Bangladesh development", 15 June 2011, http://www.future directions.org.au/publications/indian-ocean/29-indian-ocean-swa/101-chinas-investment-spurs-bangladesh-development.html .
39. Ramakant, *Nepal-China Relations,* New Delhi: Abhinav Publications, 1976; TR Ghoble, *China-Nepal Relations and India,* New Delhi: Deep Publications, 1986; Shashi Bhusan Prasad, *The China factor in Indo-Nepalese Relations,* 1955-72, New Delhi: Commonwealth Publications, 1989 and Shiva Bahadur Singh, *Indo-Nepalese Relations: Discord and Harmony,* Varanasi: Ganga Kaveri Publication House, 1994.
40. "China and Nepal", 12 April 2007, http://www.fmprc.gov.cn/eng/4402.html and Chinese Ministry of Foreign Affairs Policy Planning Division, *Zhongguo Waijiao 2006* [*China's Diplomacy 2007*]. Beijing: Ministry of Foreign Affairs, 2007.
41. "Nepali Business Leader Foresees Rosy Prospect for Nepal-China Economic Cooperation" , *People's Daily,* 24 December 2000, http://

english.people.com.cn/english/200012/24/eng20001224_58692.html and China's Ambassador to Nepal, Yang Houlan, "Growing Together", 7 January 2013, http://www.fmprc.gov.cn/eng/wjb/zwjg/zwbd/t1003198.shtml

42. This is based on Isabelle Duquesne, "Nepal: Chinese support in road construction and Investment", 30 December 2012, http://www.telegraphnepal.com/national/2012-12-30/nepal:-chinese-support-in-road-construction-and-investment.html
43. "China, Nepal sign letter of exchange on zero tariff", Xinhua, 12 November 2012, http://news.xinhuanet.com/english/china/2012-11/12/c_131968637.htm
44. Pradeepa Viswanathan, "Nepal: What is the Potential for Foreign Investment?", 21 May 2012, http://www.ipcs.org/article/india/nepal-what-is-the-potential-for-foreign-investment-3620.html
45. "China's $3 Billion Investment in Buddhist Mecca Sparks a Row", 25 August 2011, http://himalayasnepal.com/2011/09/25/chinaper centE2per cent80per cent99s-3-billion-investment-in-buddhist-mecca-sparks-a-row/
46. Thomas K Thomas, "Security agencies take guard as China invests in Nepal telecom", 19 October 2012, http://www.thehindubusinessline.com/industry-and-economy/info-tech/security-agencies-take-guard-as-china-invests-in-nepal-telecom/article4013647. ece?homepage=true&ref= wl_home
47. Manoj Rijal, "2012, year of China-Nepal friendship in retrospect", *Xinhu a,* 31 December 2012, http:xinhuanet.com/englishlchina/2012-12/31/c_ 132074343.htm
48. See Nischal Nath Pandey, "Nepal's Foreign Policy vis-a-vis India and China: The Security Imperatives", paper presented on 9 April 2003 at Banaras Hindu University, http://www.ifa.org.np/article/article10.php
49. Gopal Sharma, "Nepal clears China plan for $1.6 bln hydroelectric dam", *Reuters,* 2 April 2012, http://www.reuters.com/article/2012/04/02/nepal-china-dam-idUSL3E8F25U420120402.
50. "Nepal announces bus services to Tibet", *Indo-Asian News Service,* 2 August 2004, http://www.123bharath.com/india-news/index.php?action=fullnews&id=5273.
51. "Direct passenger bus to open between China and Nepal in May", *People's Daily,* 29 March 2005, http://english.peopledaily. com.cn/200503/28/eng20050328_178434.html
52. "China-funded Larcha dry port construction begins in Nepal", Xinhua, 20 December 2012, http://news.xinhuanet.com/english/china/2012-12/20/c_132053874.htm. As a part of this project, China will fund ($13.8 million) construction of 6.5 km road linking this port to the border, a border inspection building and a cargo warehouse. This will have a parking facility for 158 big containers and 33 cars.

53. It was reported that initially the contract was for $180 million but was raised to $305 million - raising concerns about kickbacks from China to the Maoist government. See Mei Jingya, "Chinese company bribed Nepal leaders for airport deal: Indian media", 9 October 2012, http://english.sina.com/china/2012/1008/514238.html
54. Sergei DeSilva-Ranasinghe, "China-India rivalry in the Maldives", 17 June 2011, http://www.thejakartapost.com/news/2011/06/17/china-india-rivalry-maldives.html
55. N. Manoharan, "Maldives: Indian Investments vis-a-vis Chinese Footprints", 5 December 2012, http://www.ipcs.org/article/india/maldives-indian-investments-vis-a-vis-chinese-footprints-3773.html
56. "Maldives president lauds China's foreign policy", *Xinhua*, 1 September 2012, http://news.xinhuanet.com/english/indepth/2012-09/01/c_131821248.htm.
57. A.B. Mahapatra, "China acquires a base in Maldives against India with some help from Pakistan" 27 July 2001, http://www.indiareacts.com.
58. Bandula Sirimanna, "Chinese and Indian companies dominate Sri Lanka's mega project business" *The Sunday Times*, 5 September 2010, http://www.sundaytimes.lk/100905/BusinessTimes/bt21.html
59. Cited in Saroj Pathirana, "Sri Lanka gains from Indo-Chinese supremacy battle" , http://www.bbc.co.uk/news/business-117
60. Rajeev Sharma, "China's forays in Sri Lanka", 25 October 2012, http://www.southasiaanalysis.org/node/1022
61. Jayadeva Ranade, "China gains edge in Sri Lanka", 2 July 2012, http://newindianexpress.com/opinion/article555892.ece
62. "Sri Lanka's Chinese-built port opens for business", http://india.nydailynews.com/newsarticle/4fcf66dcb1e35de57a000012/sri-lanka-s-chinese-built-port-opens-for-business
63. "China to build new international airport in Sri Lanka", 10 March 2010, http://news.bbc.co.uk/2/hi/south_asia/8560544.stm
64. "China assures more investments in Sri Lanka", 23 November 2012, http://v3.itnnews.lk/?p=3750
65. For details see "China and Sri Lanka", http://www.fmprc.gov.cn/eng/4437.html.
66. By the mid-1990s, the adverse trade balance against Sri Lanka stood at Rs. 8 billion according to the Sri Lankan Trade Ministry's statistics. See "Commerce minister leads trade team to China", *Daily News*, 26 March 1996.
67. "China assures credit to Sri Lanka", *Daily News*, 27 February 1995; "Biggest trade fair from China from April 5", *Sunday Observer*, 2 April 1995; "Singer, D. Samson sign up with three Chinese companies" , *Sunday Observer* , 23 April 1995; "China grants Rs 1 billion as economic aid: Accords signed", *Daily News*, 24 April 1996.

PART–III
CULTURAL LINKAGES AND SOFT POWER IN REGIONAL INTEGRATION

8

Cross-cultural Dialogues in South Asia

I.P. Khosla

Introduction

In this chapter the emphasis is on connectivity between the South Asian countries at the level of history, culture; and the close bonds that tie the region in terms of tradition, customs, language, ethnicity as well as other bonds like eating and dress.

Although this connectivity is evident within the region and has a background of centuries of a common culture and traditions, there are still elements within that background which have been subject to varying interpretations over the centuries. Furthermore, the attempt in the last six decades, among each of the South Asian countries, and in the effort to build unique cultures/traditions for the promotion of patriotism and national solidarity, has been to create a distance from that common background or to choose selectively from it those elements that suit a particular politico-social agenda. Even within a large nation state like India this has resulted in distance in perceptions or misunderstanding, such as with the people of the Northeast of the country; and of course this is much more so in the matter of cultural connectivity between the different nations of South Asia. It is now necessary to accept that there are many cultures in South Asia, all of which may be inter-linked; but for purposes of connectivity each has to be treated as having unique elements. Thus, it is increasingly important to embark on the development of the theoretical and practical bases for cross-cultural dialogue in the region.

While charting out these bases it is crucial that we avoid two extremes. One is the assimilationist approach in which one culture, usually that of the largest or most powerful nation, attempts to impose a uniformity of viewpoints on the others. The other assumes that the inter-cultural gulf is so wide that understanding is virtually impossible. The aims of connectivity are best served by recognition of the reality of difference combined with the certainty that mutual understanding is possible. This is especially important in South Asia, because of the ties of history and culture that bind together the regional cooperation process.

In what follows there is an attempt to suggest the kind philosophical foundations that may lead to the successful construction of such bases, and the ways in which globalisation and modernity impact on this attempt.

Ties of History and Culture

At the official level, insofar as greater connectivity and regional cooperation is concerned, the major existential driving force to take South Asian cooperation forward is, as the SAARC Charter recognises in the preamble, the consciousness of member states that they are 'bound by ties of history and culture.' This driving force is not to be confused, as is so often done, with the road to get to the objectives. The ties of history and culture are there as a driving force; the other things like the need for joint action are objectives, hopes for the future, discoveries to be made and not established facts. There was, in 1985, hardly any trade within the region, and virtually no other economic or financial ties that could act as driver, no business interest to act as driver; nor were there any strong social ties, while those existing were severely constrained by restrictions on travel; nor media ties, since newspapers and other media from one member state were not read or seen by others and even in India there was little interest in what the media of the neighbours had to say. However, the ties of history and culture have been in existence for centuries and will always, presumably, be there, to be the driver for cooperation. Over a quarter century after the establishment of SAARC, that remains broadly true.

This is what gives special coherence to the relationships and cooperation within the region as opposed to those with the outside world.

However, the charter also recognises that the need for joint action and enhanced cooperation generated by these ties has to be exercised 'within their respective political and economic systems and cultural traditions'. On the one hand these ties are, therefore, expected to carry the regional cooperation vehicle forward along a road defined by several factors, being the stated objectives of the association and which include: the need for joint action, given their common problems, interests and aspirations; the welfare and quality of life of the people of the region; accelerating economic growth; national and regional collective self reliance; and, of course, the promotion of trust, understanding and friendship among them. On the other hand, it is also true that India's neighbours stress the diversity in the South Asian region rather than the binding ties mentioned above and which are the anchor of cooperation in the region.

As a start we examine the strength of that driving force, how India and its neighbours have responded to it, and ways in which it could make for more purposeful cooperation. This could hopefully lead to the philosophical foundations necessary for eventual cross-cultural understanding.

The ties of history and culture bind the member states of SAARC has been repeated and elaborated at successive summits. At the very first summit, Dhaka, December 1985, the declaration announced that regional cooperation was the logical response to the formidable challenges faced by their countries because of the "many common values rooted in their social, ethnic, cultural and historical traditions."[1] At the second summit, in Bangalore, November 1986, the same theme was reiterated and the leaders recalled the age-old cultural, social and historical traditions which link the region, and which constituted solid foundations for regional cooperation, a phrase which was more or less repeated at the third and again at the fourth summits. Succeeding summit declarations went back to it with variations, as for example, the prime minister of India informed the one in Islamabad, January 2004, that "many of us have a shared history" and that "our forefathers fought side by side, transcending religious, regional and linguistic differences against a common colonial oppressor in our first war of independence in 1857." Or the summit at Dhaka, November 2005, which noted, "SAARC is based on the sound foundation of shared values, beliefs and aspirations."[2]

It is also not impossible to find spokesmen from other member states of SAARC emphasising the same theme, as for instance the prime minister of Bangladesh on a March 2006 visit to Delhi saying India and Bangladesh were "bound by a common history, shared values of democracy, tolerance and an ethos rooted in pluralistic and moderate traditions." Former president Chandrika Kumaratunga of Sri Lanka has voiced similar sentiments, that "India is our immediate neighbour, with whom we have been inextricably bound by ties, the origin of which have long been lost in the mist of time."

By and large, however, just as India has emphasised unity in diversity within the subcontinent, the neighbours have emphasised diversity in unity. This leads to the supposition that these ties have been weak or are being weakened.

In assessing the strength of this driving force we have to emphasise the policies of each of the smaller member states of SAARC towards India rather than towards the other countries of the region, for three reasons. Firstly, it is largely true that each of them has land and/or sea frontiers with India and India only. Secondly, India is big compared to its neighbours; it accounts for seventy five per cent or so of the total land area, of the population, the economic strength and even more of the manufacturing strength of the region. There cannot be much cooperation without India, or if India does not play its full role. Thirdly, and most important, all those ties of history and culture that bind the region are sourced in India. In terms of religion, language, traditions, and customs and values it is India that is at the starting point. At the very least it is the necessary intermediary, for even if the waves of invaders from the Northwest brought varied cultures with them, those cultures went through an Indian distillation process before they arrived in the neighbouring regions. So a lot of what follows will be about policies and attitudes towards India, even India proxying for the region, rather than the region as such.

Neighbours Policies

This being so, it can be said at the outset that India's neighbours have consistently tried to weaken, chiefly for domestic political purposes and to assert their separate identities, the cultural and historic ties binding the region. The post-1947 assertion of each of them is that very different cultural and historical traditions went into the making of South Asian politics and society. Interpretations of South Asian history and culture are thus subject, at the extremes to–two kinds of thinking. Where it is agreed that there is such a thing as a South Asian history and culture, historians dispute the nature of its origins and what went into it. Where, on the other hand, the smaller states wish to go further in establishing distinct identities, they dispute the very idea that there could be a history and culture of the region, which would therefore, according to them, have to be an Indian history and culture, as well as separate and distinct Pakistani, Bangladeshi, Sri Lankan, Nepali and so on, histories and cultures. Needless to say, the first kind of thinking feeds and strengthens the second.

If we take religion as an important starting point to examine how far this trend has gone Pakistan was, of course, created as an Islamic state; in

Bangladesh, too, Islam has been declared the religion of the state by the eighth amendment to the constitution, June 1988; even Sri Lanka, with its generally secular traditions, opted for Buddhist and Sinhala status under the constitution in 1956; while in Nepal, taking the opposite direction, the erstwhile Hindu status of the state, which had been highlighted since 1960, has now been abolished. The link between religion and the building of a nation state is typically seen in the case of Bhutan, from a Bhutan Planning Commission document of 1999. This put it as follows: "The emergence of Bhutan as a nation state has been dependent upon the articulation of a distinct Bhutanese identity, founded upon our Buddhist beliefs and values, and the promotion of a common language. These have been defining elements in our history and have made it possible to unify the country and to achieve national homogeneity and cohesion among the various linguistic and ethnic groups".[3]

In each case the religious minorities became less than equal though in each case also the constitution recognised the equality of all citizens. Further the secular character of India was doubted by the neighbours. Pakistan has never accepted that India is secular, and among other neighbours also there is considerable doubt reinforced by events like the occasional communal violence and the rhetoric about constructing temples where mosques are located. It is not so important here that India remained secular, though it did; the point is that the shared civilisational/cultural character of the region was eroded, questioned, and no longer, if it ever was a strong basis for cooperative endeavour.

Another substantial obstacle to developing good neighbourly relations in South Asia is the politically different development. India has by now a deeply entrenched democracy, while the same cannot be uniformly said of its neighbours, although all are making efforts in this direction. Nevertheless, over the years since independence, India became an example for the democratic forces in those countries, so that there is a temptation for the governments there to label any group which strives for democracy as anti-national and pro-Indian; all such groups are put into the same basket as non-democratic forces which oppose the government, and even Indian agents; as such they have to be suppressed if necessary by force. Looked at from the long-term view, there has been progress towards democratisation in South Asia, but the repeated hiccups in this trend are not unrelated to the state of mutual relations among the states.

Coming to ethnic unity/divergence, where populations in the smaller states of the region are close kin in language, religion, ethnicity and culture to groups in India, which groups are often seen as demonstrably more advanced in terms of identity building, in prosperity and economic welfare, in political strength, neighbouring governments wish to look at their history (for instance) in Indo-centric terms, categorising periods of resistance to India as the most significant.

Then there is economic divergence. On the whole India's strength has grown in proportion to that of its neighbours, and this trend is likely to continue. The comparatively rapid industrialisation and growth rates of India needs to be contrasted with the slow growth of industry in the neighbours leading to fears that their economies would be overwhelmed if they opened their market to Indian products. Any attempt to use economic cooperation as an instrument to promote better political relations thus comes up against the smaller neighbours fear that Indian products will swamp their markets and reduce/prevent industrial development.

Overcoming the effects of the above trends in the interests of creating a regional history and culture which are acceptable to both India and its neighbours have domestic Indian implications, on the one hand, regional implications, on the other. All these modes of resolution involve acceptance that it is only through benign intra-South Asian cross-cultural encounters that we can give the necessary broad legitimacy that can make the ties of culture and history serve the purposes that the founders of SAARC intended.

In order to consider the theoretical and practical bases of cross cultural encounters in any region, an essential point is that they have to occur within the context of a broader background of world developments which cannot be ignored; they stand at the meeting point of globalisation and post-modernism. These two apparently contradictory trends are pulled together within the encompassing arenas of history as well as culture or religion. Globalisation is, in essence, about the modern, taking that to have begun with the spirit of inquiry, of human self-reliance and the defiance of customs which launched the renaissance spirit, and whose exploits paved the way to the enlightenment and then the industrial and technological revolutions of modernity.

Globalisation

Among the many definitions of globalisation, the most apt is that it is the recent rapid expansion of the areas of inquiry where the global system is necessarily the main unit of analysis. This does not mean uniformisation, or the spread, unaltered, of universalisms; as they spread, they are particularised; difference exists, but needs to be seen in the context of a globalising process; the latter shifts and changes as it receives inputs from the former, which in turn is influenced towards uniformisation but never achieves it, because the globalising process itself generates resistance as the identity of difference seeks to assert itself. Simultaneously, therefore, in Roland Robertson's phrase, there is the universalisation of particularisms, and the particularisation of universalism.[4]

The main characteristics of the globalising process, as brought out by Niklas Luhmann and others like Roland Robertson, are best described by starting with pre-modern society.[5] This is stratified, while modern society (modernisation and globalisation are intimately linked) is functionally differentiated. In a stratified society, status, clan, the rural/urban divide, belonging or not belonging to this or that class, the domination of the nobility and the upper strata – these are of primary importance. Modernisation meant a shift to functional differentiation, to the importance of political, economic, scientific, or educational, or other subsystems of society rather than of the nobility, the peasants, or other localised classes. Who one was in terms of clan or village becomes less important than what one can do in terms of skills in management or medicine or teaching or the other professions. Access to wealth, power and knowledge is determined not by ones membership of one or other status group, but by functional competence in one or other functional area. The shift to functional specialisation started in the west and increased western communicative capacities to the extent of generating institutionalised techniques, forms of organisation, sophisticated technology and military apparatus that, all put together, enabled western expansion.

So there are three inter-related aspects of globalisation: modernisation, meaning the progress from a traditional to a developing to a developed society; functional differentiation, meaning the replacement of ties to clan or locality by those to groups defined by the system, such as a profession or a skill; and the spread of standardised patterns across the world, which would include value systems like democracy and a commitment to uphold human rights, mass culture and consumption, or the ethos of transnational associations and groups. The third aspect is central to globalisation, since it builds on universals; John Meyer, for instance, says that nation-states around the world exhibit significant isomorphism in their constitutions, they pursue the globally legitimated ends of progress and equality, they conform, in other words, to the norms of world polity.[6] And it is the growth of a world culture that holds this decentralised world together. Progress from one level of a hierarchical system to the next within a stable order, which is the key component of the project of modernity, reappears therefore in the globalisation discussion; as Robertson says the problem of modernity is in a sense subsumed by the problem of globality.[7] He argues that the modern state is impossible without its becoming heavily involved in the production of a high culture which is needed both to handle internal administration and to deal with the problem of identity. Challenges to the world system may come from areas peripheral to the system and may even try to provide a new vision of ultimate reality on which world order should be based. Hence the global field is pluralist, with a proliferation of civilisational, continental, regional and societal definitions of the global-human condition; but it does not follow, as Robertson argues, that difference has value. In fact the validity of the argument that the value of cultural diversity, with particular references to the idea that such diversity is in and of itself good both for the system and units within the system, is not recognised.

There is something inexorable about the retrogression from the laudable target of such recognition, for technology translates into more than just the politics and economics of power; it irons out diversity, thus reinforcing the standardisation of presuppositions leading from politics to economics to culture. Firstly, a world culture of political and economic value systems leads to the widening acceptance of a particular type of political pluralism and democracy as the ideal; to liberal neutralism and the minimal engagement of the state in areas where the deepest beliefs of the people lie. A thin layer of fixed rules, often imported (an aspect of globalisation), substitutes for a flexible regulatory framework within which conflict can be mediated. This leaves cultural or religious differences untouched while encircling them with a band of abstractly formal procedures, which, of course, are also heavily influenced by those imports. The philosophy, the symbolism and the theology of tolerance in the faiths of the citizens is ignored, while religious and moral beliefs (which most often show signs of great flexibility and accommodation) are subordinated to a rigid and overarching liberal neutral code of state action, conflict is left unmediated and, perhaps equally important, nation-building is either ignored or distorted.

This culture incorporates human rights norms which are of recent origin even in the west, being the result of deontology suppressing consequentialism and of placing the individual being above the state. Since the privileged write out the charter of rights, this automatically leads to the suppression of the underprivileged. These norms are part of a standard of civilised behaviour and even of civilisation itself, developed by the European states, and now accepted, or at least expected to be accepted, by all.

Economic Globalisation

The globalisation of trade and finance ensures that norms evolved in the west are incorporated by those who do not wish to be ejected from the system; the basic norm is the link between democracy and the market; there has been a fundamental conviction that democracies do not go to war against other democracies, and that real cooperation will be possible only between real democracies, those which are supported by the people, which in turn can only flourish in an adequately functioning world economy based on an open world market. And the expansion of multinational companies ensures the uniformisation of culture within business and management ethics and practice, working in an environment of uniformised laws and rules relating to business.

Secondly, functional differentiation ensures that in specific areas such as political action, the medical or legal practice, in academic disciplines, even in some of the arts (writers and artists from the peripheral areas desire most of all to publish or exhibit in the core areas) cultural hegemony strengthens a globalised system built in the west. The medical profession, for instance, develops its own driving mechanisms and culture for progress; this is entirely created in the west and it has more in common with that profession in other parts of the world, and is less and less in tune with any component of indigenous culture. Another is the case law developed by legal systems around the world which, in the balance between indigenous and global traditions, has a heavy dependence on the latter.

Just as the basic structures of modernity were isomorphic but autonomous, so the differentiation process creates functional areas or subsystems which have a certain similarity of structure, but are autonomous enough for the doctor or lawyer to have more in common, where his professional culture is concerned, with a doctor or lawyer from a different part of the world, than with someone from a very different profession or calling who belongs to his own part. Subsystems develop a transnational world view, including on work ethics, the acquisition of knowledge and the internal management of the subsystem itself, which reduces the role of indigenous culture. Self-identity is increasingly seen in the context of the subsystem; the central regulatory role of traditional moral codes is weakened: the businessman, now competing internationally, puts profit above moral codes, the politician puts power.

Thirdly, mass culture, including the culture of mass consumption and mass news, which is fuelled by the speed and reach of information technology, has ensured a steadily widening cross-cultural standardisation of the hermeneutics of products, events and images, for which again the norms are developed in the West. Globalised culture – values, functions and mass culture – has two characteristics that bear on cross-cultural dialogue. Firstly, it is not deep; it is confined to a few, especially in Asia and other parts of the third world: the politicians, the academics, the professionals, the bureaucrats and the middle class.

It is carried by the cosmopolitans, those willing to engage the other, people at home in the cultures of other people almost as much as their own. Their ethical and moral codes and cultural values derive from the functional subsystem to which they belong, and these are already cross-cultural. Where the potential for inter-cultural conflict does exist, secondly, the problem arises that the global mass media and consumption culture is contextless and historyless, particularly for those in the recipient areas. Instant judgment rather than a contextualised tolerance based on understanding, instant gratification rather than the fitting into an organic life, are its important components. Constantly changing fashions, particularly in industries like clothing and music, the pressure of advertising to re-buy what you already have, fleeting beguiling images of very different life styles, are what comprise this mass culture.

Modernity, however, taken as that essence of western civilisation that made it stand apart from its predecessors, had a narrower base and a far more elaborate superstructure than that: a base of logically infallible truths; and a superstructure of timeless and incontrovertible universals covering every field of human thought and activity, from philosophy and the law to natural science and technology, from societal development to ethics; but most notably the Cartesian supremacy of reason, the Newtonian origins of modern scientific thought, a hierarchical theory of societal development, and a decontextual ethical structure, whether deontological or consequentialist.

Steady progress, hierarchical ordering, and stability were supposed to shadow the project of modernity; three normative interrelated concepts that had no logically necessary connection with the edifice, but were considered indissociably bound to it. The logic of pure reason, the structure of the material world, the social order, and the concept of the good or the just, were not independent; they were inter-dependent, though autonomous.

The Post-modern Condition

Analysts of the post-modern condition tried to break the edifice of modernity at its foundations, hence also, of course, to undermine the entire project of globalisation. This is a programme which is more elaborate than the preoccupation with 'difference' or 'otherness' which is so much a concern of modernity. This should help destroy that hierarchical ordering of inter-societal or international relations which had enabled and justified orientalism in the intellectual currents of western thinking about the east or, coming to South Asia, assertions that, on the one hand, regional culture is a single stream originating in ancient times and with some variations, or, on the other, that it has always been about multiple streams, which have had something in common. On the contrary, both at the global as well as the regional levels, and even with the loss of faith in modernity, or the end of the era of modernity itself, there was a reinvigorated analysis of that expanding uniformity of pre-suppositions, aspirations and values in political, economic and social constructions which is included in the term globalisation–if modernity was not moving forward in the west, it was spreading horizontally to other parts of the world; and despite avowals by its theorists and exponents about the plurality of definitions of the global-human condition that must necessarily be included in the term, a somewhat less clearly defined hierarchy still pervades these analyses, since such ordering continues to define the reality of the global political, economic and social systems. The challenge to the west-centric view of the world and the increasing activity of non-western cultures and societies in shaping its future has not really had much impact.

It is in this broad framework that we have to examine whether, in our region, culture has escaped the rigidities of the project of modernity, for it is where the liberating influences of post-modernism made their earliest impact worldwide. It should, therefore, be possible to find areas where inter-cultural differences, different interpretations of our respective histories and cultural traditions, are not so wide as to be unbridgeable, nor so narrow as to produce identity. The problem is that every successful effort at understanding carries the germ of assimilation, which India's neighbours fear and resent; and to solve this it is necessary to negotiate the kind of understanding that leaves blank spaces, does not try to go all the way, and that is aimed equally at self-knowledge, even self-transformation. This is the route developed by Fred Dallmayr.[8]

To find this negotiated path we have to ask firstly whether, at all, there can be such areas; more practically whether principles exist for locating them; secondly how we should go about finding the framework, such as an agreed human teleology, from which these principles can be derived; and thirdly, whether there is a guiding reality, such as a supreme being, behind that framework. Or, more mundanely, who constructed it?

Dallmayr's study of eastern and western philosophy reveals a wealth of areas for the kind of cross-cultural encounters he recommends, and he is able to find principles that could help in the search for more. The framework is the departure from modernity which characterises western thinking today, and this signals the entry of a nagging doubt about whether we still have reason to be suspicious of western efforts at cross-cultural understanding. Cultures trying to understand each other need starting points, concepts on which there is agreement; if not a guiding reality, another abstract or metaphysical necessity for understanding should construct and show the way to the framework.

Since the metanarratives of modernity played an essential enabling role in the construction of a technologically advanced western society, which in turn became a sufficient condition for imperial policy, there is some ground for the view that once the metanarratives are exhausted, hegemony will automatically come to an end. On other hand, the search for new ground could be read as an attempt to revive orientalism in an unrecognisably different form, but in those of Dallmayr we feel there is sincerity in suggesting that benign cross-cultural encounter can provide an alternative. And here we nevertheless have to note the continuing intensity with which western studies of eastern culture in particular are non-reciprocally pursued, but also that in South Asian region it is not true that India's studies of its neighbours overwhelm those in the opposite direction.

The Principles for Cross-cultural Understanding

Culture, in historical terms, has followed the pattern of modernity. Within a society there was high culture, middle class culture, and low or mass culture, in a hierarchy which was repeated inter-societal, with some societies being more advance or 'high', culturally, than others: this is a pattern within which cross-cultural understanding presented no problems.

Modernity divides culture into two segments, of which the first includes areas subject to globalisation, such as functional differentiation. There is the culture of the medical world, for instance, which applies the same norms or value systems from one part of the world to another; or that of the legal world, for instance that of the Wall Street law firm which, with the globalisation of business and financial services, has spread to Europe, the Indian subcontinent and East Asia; and in the same category, though at a different level, there is the cultural area of political and economic value systems: the spreading acceptance of a particular form of democracy in which the citizen increasingly withdraws from active participation in politics which is left to the professional politician; or of a Kantian deontological version of human rights and a similarly based economic philosophy which goes briefly by the name of the supremacy of the marketplace. The power of technology holds this segment in place, despite local aberrations.

The other segment is more recalcitrant, and includes the belief in religion, the philosophical world view with which a people's tradition endows them, the teleology of human existence; and percolates to art and literature, music and dancing. This segment, especially the philosophy and world view of a people, is the one that can be tackled through the post-modern approach. If de-differentiation, a signpost of the post-modern approach, leads to the abandonment of borders between high and low art, high and low culture, assimilatory possibilities are reduced or eliminated, and even understanding changes itself to a kind of co-being. The post-modern condition showed incredulity towards universal schemes and metanarratives, and stressed difference, heterogeneity and local determinism. In this context the most desirable cross-cultural encounter is dialogic interaction or engagement; not the Habermasian dialogue which presupposes universal rules for dialogue which are west-oriented; but one which one recognises 'the Other' as interlocutor, but also as a fellow human being, one that can be loved and respected; a dialogue which steers between atomism and assimilation, between absorption and repulsion. The focus has to be on the search for principles enabling the dialogue; without some common ground, a minimum shared understanding of language, there can be no dialogue. But if the common ground is expanded too far there will be an erosion of difference with the latent threat of assimilation or at least acculturation. The precarious middle path, or, put another way, the precarious course between (or beyond) assimilation and atomism, is the one that is most genuine and normatively commendable. We have to ask, once we embark on the project of cross-cultural dialogue, whether there is a space where two or more different modes of thought can meet for mutual understanding; whether there are modes of thought in each culture which are neither identical nor so radically apart as to bar communication. Such modes should not start with the polarisation between, for example, western rational-scientific and South Asian or Indian intuitive-mystical thinking; or western materialism and South Asian and Indian spiritualism; or western freedom of thought and how we in our region cling to the text.

But they can start with the distinction between text and context, rational discourse and life-world. South Asian thought generally and Indian thought in particular, is contextualised, life dependent, while that of the west is context free, categorising or bracketing geographically confined cultural contexts. The cultural and inter-religious engagement of Akbar and the widespread inter-cultural engagement in the development of East Asian civilisation, are examples of the cross-cultural dialogue to be aimed at. This effort should result in the exchange of words and silences, but both words and the silences in between will have multiple meanings which are not meant to be fully grasped. This does not mean the effort should not be made, but that the effort will yield a blend of understanding and non-understanding, the latter giving way slowly, but never completely, to the former. We must be ready to seek understanding, go as far as possible, yet respect the blank spaces that will always be there. This is the middle way between total understanding which means appropriation and destruction of the other, and no understanding, meaning total segregation or atomism; a way which places understanding in a framework of a common world and a common humanity, a multiple universe of hermeneutics where the self is de-centred but not erased.

Worldly situatedness means less distantiation, more contextuality, embeddeness in history, culture, the environment. It makes one ready for co-being with others. Here again it is necessary to steer between an isolating parochialism and the temptation to absorb the other in an effort to achieve standardisation of global homogenisation. The general point is that in the west, metaphysical dichotomies are increasingly being taken from the world of epistemologically possible certainties to that of metaphor, imagery, transcendental poetry. The context underlines the many approaches to understanding, the multitude of meanings and the desirability of leaving some things not understood. Diverse national and cultural traditions, identities and life-forms become, in this philosophical turn, part of the general ascendance of local, national and regional life forms, and this recognition of diversity is a precondition and enabling warrant for an ecumenical order which may extend throughout the region, or even beyond.

The importance of India in this context cannot be over emphasised. India's central position embroils it deeply in regional events without being able to control them. It does not have the option of standing aloof nor is it the capital of the region where all decisions will be made. India must therefore re-identify itself by responding to the call of its own real memory (which is of diversity and the tolerance of difference), but at the same time reach out to the other. In doing so, its own identity will evolve, and it will be able to engage the other through dialogue and reciprocal learning, an agonal process in which silence is as effective a means of discourse as any other.

Eastern Openings

In the philosophies of Radhakrishnan and J.L. Mehta, Dallmayr finds further opportunities for benign dialogic encounter. He also explains their philosophies in some detail as his own contribution to an opening; and goes beyond philosophy to learn from their life worlds, making one think of the possibility that, apart from a benign wish for dialogue, eclectic essentialism or disillusionment with the west's cultural tradition could be involved in the crossing of cultures.

Radhakrishnan combines the abstractions of logical thought with spiritual aspiration; and autonomous reflection, which is a characteristic of both, with experiential reality, a life lived.[9] He combines western and Indian culture as well as tradition and modernity, and goes to metaphysics. Being is the foundational concept and the existential world derives from it; but being itself does not exist, it is free and unconditionally active, hence gives rise to the world. So Being is absolute, or Brahman; and it is unceasing activity, or Ishvara, which appears as the agency which creates, sustains or destroys (Brahma, Vishnu, Siva), and in this world, which is a dependent reality, an appearance (Maya), man is a wanderer, free, moving from one metamorphosis to another, but always immersed in the creative intention of the cosmos. Human suffering leads to deeper insights; through solutions to ones problems we move to another metamorphosis, and thereby collectively to Brahmalok, or the Kingdom of God. Radhakrishnan's philosophy provides the grounding for a dialogue made possible by Indian teachings in the (actualisable) domain of practical life, that of Karma Yoga construed as a non-attached mode of life. Mahatma Gandhi is a typical Karma Yogin who combined simple goodness, patience and an active engagement on behalf of the oppressed and underprivileged of society, qualities which uniquely entitled him to reach out to and understand others, whatever be the different cultures to which they belong.

As for the philosophy of J.L. Mehta, three aspects are relevant.[10] First, the need to overcome the modern metaphysics of the cogito which, following Descartes, was taken up by Kant in his transcendental consciousness, and others like Fichte in the infinite ego; and most of all in Hegel in the absolute Spirit. Cogito leads to subjectivity, to privileging the conscious and self-conscious. It was Heidegger who showed the way out through the idea of Dasein, or being, thus undermining modern epistemology with its dichotomies between subject and object, knower and known. Secondly, in its historical development (per Hegel) Cogito led to a view of history as progress from obscurity to ever higher analytical levels of thought, but in the process of the self realisation of human reason at the expense of myth and the imagination (which faculties accompany the human as Being) there was the Europeanisation of the world, the west comprehending the east on its own terms but not vice versa. Hermeneutics came to be used as a western weapon in this interaction. Nietzsche, Heidegger, and Gadamer broke away from this tradition, opening the path to a hermeneutics of 'letting be'. Thirdly, therefore, on this path, the hermeneutical understanding of cross-cultural interaction needs to be an experience of understanding-self-understanding or even self-transformation, an ontological process, a truth-event in which exchange by words and experience leads to both comprehension and the possibility of change on each side. Such an approach is especially important for South Asia, where atmosphere is continuously clouded by suspicions of homogeneity and hegemonism. Play, participation, opening oneself to the other, self change, a mutual sharing of horizons rather than trying to grasp the concept of the other – these are the characteristics of understanding.

As with Radhakrishnan, Dallmayr looks at Mehta's views and example on a life lived for clues to further openings for dialogic reciprocity. Mehta, he says, linked the classics with current Indian lived reality, particularly the Rig Veda as the founding origin and source of Indian experience, a text which is used constantly to resume that experience in the light of all that has emerged since then. A whole stream of sacred texts and insights were based on the Rig Veda, including the poetic formulations, the wisdom that gave rise to the Upanishads, or the status of Vedic Gods like Agni, Rudra or Varuna, who formed part of a poetic world disclosure, not a personification of the forces of nature, nor the embodiment of abstract concepts. These Gods are not out there, separated from us, but are a part of everyday being and a channel into a part of our everyday world. Mehta's involvement with popular and devotional Hinduism or Bhakti, concerns an immediate living relationship with the sacred which the Hindus never abandoned. This is illustrated by his comments on the Ramayana, the progress of Rama from the human to the divine; and on the Mahabharata, that treasure house of stories, gods, heroes, sacred symbols and values like non-violence, and that every being, during its life, is backed up by a divine power. Bhakti means feeling, the unity of heart and mind, going beyond the division between faith and reason, which is a necessary prerequisite for abandoning the dichotomies that bar cross-cultural understanding.

Conclusion

The cultural protectionism practised by nations, minorities or ethnic groups in South Asia, even the nationalisation of culture as a reaction either to the relativisation implicit in globalisation, or to the fear of Indian assimilationism, or both, provide an assurance of genuine plurality.

In this region the awareness of difference strengthened the struggle against colonialism and led to an understanding of the ways to resist the metanarratives of modernity. Equally important, it was the rigidities of modernity that helped to ensure that those weapons were effective during a struggle that was usually protracted. Similarly, it is the rigidities of globalisation that facilitate an understanding of its weaknesses, and enable resistance and the assertion of the local. These various struggles, against colonialism, modernity and globalisation, have given the diverse national, ethnic and other groups within the region the experience and the weapons needed to fight against any kind of assimilation, but they have also encouraged deliberate policies of distantiation from the central cultural foundations.

On the one hand, if these rigidities are removed by the absence of framework, if the post-modern meets globalisation, the imposition of the uniformities of presupposition that have so far characterised political and economic constructions and only recently began being extended to culture would, driven by the force of performative technology, be the more rapidly so extended. In other words, if we agree with Lyotard that performative technology subordinates the metanarratives of modernity at a time when they are already under attack, then it can also subordinate the creative openings provided by post-modernism for cross-cultural dialogue; then such openings become the place where globalisation meets and takes advantage of post-modernism.[11] In other words the impact of globalised value systems or functional subsystems/subcultures, or of the spread of a global culture through the technology of the media and mass consumption can lead to the slow but inexorable absorption of traditional and deeply rooted indigenous culture. Perhaps this can only be avoided by a reassertiveness which resembles fundamentalism, a reassertiveness which cannot help cross-cultural dialogue.

On the other hand, if we go with the internal logic or the internal framework of post-modernism itself, it has to be contextualised, and that historical context can only be the relative and historic decline of the civilisation that produced it. At the same time, while it is not necessary that the origins and logic of post-modernism should have had anything to do with a programme of cultural expansion or assimilation, and this has probably not been the case, but going again by its internal logic which conflates intent and result, a nagging doubt seems not unjustified. In that case our cultural roots will still remain intact, though in attenuated form. Nevertheless there will be many areas of culture, from all parts of our region, where cross-cultural understanding is not redundant because it has already become part of a uniformised global process, nor problematic because of the impossibility of understanding or inevitability of disjuncture. These areas include most prominently religion and belief in a traditional heritage, of daily life and ritual and the family.

It is true that through the openings created for such cross-cultural dialogue traffic can move both ways: towards the enhancement of cultural pluralism through benign cultural dialogue; or towards gradual acculturation or assimilation if one or other partner in the dialogue has or develops non-benign intentions. This underlines the importance of additional guiding principles to separate the benign from the non-benign, guiding principles which have to be fully aware of the power of technology and the technology of power.

References

1. Cited in Davinder Kumar Madaan (ed), *SAARC, Origin, Development and Programmes,* New Delhi: Deep and Deep Publications, 1997, p. 132.
2. Texts of the SAARC summit declarations and of the statements made by heads of delegations at those summits can be accessed at the SAARC Secretariat website and in the various issues of *South Asian Survey.* For the first nine summits the declaration texts are also in Madaan, *ibid*.
3. Cited in Daniel Schappi, "Cultural Plurality, National Identity and Consensus in Bhutan", *Center for Comparative and International Studies*, Working Paper no. 6, University of Zurich, p. 6.

4. Roland Robertson,"Internationalisation and Globalisation", *University Centre for International Studies Newsletter,* University of Pittsburg, Spring 1989.
5. Niklas Luhmann, "The World Society as a Social System", in *Essays on Self-Reference,* New York: Columbia University, 1990, pp. 175-190.
6. John Meyer, "The World Polity and the Authority of the Nation-State", in Albert Bergesen, (ed.), *Studies of the Modern World System*, New York: Academic, 1980, pp. 109-137.
7. Robertson, n. 4.
8. Fred Dallmayr, *Beyond Orientalism, Essays on Cross-Cultural Encounters,* New York: State University of New York, 1996.
9. The two best known and most accessible of the works of S. Radhakrishnan are, *The Hindu View of Life*, London: George Allen and Unwin, 1927; *An Idealist View of Life,* London: George Allen and Unwin, 1932.
10. J.L. Mehta, *Philosophy and Religion, Essays in Interpretation,* New Delhi: Indian Council of Philosophical Research and M. Manoharlal Publishers, 1990.
11. J-F. Lyotard, *The Post-Modern Condition: A Report of Knowledge,* Manchester: Manchester University Press, 1984.

9

Cultural Diplomacy and Regional Integration in South Asia: Relevance and Importance of India's Role

Rabindra Sen

Cultural diplomacy has acquired a great deal of relevance, especially in recent years, as a tool of foreign policy. This chapter seeks to highlight the role of cultural diplomacy as an instrument of India's foreign policy in general and for promoting goodwill and understanding in relations with its South Asian neighbours in particular.[1] The chapter is broadly divided into two parts. In the first part, the importance of cultural diplomacy is highlighted, with special emphasis on India's rich cultural heritage and tradition. The second part of the chapter deals with the importance of cultural diplomacy in India's South Asia policy. Relating cultural diplomacy to our 'South Asia' policy, an attempt is made in this section to bring out the salience of cultural diplomacy in underpinning efforts towards the objective, howsoever remote or unattainable it may appear or in reality be, of genuine regional cooperation.

Cultural Diplomacy and Indian Foreign Policy

Let us first of all consider the importance of culture and cultural diplomacy, the contextual significance of which for India's foreign policy in general is provided by the richness of its cultural heritage. The culture of a nation manifests itself through language and art, philosophy and religion, education and science, films and newspapers, radio and television, social habits and customs, political institutions and economic organisations.[2] Culture is an important factor in determining the status of a country in the international community.[3] It is increasingly axiomatic today that the old calculations of 'hard power' are no longer sufficient to guide a country's conduct in world affairs. 'Soft power' has also become important.[4] Needless to say, a nation's cultural appeal would go a long way towards bolstering its 'soft power'.

Cultural diplomacy would imply the use of the art of diplomacy in promoting culture which would amount to projecting a particular group to another, creating awareness of one another.[5] The task of cultural diplomacy would be to produce understanding that goes beyond stereotyped images and to mould perceptions in a favourable way.[6] The Indian Council for Cultural Relations (ICCR), set up in April 1950, is India's preeminent instrument of cultural diplomacy. The ICCR has taken upon itself the twin tasks of promoting and interpreting Indian culture abroad in its widest sense as well as in establishing, reviving and strengthening cultural ties between India and other countries.[7]

India is culturally rich and powerful. In June 2008, at the inauguration of the Rabindranath Tagore Centre in Kolkata, the then external affairs minister Pranab Mukherjee referred to India as a cultural superpower[8] and said, "Our culture goes back to the dawn of time.[8] It is distinguished by antiquity, continuity, refinement, diversity and an ability to assimilate the best from outside without losing its own inherent character and authenticity".[9] In the same speech, Mukherjee highlighted the greatly increased importance of cultural diplomacy and referred to India's unique position for facilitating cultural interaction among nations.[10] While India still has miles to go in its quest to be a global power, the world indeed is already embracing it as a cultural giant. As Swami Vivekananda had emphasised long ago, other nations may have an unquestionable command over material resources, but they have to turn to India for the cementing spiritual force.[11]

Endowed with a very powerful heritage in every sphere of cultural activity, it is hardly surprising to see cultural diplomacy evolving into a significant Track II, and India realises how important it is to go all out to leverage this thrust.[12] Indian cultural centres are important platforms to promote India's cultural diplomacy in South Asia and other parts of the world. The main activities of these cultural centres are to provide the local population an opportunity to learn about Indian culture.[13] Also important are the formal cultural agreements India has signed with a number of South Asian countries.[14] Educational assistance forms another element of India's cultural diplomacy, offering opportunities to visit India, acquire education and learn about Indian culture.[15] Technical assistance is also provided under the umbrella of the Indian Technical and Economic Cooperation Programme.[16]

While crafting a new cultural diplomacy and rebuilding its soft power, however, we should be careful not to keep our eyes off the important tasks and challenges ahead. While reinventing its cultural diplomacy in Asia, India needs to focus more on the two-way interaction and avoid the past crude emphasis on what India gave to the rest of Asia,[17] projecting itself as it did in the past as the 'mother of all civilisations'. As former Indian foreign secretary Muchkund Dubey has observed, "We should eschew the tendency too frequently on display among Indians to rub in commonalities or overstate them. We should generally leave it to them to highlight their commonalities with us."[18] The policy prescription, albeit a general one, is particularly relevant to the cultural plane. In many places, domestic politics often prevents an acknowledgement of the common cultural past, let alone building on it. We should make it easier for the countries both in our immediate and extended neighbourhood, to explore, discover and preserve the shared history.[19] This would necessarily involve a return to greater cultural openness, which lies at the core of India's soft power tradition.[20] The road to rejuvenation of India's soft power in Asia lies though mutual cultural rediscovery.

India needs to develop new instrumentalities in leveraging its widely acknowledged soft power strengths. What is required is a cohesive and consistent policy to maximise the gains. For this the foreign office and the ministries of tourism and culture need to work with greater synergy.[21] Other ministries such as information and broadcasting, communication and information technology, and human resource development also have to join in and pool their efforts to concertedly promote India's public and cultural diplomacy.

Cultural Diplomacy and South Asia Policy

In this part of the Paper, the focus is on the most pertinent question as to how important cultural diplomacy is and should be in the formulation and implementation of India's 'South Asia' policy and in bringing the countries closer together to realise the objective of regional cooperation without which South Asia will but continue to be one of the volatile and peace-starved regions of the world.

With regard to the issue of regional integration in South Asia, there are four basic questions which are relevant. How integrated is South Asia? What are the obstacles to regional integration in South Asia? What are the notable achievements, if any, of South Asian Association for Regional Cooperation (SAARC)? What are the weaknesses of SAARC?

The above questions are not going to be taken up for a detailed discussion. But a few comments on the level of integration in South Asia and the role of SAARC will not be out of place. The purpose of mentioning the questions is to establish the significance and relevance of cultural diplomacy and connectivity for moving forward towards the objective of regional cooperation.

Regional cooperation in South Asia has been handicapped by the trust deficit, especially between India and Pakistan.[22] Even the historic election in Pakistan in 2013, which gave rise to expectations of the dawning of a new era in India-Pakistan relations, has not made much of a difference. To apply one of the most important yardsticks of measuring regional cooperation, i.e., intra-regional trade, more than two and a half decades after its formation, SAARC is way behind the European Union, NAFTA and ASEAN. There is no gainsaying the fact that SAARC has not achieved much and, as Smruti Pattanaik rightly observes "is found wanting both in terms of forming a regional identity and of forging any sense of a regional belongingness."[23] However, in spite of the failure of SAARC to live up to the expectations, it is perhaps too early to.completely write it off.[24]

One of foremost objectives of India's South Asia policy should be to relentlessly try to promote cooperation among the countries in the region. While seeking to further its interests, India should not overlook the importance of looking both in and around. A strategy of looking at other regions can only supplement and should not be thought of as a substitute of the need to improve and strengthen relations with our immediate neighbours irrespective of the nature of our relationships with them. Muchkund Dubey, in fact, goes to the extent of arguing that India's neighbours are its best and natural partners for economic cooperation.[25]

There are, of course, valid reasons to be skeptical about the state of affairs in South Asia and India's own position in the region. Former prime minister Manmohan Singh himself said that we live 'in a difficult neighbourhood'.[26] India's own position in the region also has become weaker.[27] Subhash Kapila observes:

> India has achieved a fair measure of foreign policy successes as far as South East Asia and East Asia are concerned and could be said to be following a well calibrated strategy in these regions with long term gains in mind. Regrettably, in South Asia right under its nose, *where Indian foreign policy successes are most needed,* India seems to have been totally outmanoeuvred by China's grand strategy and diplomatic moves.... India's national

attributes of power abundantly bestowed on it should have facilitated India to create enough political, economic and strategic leverages to back up its diplomacy in South Asia. The picture however is otherwise" (emphasis added).[28]

The problems have recently been compounded by uncertainties and doubts even with regard to the Maldives and Bhutan, with which India's ties have long been very close and strong. Given the problematic of regional cooperation in South Asia and specifically the problems faced by India in its relations with its South Asian neighbours, it is an imperative that India gears its efforts to tide over the problems and hurdles.

India, therefore, has to apply itself to the task of rebuilding and strengthening its soft power both in and beyond South Asia by fashioning an appropriate and 'mutually' rewarding cultural diplomacy. India's rich cultural diversity and tradition gives the country the in-built strengths on which to base its efforts.

Culture, which is a very important component of a nation's soft power, can circumvent national boundaries. For instance, noted singer Runa Laila has stressed that 'like music itself, a singer has no boundaries'.[29] Cultural diplomacy, however, should not be viewed as a magic wand and obviously has limitations. Keeping the cultural window open may not be possible if the political climate is not quite conducive to cultural and people-to-people ties. Two instances will suffice. In January 2013, following growing tension between India and Pakistan due to incidents at the border, at least twenty-four Pakistani artists who were set to stage a play in Jaipur for a theatre festival organised by the National School of Drama and the ministry of cultural affairs had to return home.[30] In the same month, the Jaipur Literature Festival was marred by some unfortunate developments.[31]

What is important, however, is that contacts at the Track II level involving all the segments of society including artists, academia, business community and students may contribute a lot to enlarging the peace constituencies and keeping alive hopes for 'aman' when darkness envelops the political relationship and allows very little or virtually no progress on the Track I level.[32] Herein lies the importance of cultural diplomacy.

While reviving up cultural diplomacy as it should, India should tread cautiously so as to make sure that the use of the instrument is not misunderstood by its neighbours in South Asia as an attempt on the part of India to dominate and swamp their own cultures. Such a denouement would be wholly counterproductive. The goal should be to strive for recognition on the part of our neighbours of the importance of their cultural ties with India.[33]

Peaceful coexistence of diverse ethnic, religious, and linguistic groups has historically been a hallmark of South Asian cultures. For this reason, many have referred to the region as a "salad bowl" of culture: a hodgepodge of different peoples, beliefs, and behaviours.[34] Under the layers of diversity, however, lies a solid core of South Asian tradition. Onno Ruhl, director of World Bank India, has rightly pointed out that South Asia truly is a common cultural space.[35] To quote Ruhl,"...South Asia is the least integrated region in the world. Yet, it could benefit from regional integration. Culturally, there's great commonality amongst South Asians."[36]

Needless to say, frequent exchanges of ideas, personalities and groups of people representing art, culture, music, literature and sports across state borders, greater interaction at the level of common people and not just formal summits and meetings between governments, would surely go a long way in fostering friendly ties, generating a sense of belonging and also facilitating a better understanding and appreciation of each other's traditions.

Greater cultural connectivity is likely to enhance the prospects of eroding the barriers that threaten to hinder friendship and cooperation among countries in the volatile South Asian region. It is pertinent to point out that the importance of the region's cultural heritage for the SAARC process was duly acknowledged at the tenth SAARC summit in Colombo in 1998. Again, at the fifteenth summit in 2008, the leaders directed that the agenda for culture be implemented in full.[37]

It will not be out of place to mention some encouraging developments which stand out as islands of hope in a sea of despondency. The Bengal Foundation of Dhaka and the ITC-SRA of Kolkata have forged a unique partnership, that of helping each other preserve indigenous music of Bengal.[38] In January 2013, bonhomie between India and Bangladesh marked the thirty seventh Kolkata Book Fair, where India's eastern neighbour was the theme country.[39] Also worth mentioning is Maitree Bandhan, an initiative of *The Times of India* and *Prothom Alo* – two leading newspapers respectively in India and Bangladesh.[40] And truly remarkable and exhilarating has been the decision to celebrate the linguistic and cultural oneness along the India-Bangladesh border.[41]

Conclusion

India is committed to making the Twenty first Century truly an "Asian Century". But is the actualisation of the vision of an Asian Economic Community i.e., an integrated market linked by efficient road, rail, air and shipping services possible without a vigorous and successful effort as the first step to achieve the goal of regional cooperation in our immediate neighbourhood.

Seeking a peaceful South Asia, India as the largest country in the subcontinent has to take the lead in efforts toward promotion of mutual understanding and regional cooperation. For achieving this goal India's rich reservoir of cultural heritage should be tapped not simply to expand its influence and power, but more importantly to promote regional cooperation by fostering a feeling of togetherness. The lack of funds needed by the ICCR and the MEA to bolster India's cultural diplomacy is no doubt a matter of grave concern, but the objective should still be to do the best under the circumstances.[42]

India is not oblivious of its cultural footprint in and beyond South Asia. However, it is necessary to wipe off the dust accumulating on it through the years due to lack of goodwill and misperceptions. The rationale behind cultural diplomacy is not just to showcase India, but to stress the importance of the cultural window, especially when the political window is more or less shut, for seeing and understanding each other. The objective is to win the hearts and minds of people of the different countries across the region and the globe so that they understand and cooperate with India at bilateral and multilateral levels in ushering in a peaceful atmosphere not clouded by mutual suspicions and threat perceptions. "Do not protect yourself by a fence, but rather by your friends", a Czech proverb, seems quite appropriate and worthy of a mention.[43] The goal should be to strive for greater cultural connectivity to promote each other's acceptability, mutual understanding and finally, and most importantly, to pave the way for a transformation of South Asia from a troubled and fractious region to a peaceful one. The idea may be pooh-poohed as a dream never to come true. But the author still is optimistic of the future.[44] The goal should be to be tolerant of each other's cultures and weave the cultural identities into a whole and minimise as much as possible the 'Culture Wars' within and across national boundaries in South Asia.[45] Kapila Vatsyayan's quintessentially appropriate observation, albeit more than a decade old, about our cultural tradition was, "The tradition is too precious not because it is old or *ours it* is precious because a *worldview based on the principles of the interconnectedness* and of a unified vision and multiplicity and diversity of expressions in life-style, philosophy, languages, culture and the art alone can inculcate mutual respect and be the basis of a harmonious world of just balances and equilibrium for the future"(emphases added).[46]

The goal should be to promote cultural togetherness within the country as well as in our relations with countries far and near, and it is this that can act as a pillar for intra and inter-state cooperation. The goal should be to establish a regional cultural community. It may be relevant to point out here that one of the three pillars of the ASEAN Community envisioned by the countries in South East Asia is the ASEAN Cultural Community.

Not long ago, during her visit to India, former US secretary of state Hillary Clinton said, "We understand that much of the history of the twenty first century will be written in Asia. And much of the future of Asia will be shaped by decisions not just by the Indian government but by governments across India and by the 1.3 billion people who live here".[47] Why only India, let us together with our neighbours, big or small, resolve to shape Asia's future, a future in which we will have common stakes. The destiny of South Asia and Asia as a whole is in our hands.

References

1. Rabindra Sen, "India's South Asia Dilemma and Regional Cooperation: Relevance of Cultural Diplomacy", *Strategic Analysis*, Vol. 38, No. 1, 2014, pp. 68-78. For a discussion of the importance of cultural diplomacy in India's Look East Policy, see, Rabindra Sen, "Cultural Diplomacy and India's Look East Policy", in Ganganath Jha and Vibhanshu Shekhar (eds), *Rising India in the changing Asia-Pacific: Strategies and Challenges*, New Delhi: Pentagon Press, 2012, pp. 187-207.
2. P.S. Sahai, "Cultural Diplomacy: India in Singapore", cited in Sen, "Cultural Diplomacy and India's Look East Policy", *ibid*, pp. 195-196. Culture, a whole way of life, includes art, music, dance and drama. We should include sports as well. For an excellent discussion of the extent to which sports can be beneficial from the point of socio-political identity building and integration, see Boria Majumdar, "Breaking Through Barriers", The *Times of India*, 9 July 2013, p. 12.
3. Sahai, *ibid*, p. 2.
4. Cinema, dance, music, literature, yoga, ayurveda, Mahatma Gandhi, Rabindranath Tagore and even IT industry constitute a formidable array of India's soft power assets. See Navdeep Puri, "Public Diplomacy in India's Foreign Policy", *Strategic Analysis*, Vol. 35, No. 2, March 2011,

p. 299. Needless to say, our 'cultural' ambassadors have made great contributions in earning for India a place in the minds and hearts of people all over the world. Referring to the Indian beauties, a source from Loreal, the official make up partner at the Cannes Film Festival, said, "The role of our Indian ambassadors at Cannes has grown....", see Bharati Dubey, "Four Indian movies to premiere at Cannes fest", *The Times of India,* 13 May 2012.

5. Sahai, n.2.
6. *Ibid.*
7. For the objectives of the ICCR see *ibid*, p. 3.
8. The author, however, is not quite comfortable with this term because of antithetical implications arising out of its association with 'dominance'.
9. *Bharat Bichitra* (A High Commission of India Publication), Vol. 4, Issue 4, June 15, 2008.
10. *Ibid.*
11. Swami Gambhirananda, "Swami Vivekananda's Conception of World Peace", *Bulletin of the Ramakrishna Mission Institute of Culture,* Vol. 64, No. 2, February 2013, p.54.
12. Saurabh Shukla, "Soft Power", *India Today,* 30 October 2006, cited in Sen, "Cultural Diplomacy and India's Look East Policy", n.1, p. 205. In 2009, Virendra Gupta, the then Director General of ICCR, said, "It is India's long-term objective to promote cultural connectivity with neighbours, as also with countries beyond the region." "Cultural diplomacy in mind, India plans 15 centres in 2 years", http://www.thehindu.com/arts/history-and-culture/article61729.ece.
13. Pranav Kumar, "Contours of India's Cultural Diplomacy in Southeast Asia", *Institute of Peace and Conflict Studies,* New Delhi, Article no. 2559, 6 May 2008, http://www.ipcs.org/article_details.php?articleNo.=2559, p. 2.
14. For a list of countries and other relevant information provided by the Ministry of Culture, see indiaculture.nic.in/indiaculture/cultural-agreement.asp.?
15. Kumar, n.13, p. 2.
16. *Ibid.*
17. C. Raja Mohan, "Soft power, hard facts", cited in Sen, "Cultural Diplomacy and India's Look East Policy", n.1, p. 206.
18. Muchkund Dubey, India's *Foreign Policy: Coping with the Changing World,* Delhi: Pearson, 2013, p. 61.
19. Mohan, n.17, p. 3.
20. *Ibid.*
21. Shukla, n.12.

22. The grouping has a long way to go to reduce the "trust deficit" among its members. See John Cherian, "Miles to go", *Frontline,* 20 April 2007, pp. 27-30.
23. Smruti S. Pattanaik, "SAARC at Twenty-Five: An Incredible Idea Still in Its Infancy", *Strategic Analysis,* vol. 34, no. 5, 2010, p. 671.
24. *Ibid,* p. 676.
25. Dubey, n.18, p. 51.
26. *The Times of India,* 24 May 2013, p. 1.
27. Dubey, n.18, pp. 52-60. Dubey puts forward some invaluable suggestions for improving India's image in the region. For strongly worded comments about India's weak position in South Asia, see M.J. Akbar, "India has never seemed as helplessly weak as now", *The Times of India,* 5 May 2013, p.18. The comments may be viewed as too critical and highly exaggerated, but as a pointer to the weakening of India's position in South Asia, should nonetheless be taken seriously.
28. Subhash Kapila, "China Outmanoeuvres Indian Foreign Policy in South Asia", Paper no. 5213, 13 September 2012, www.southasiaanalysis.org/node/972, cited in Sen, "India's South Asia Dilemma…", p.75. Also see Suhasini Haidar, "In the neighbourhood, it's 'India fading'", *The Hindu,* 3 January 2013.
29. *The Times of India,* 2 January 2013. The author was indeed greatly moved by the following lyrics a song by a Bangla band created by a group of Bengali professionals in the United States – 'A boundary line divides us, cross it and you will be caught, but you don't need a visa to visit the land of the Bengali songs', *The Times of India,* 26 December 2012, p. 2.
30. Ashish Mehta, "Curtains for Pak actors at Jaipur fest", *The Times of India,* 17 January 2013.
31. Sachin Parashar, "Two Pak diplomats barred from attending Jaipur literary festival", *The Times of India,* 25 January 2013.
32. We may in this connection refer to the out-of-the-box solutions on Sir Creek proposed by an Aman Ki Asha seminar held in December 2012. Although rightly emphasising the point that only official dialogue between India and Pakistan is needed to resolve the issue, B.R. Rao argues, "Till then, however, the options … could help towards easing the problem, reducing both the tension and the trust deficit." See B.R.Rao, "Ripe Fruit That's Hanging Low", *The Times of India,* 4 January 2013, p. 14.
33. It is gratifying to note that the close cultural relationship between the peoples of Nepal and India has been described by the Nepalese embassy in India as a 'great asset for both countries', http://www.nepalembassy.in/socioculrel.htm
34. "South Asia: India and Beyond", www.ushistory.org/civ/8.asp?.
35. *Times of India,* 4 January 2013, p. 14.

36. *Ibid.* A few years ago, Nirupama Rao, former Indian foreign secretary, said, "South Asia is one concept, culturally and geographically, though not politically." See Rita Pearson, 'Indian Ambassador Addresses South Asian Identity', http://www.thehoya.com/indian-ambassador-addresses-south-asian-identity-1.2617300.
37. See for details, "SAARC Cultural Centre Mandate", www.saarcculture.org
38. Jhimli Mukherjee Pandey, "Musical event helps trace classical heritage", *The Times of India,* 2 December 2012.
39. *The Times of India,* 20 January 2013.
40. *Ibid,* 7 December 2012.
41. *Ibid,* 26 June 2013, p. 2.
42. For details of the acute financial constraint, see Devirupa Mitra, "Cash-strapped ICCR puts culture on hold", 16 June 2013, newindianexpress.com/thesundaystandard/Cash-strapped... -
43. *The Times of India,* 29 October 2007.
44. The following is just one of many examples that can be cited of how something totally unimaginable actually may happen. Britain's most iconic naval commander Nelson had once said, "You must hate a Frenchman as you hate the devil." Kounteya Sinha, "Irony: UK to lend Nelson's Trafalgar uniform to Paris", *The Times of India,* 9 February 2013. Could anyone ever imagine that the English would one day decide to loan to France the uniform which Nelson was wearing when he was fatally wounded after a French musket ball pierced his shoulder at the great Battle of Trafalgar more than two centuries ago? An additional support for the author's optimism is the following very interesting comment from a recent report in *The Times of India:* "Peace between India and Pakistan has been stubbornly elusive and yet tantalisingly inevitable", *The Times of India,* 22 June 2013, p. 9.
45. Lamenting over the rapidly increasing manifestation of the problem and cautioning us quite rightly, Kanti Bajpai, raises the question, "Why is the Indian culturescape so tumultuous?", See Kanti Bajpai, "The Era of India's Culture Wars", *The Times of India,* 2 February 2013. Unbelievable though it may be, there were even attacks on Pandit Ravi Shankar for blending Indian ragas with western music. See Dileep Padgaonkar, "Shankar's Passionate Tryst With France", *The Times of India,* 15 December 2012.
46. Kapila Vatsyayan, *Unity in Diversity As The Main Tenet of Indian Culture* (Foundation-Day Oration), Ramakrishna Mission Institute of Culture, Calcutta (Kolkata), 29 January 2001, pp. 21-22.
47. *The Times of India,* 21 July 2011.

10

Winning Hearts and Minds: The Role of Soft Power in India's Regional Strategy

Rashmi Bhure

The most remarkable development of the twenty-first century is the global power shift to Asia. The comparative decline of America and the rise of India and China have become fascinating subjects for scholars all over the world. Many reports and studies published have predicted that soon China would replace the United States as sole superpower and by 2030 India would be amongst the first three major powers in the world.[1] This implies that China and India would play a larger role in global governance in the near future. Certainly the Asian giants require playing correct moves to make these futuristic projections a reality.

In case of India its power index in future depends mainly on three factors–firstly, on India's domestic stability; secondly, its equation with the United States and the fast growing global giant China and thirdly, its relations with its neighbours.

Peaceful and stable South Asia would be critically imperative for India's ascending power. India's economic growth cannot rise to its potential if it is embroiled in conflicts or has strenuous relations with its neighbours. In tandem India also has to take cognisance of the 'China factor' and its 'hegemonic' behaviour in the region. China has over the years adopted the 'Kautilyan strategy' while developing relations with India's neighbour Pakistan. Much of literature has already been churned out by the Indian scholars regarding China's 'Pearls of String' theory. China's policy in South Asia can be analysed within the framework of the realist approach to international relations that is the desire to dominate other states increases as a state's power capabilities grow. However, post cold war international politics is characterised by major shifts in approach from traditional realist perspective on 'power' (hard power).[2] In accordance with China made deliberate attempts to transform its policy towards South Asia. Beijing downplayed its hard power and increasingly started using the instrument of 'soft power' to expand its influence in the South Asian region. Apparently, India lags well behind in projecting its soft power in its neighbourhood. In the new emerging global scenario the Paper argues the significance of soft power in India's regional strategy and discusses the need to further leverage India's soft power in the coming decades.

Paradigm Shift in International Politics: From Hard Power to Soft Power

In the twentieth century, power in world politics was seen in terms of military power but gradually the futility of this power became evident. By the end of the millennium the realist notion of power itself was challenged. The US wars in Vietnam, Iraq and the war on terror are classic examples of the limitations of the military power to win asymmetrical wars.

In 1990s the security parameters altered and it was difficult to deal with these new threats with only hard power. As a consequence, world over the governments recognised the need to implement innovative strategies to deal with the new challenges.

Soft power then was seen as the alternative or complimentary to the traditional hard power. Countries like the US soon realised the importance of investing more in the soft power tools. The term 'soft power' was itself coined by the Harvard University professor, Joseph S. Nye Jr. in 1990. For Nye soft power meant getting others to want the outcomes you want through co-opting people rather than coercion.[3] Soft power resources are the assets that produce attraction which often leads to acquiescence. According to Nye a country's soft power arises mainly from its culture, political values and the manner in which its foreign policy is conducted. Largely the success of soft power depends upon the image of the country in the international community or the world's perception of that country. In this regard, Shashi Tharoor says "hard power is exercised; soft power is evoked".[4] Soft power of a nation helps to narrow the differences between troubled countries besides creating attractiveness and winning hearts and minds. What is more is that the nation can afford to reduce its massive expenditure on the hard power that can then be utilised for development.

India's Regional Strategy-Search for Alternative

Centrality of India in South Asia is an entrenched fact that cannot be wished away. By virtue of its geostrategic location, size and economic potential, India has acquired this unique position. India's relations with its South Asian neighbours have been always asymmetrical as most of its neighbours are very small in comparison- geographically, demographically and economically. South Asian nations share civilisational, cultural, linguistic and ethnic ties that are deeply rooted in their history. Ideally these linkages should have struck a harmonious cord amongst the South Asian countries but in reality some of these factors have in fact drifted the neighbours apart. The countries in the region typically have perceived India as a 'hegemon' or 'big brother' that is overshadowing their identities. This is causing an insecurity dilemma among the smaller nations. Hence to counter or balance India's weight in the region they have looked up on external powers like China and the US. China's growing footprints in South Asia and attempts to bring peripheral states into its area of influence is a cause of concern for the rising India.

For more than a decade now, we can witness clearly India's ambition to play a larger role in the global politics. India's unprecedented economic growth in 1990s coupled with the 1998 nuclear tests and the US recognising India as a nuclear power, India's claim for the permanent seat in the United Nations Security Council, and its participation in the various international institutions are indications of India's changing status from a benign power to a rising major global power. However, India's global aspirations are starkly contrasted by the challenges that it faces domestically and regionally. In contemporary times these constraints make India the most misunderstood country and land of paradoxes. Thus, mixed reactions are given in different opinion polls regarding India's emergence as a dominant player in the global politics in the near future.[5] Therefore, to be recognised as a global power in the due time, the key question is what strategy should India adopt to build its image or position?

The old paradigm of minimal contact and cautious engagement with neighbours will have to be changed by India.[6] This policy apparently is outdated in the days of globalisation where interdependence and transnational threats is a reality that demands proactive participation by the global players. In the twenty first century South Asia faces many non-traditional security issues such as terrorism, climate change, food and water security, migration etc. These challenges cannot be addressed within the framework of national interest but through regional initiatives.

India is now in a position to develop strategy that would accommodate its neighbour's politico-security concerns while constructing common grounds to deal with vital issues affecting the regional stability. As a largest country in South Asia, India can play an important role in building bridges across the region. This initiative is significant not only for the rise of India but equally so for the region's progress, prosperity and development. For this, India will have to systematically and effectively harness the soft power tools in its regional diplomacy.

Historical Background: Soft Power in India's South Asia Policy

In the South Asian context, the concept of soft power per se operates very intricately.[7] It is ironical that the countries in the region share the soft power resources but have not adequately harnessed these resources for the regios's prosperity or stability. One of the reasons could be the troubled borders that have divided and kept the region bleeding forever. The strokes across the map drawn by the British empire have been the major source of conflict and tension amongst the countries in the region. However, the process of globalisation and information revolution has dramatically changed the politico-security environment of South Asia where the cost of attractiveness (soft power) outweighs the cost of coercion (hard power) in the big power's diplomacy.[8] However, the western definition of soft power may not be appropriate to the heterogeneous region, which despite of many commonalities has occasionally turned into conflict zone and is heavily militarised. In the South Asian context, soft power should be understood as an 'ability to accommodate others concerns' rather than 'ability to influence'. It would also mean accommodating contradictory forces and ideas instead of 'Indianising' the region.

The roots of India's soft power in its regional policy can be traced to the Nehruvian era. Nehru attempted to demonstrate India's leadership at global and regional level by projecting ideals of non-violence and mutual co-existence (Panchsheel). In the early years after independence India invested considerably in cultural exchanges, dialogues amongst nation-states and built an image of moral persuader. The Non-Aligned Movement (NAM) gave a forum to the decolonised developing countries. India's policy of disarmament and its participation in the UN peace keeping forces not only gave India high moral authority worldwide but its acceptability as a peacemaker nation in international conflicts and crisis also became greater. There is much that the present Indian foreign policy makers can learn from Nehru's soft power ideas. Nehru's policy gave India a distinct identity in the world affairs. Unfortunately flaws in Nehru's soft power approach became evident in 1962 with China's attack on India. India's defeat in the war demonstrated that soft power is ineffective without the back up of hard power capabilities. What is more is probably the time (cold war, arms race and nuclear power) was not right for Nehru's soft power policy. As fallout in the later years until the end of cold war India adopted the hard power strategies in South Asia. This was seen in India's role in East Pakistan in 1971 and military intervention (involvement) in Sri Lanka in 1987 as well as in the Maldives in 1988.

With the new emerging world order in the 1990s India had a paradigm shift in its foreign policy. Acknowledging the fact that the traditional hard power will not be sufficient to attain national interests and enthralled with Nye's concept of soft power, India crafted its new regional policy. For the first time the soft power approach was evident in India's regional policy (Gujral doctrine). The Gujral doctrine advocated that India does not ask for reciprocity among asymmetrical partners in South Asia and emphasised on non-interference in internal affairs of the countries in the region. The Gujral doctrine has been continued by the United Progressive Alliance (UPA) government since 2004. In February 2005 the then foreign secretary Shyam Saran and prime minister Manmohan Singh tied up more explicitly to the Gujral doctrine and stressed the need for increased economic relations and promoted the idea of partnership with the neighbours.[9] India's regional policy has certainly seen new trends since 1990s but the historical legacies are still lingering around. India's hard power approach in 1970s and 1980s is deeply rooted in the region leading to mistrust and animosity. India will have to design a systematic strategy to change these perceptions and build an identifiable soft power image.

India's Soft Power Resources

Political Values: India is a country full of paradoxes, yet India's values and institutions have sustained its democracy for more than six decades. India is the only South Asian country with such a long record of democratic form of government (except during the period of emergency in 1975). The institutional structures of parliamentary democracy, federalism and secularism have managed the multi-ethnic, multi-religious and multi-lingual India for over a half century. Though late but finally in the post cold war period the world recognised India's political achievements. India having a stable democracy in a region that is one of the most volatile in the world probably helped it to gain the global attention. In the 1990s the world's oldest democratic country the US recognised India's economic growth and the common democratic values shared by both the nations and changed its stance towards India from 'estranged democracy' to a 'natural ally'. India's democratic model though different from the western model was now accepted by the world. While India's democratic model is valued across but is not considered to be perfect or ideal. Despite its long cherished democratic traditions, Indian government has not regarded the promotion of democracy as a foreign policy tool. Post-independence Indian foreign policy was based on the principles of non-alignment or non-interference. Keeping in lieu with its policy of 'non-interference in internal affairs' of other countries India made some modest efforts since 1964 for promotion of democracy through the Indian Technical and Economic Cooperation (ITEC) programme. ITEC is demand-driven technical cooperation programme of India mainly for developing countries. It symbolises India's contribution to South-South cooperation.

Till 1990s India's regional policy was security-centric thus exporting the democratic model in the neighbourhood was not on the list of Indian foreign policy-makers. After the historic visit of the American President Bill Clinton to India in 2000, the US perceived India as a partner in promotion of democracy. In 2006, the US president George Bush during his visit stated in New Delhi that "as a global power India has an historic duty to support democracy in Iran, Cuba, Syria, North Korea and Myanmar".[10]

In the regional context, question of promoting democracy has played a greater role as well. In 2005, when the Nepalese king declared the state of emergency, India imposed a series of sanctions. Foreign secretary Shyam Saran explained in this regard that India was giving greater support to democracies in Southeast Asia.[11]

Recognising democracy as a global aspiration and a fundamental to establish peaceful societies, India in 2005 became the part of the Global Democracy Initiative (GDI) started by the US. Also in the same year India participated in the UN Democracy Fund that worked for building democratic structures and protecting human rights across the globe. India has contributed $15 million to this fund and is the second largest donor next to the US. India's massive contribution to the post-war reconstruction work in Afghanistan is under the same agenda. India's initiatives in promoting democracy as a foreign policy tool have always been sporadic.

Economic and Development Aid: Economic and Development assistance or aid is a tested instrument of the western nations for attaining their political objectives or promotion of democracy. India has been the largest beneficiary of the western aid for more than half century. However, as a consequence of its economic rise from a largest recipient country

India today has turned to be a generous global donor and specifically is the largest donor to SAARC member countries. The aid effort as a whole is divided between bilateral grants, loans, and guarantees designed to further relationships with particular nations and contributions to multilateral institutions with the objective of building India's influence within forums such as the International Monetary Fund.[12]

India's Overseas Development Assistance (ODA) is primarily focused in its neighbourhood mainly in Bhutan, Nepal and Afghanistan. Infrastructure, health and education are the focus of Indian development assistance in South Asia. Further within the framework of ITEC India provides educational and training programmes. This programme provides for good future relations with the recipient countries.

India is also involved in development and humanitarian aid efforts during natural crisis. In 2004, in the wake of tsunami Indian navy participated in the humanitarian assistance work. Similarly in the aftermath of the floods in Pakistan in 2010 India gave humanitarian aid to a country with which it has fought three wars. India has been one of Afghanistan's top five donors since 2002 with commitment of over $ one billion. India donated one million metric tonnes of wheat in 2002 (remarkable achievement from PL 480 programme), which is the single largest donation in the history of the UN World Food Programme (WFP). India is a major contributor to the SAARC Development Fund to promote actions on social, economic and infrastructure areas.

India's larger strategic ambitions have also influenced its development assistance. It has bolstered its aid programmes in Nepal and Bangladesh in an attempt to curb the Chinese influence. Moreover, the Indian foreign policy-makers have reckoned with the fact that India's image in the neighbourhood is not what it should have been. Through the aid's programme, India plans to transform its image from a 'regional bully' to 'a partner in the region'.

India has emerged as the fifth largest donor in Afghanistan as it works here consistently to keep Pakistan on the periphery. Its grants are focused on creating goodwill rather than influencing the recipient nations. Hence India attaches far less conditionality to its aid as compared to other donor nations this makes Indian aid more attractive to recipient countries. India's aid thus has greater legitimacy in the developing world and this is likely to strengthen its soft power.

In contrast to the western countries, India's development assistance has been little known or much is not there in the public domain. The awareness regarding the American values and foreign policy goals around the world is through the USAID (United States Agency for International Development). Whereas till recent times India was not even having a single agency for implementing its aid. Ministry of External Affairs (MEA), the Ministry of Finance and the Export Import Bank of India (Exim Bank) were involved in administering the Indian aid. It was only in 2012 when India realised the importance of aid as a soft power tool that it has set up a coordinating unit, the Development Partnership Administration (DPA) as a division within MEA.

Culture: Culture is certainly an important part in creating and promoting national images.[13] India is a land of rich diversities with a unique culture. It is one of the ancient civilisations that has offered refuge and more precisely religious and cultural freedom to Jews, Parsis, Christians, Muslims etc. The Jews viewed India as a safest place for refuge after the tragedy of holocaust.[14] India has truly embraced the world this reflects from the fact that city like Mumbai has all religious places like Church, Mosque, Synagogue, Hindu and Buddhist temple, Gurudwara etc. British historian E.P. Thompson wrote that this heritage of diversity is what makes India 'perhaps the most important country for the future of the world'.[15] At the same time we cannot ignore the contemporary reality, where cultural and religious identities have become sensitive issue in India. These differences are inevitable and are part of the process of evolution of a pluralistic democracy.

Twenty first century is the age of information where how a country projects (through modern communication techniques) its soft power globally and how other global players perceive it is very significant. The Indian government undertook various efforts in recent years in order to insert 'culture' into foreign policy. It can be said that India by the means of 'cultural diplomacy' attempted to attain the goals of 'political diplomacy'. In order to promote awareness of India's composite cultural heritage the ICCR was established way back in 1950. Since then thirty five cultural centres have been setup in different parts of the world. ICCR is planning to start fifteen more centres in order to promote India's soft power in Asia. These centres would be in India's immediate and extended neighbourhood. Compared to other countries this number is insignificant. For instance, China has given a push to its soft power by starting the Confucius Institute in 2004 to promote Chinese language and culture. Already it has 350 institutes across the globe and plans to start 200 more.

ICCR numerous activities range from film festivals to book fairs, classical music and dance programmes, art events, yoga teachings etc.

These initiatives illustrate India's endeavour to use soft power in the foreign policy. Besides this, the Indian government is also propagating the use of Hindi abroad. Various events are being sponsored every year like the World Hindi Conference and Hindi language classes are offered in different centres.[16] ICCR since 1980's has been organising festivals of India abroad with an idea to promote 'people's diplomacy'.

Understanding the importance of soft power, the MEA, in 2006, started a new division for public diplomacy. Its main goal is to foster a greater understanding of India and its foreign policy concerns in the country and abroad.

Bollywood is the most important medium of expression of India's popular culture. Bollywood films are now viewed by wider international audiences. In the twentieth century Hollywood movies created a glorifying homogenous picture of an ideal type of middle class consumer society in the US. It shaped ideas and images of economic, political and societal development that became the core of modernisation theories in the 1950s and 1960s.[17] Bollywood 'brand' today has become popular amongst the Indian diaspora and others. So is the case of TV soap operas there profit index are rising every year. The family values and the emotional base of these soap operas appeal to the people widely across the world. The Indian tele-serials are shown in more than twenty seven countries such as Africa, America, European countries, South East Asian countries, Pakistan and other South Asian countries. Besides this, the Indian cuisine is winning the hearts and stomachs of people from Seattle, Singapore to Shanghai. The influence of Indian culture is presently growing even in Pakistan despite of the reality that the diplomatic relations between Delhi and Islamabad has hit a sour note. Pakistanis are in awe with Indian fashion designers, bollywood stars and goods.

The cultural diplomacy of the government has certainly helped to promote a new and modern image of India abroad. India now appears to be more attractive to the overseas public, a country with potential market and knowledge power. Therefore, the increase of foreign direct investment in recent years can be partly attributed to India's soft power diplomacy.

Interestingly, Indians are very modest in their self-assessment. Despite of the fact that the Indian culture is becoming popular globally, it is not seen as a societal model by Indians themselves. A survey on 'World Powers in the Twenty-First Century' showed that only seven per cent of Indians had the confidence regarding their own country as a social or cultural model for others.[18]

Surely to create that 'India Brand' India has to work vociferously. Much more needs to be done in terms of tapping media resources. Indian diplomacy has been slow in recognising the importance of social media in the area of foreign policy. Though currently the social media is gaining some ground and MEA's Public Diplomacy Division (PDD) is engaging by starting a new web portal for Indian public diplomacy. PDD is connecting with young tech-savvy generation in and outside India through twitter, blogs, facebook, etc. Yet Indian public diplomacy is in infant stage.

India needs to deploy the social media at different governmental levels more effectively and transparently; there is lot of scope to grow. Similarly though new cultural centres are in the pipeline, many more will be needed in the coming decade to increase India's outreach. The ICCR also facilitates scholarships and exchange programmes for students and scholars. It annually offers about 2325 scholarships to foreign students at Indian universities.[19] Students from around eighty countries are studying in India under these schemes. Most of the scholarship gainers are from Asian and African countries. India has to further expand these activities to familiarise the young generation in different countries with the vibrant India of the twenty first century. In addition to this more academic Chairs' need to be set up in various universities abroad for Indian studies. India to attain its ambition of becoming a dominant power in the near future yet needs to invest more in cultural diplomacy.

Conclusion

India an aspiring major power has certainly begun to embrace with the soft power strategy in its foreign policy though in a limited way. If India wants to remain as a source of attraction to others it is not merely enough to build image but rather to transform it into reality. For this firstly, India has to put its house in a better order. Secondly, internal cracks require to be cemented by the spirit of 'Indianism' or the larger idea of India. India has tremendous resources of soft power but has not fully harnessed them due to lower self-esteem or modesty. This means that more systematic development of soft power strategy will be required by India. In short, capacities have to turn into capabilities. Here, India has to explore adequately the role that the Indian diaspora and its young tech savvy generation can play for disseminating India's soft power assets globally.

On the regional level, Indian foreign policy-makers seem to have acknowledged the value of soft power in recent years. Different initiatives taken since 1990s indicate that India is re-defining its image as a benign economic power in its neighbourhood. Soft power emanates from people and not merely from South Block, thus, India is encouraging people-to-people contacts to overcome the trust deficit in the region. To build sustainable relationships in the region this initiative is welcomed but it needs to be broad-based.

Nevertheless, in contrast with the US, UK or China, India has to go a long way leveraging its soft power potentials as an instrument of foreign policy. The biggest limitation here is that soft power is still not in the public discourse in India.

References

1. US National Intelligence Council Report, *Global Trends 2030: Alternative Worlds*, 12 December 2012, http://publicin telligence.net/global-trends-2030/; Fareed Zakaria, *The Post American World*, New Delhi: Penguin, 2008; James F Hoge Jr., A *"Global Power Shift in Making", Foreign Affairs*, Vol.83, No.4, July-August, 2004.
2. Uma Purushothaman, "Shifting Perceptions of Power: Soft Power and India's Foreign Policy", *Journal of Peace Studies*, Vol. 17, Nos. 2 and 3, April-September 2010.
3. For the concept of soft power see Joseph Nye, *Bound to Lead: The Changing Nature of American Power*, New York: Basic Books, 1990.
4. Shashi Tharoor, *Pax Indica: India and the World of the 21st Century*, New Delhi: Penguin, 2012, p. 278.
5. GlobeScan, "Global Poll" (2006). http://www.globescan.com/news_archives/bbc06-3/index.html.
6. Asif Ahmed, "Emerging Chinese Security Threats in Indian Context: Need for India to Review Security Strategy", 8 August 2012, http://www.eurasiareview.com/08082012-emerging-chinese-security-threats-in-indian-context-need-for-india-to-review-security-strategy-analysis.
7. J Jegannathan, "Alternative Regional Strategy for India: Exploring Soft Power Options", *IPCS Issue Brief*, no.180, January 2012, http://www.ipcs.org/pdf_file/issue/IB180-Jegan-SoftPower.pdf
8. *Ibid.*
9. Christian Wagner, "From Hard Power to Soft Power: Ideas, Interaction, Institutions and Images in India's South Asia Policy," Heidelberg Papers in South Asian and Comparative Politics, Working Paper, No. 26, March 2005, p. 3.

10. Amit Baruah, Bush's Remarks on Regime Changes put India in a spot, *The Hindu*, 5 March 2006, http://www.hindu.com/2006/03/05/stories/2006030504350900.html
11. As cited in Christian Wagner, *Promotion of Democracy and Foreign Policy in India*, Berlin: Stiftung Wissenschaft und Politik, October 2009, p.10.
12. Ian Hall, "India's New Public Diplomacy: Soft Power and the Limits of Government Action", *Asian Survey*, Vol.52, No.6, November-December 2012, pp.1105-1106.
13. Christian Wagner, "India's Soft Power: Prospects and Limitations", *India Quarterly: A Journal of International Affairs*, Vol. 66, No. 4, December 2010, p. 335.
14. In personal interaction with holocaust survivors in Jerusalem in December 2012.
15. Cited in Tharoor, n.4, p. 280.
16. Nicolas Blarel, "India's Soft Power: From Potential to Reality", p. 31, http://www2.lse.ac.uk/IDEAS/publications/reports/pdf/SR010/blarel.pdf
17. Wagner, n.13, p. 336.
18. A survey report, *World Powers in the 21st Century*, 2 June 2006, Berlin: Bertelsmann Foundation, p.12.
19. "The Many Scholarship Schemes of ICCR," http://www.iccrindia.net/scholarshipschemes.html.

PART–IV
BILATERAL RELATIONS

11

Connectivity, Development and Regional Integration: The Case of Kaladan Project between India and Myanmar

Santishree D. Pandit and Rimli Basu

Introduction

If understanding the links between environmental sustainability and equity is the most crucial and critical factor to expand human freedoms for the current and future generations, as envisaged by the 2011 UN Human Development Report, then connectivity is one of its core variables. The report also states that the global human development progress, as witnessed and documented cannot continue without bold global steps to reduce both environmental risks and inequality. Therefore, stressing the global connectivity through regional linkages as one of the foremost gizmo for the future generations. Further, identification of pathways for people, local communities, countries and the international community to promote environmental sustainability and equity in mutually reinforcing ways will be stressed for the coming years.

At the fragmented regional level, focusing on Southeast Asia, India is trying to pragmatically implement this theoretical framework through various connectivity programmes with Southeast Asian countries. As one of the strongest civilised states with greater capabilities and broader visions, India is certainly expected to surge ahead with this goal.

As the land bridge to Southeast Asia, India therefore, did forge ties with Myanmar through various connectivity linkages like Asian Highway

Project, Kaladan Project, Moreh-Tamu link road, opening of 'Border Huts'. To be specific, "Kaladan[1] Multi-Modal Transit-Transport Facility" (called Kaladan Project) is to be established through the Kaladan River in the Arakan [Rakhine] state of western Myanmar and through the state of Mizoram in India. The work of this $ 120 million (INR 545 crore) project, funded by the ministry of external affairs, Government of India began in 2008, and was scheduled to be completed in 2014. After completion, this project will connect the eastern Indian seaport of Kolkata with Sittwe port in Myanmar by sea. It will then link Sittwe (in Myanmar) to Mizoram (in India) via river and road transport. The completion of this project will reduce the distance from Kolkata (in India) to Sittwee (in Myanmar) by approximately 1328 kms. It will also reduce the transport burden on the narrow Siliguri corridor, also known as 'chicken's neck', in Jalpaiguri sub-division of Northern Bengal of the state of West Bengal in India. Kaladan project, after completion will prove beneficial for India in creating greater connectivity with its north-eastern states, and beyond to Southeast Asia through Myanmar.

This paper seeks to address, thus, whether connectivity of India-Southeast Asia through Kaladan project of India-Myanmar would prove beneficial or detrimental for the overall development and integration of the region from a global perspective. Further, it would be able to minimise the country-wise/region-wise disparity in the region, as envisaged by the UN Human Development Report.

Integrating development through convergence of economies, although sounds an anti-thesis to 'territoriality', is going to be the official Political agenda for the future. Human development, as envisaged still remains in the core, which reminds us that all future development and integration will pivot around it. The political dynamics of integration embraces the above idea through 'connectivity'.

Conjoining Southeast Asian region, which is widely separated on the basis of 'territoriality', was the main theme of India through its 'Look East policy'. That in itself has paid rich dividends today, almost a decade later. According to some scholars, the Look East Policy is considered as the 'master stroke' of Indian foreign policy. However, the land-bridge country (read Myanmar) between India and Southeast Asia is widely neglected in terms of 'connectivity'. Geographically, Myanmar is a gateway to Southeast Asia and can be a central hub for exchange of goods, services and technology. Underdeveloped infrastructure and unfavourable institutional and business environment seriously limit participation of the economy into regional and global networks. Thus, cross-border connectivity will play a very important role in this scenario. Establishing better connectivity by all means namely, material, institutional and 'people-to-people connectivity' will allow Myanmar, India and then, the other Southeast Asian countries to raise possibilities for collaboration between and among themselves and to expand economic synergies for development in the region. Moreover, regional interconnectivity through infrastructure development, trade facilitation and regulatory harmonisation among the respective economies such as India, Myanmar and other ASEAN members can make each economy more dynamic and bring enormous benefits to the entire region.

Linkage projects between India and Myanmar are several in numbers. Some of the important ones are: BLO (Border Liaison Office), Kaladan Multi-Modal Transit Transport (KMMTT), Sittwe port development to improve land/water communication links, Tamu-Kalewa-Kalemyo road, Rih-Tiddim (80.17 km) and Rih-Falam (151.5 km) roads, Tamanthi and Shwezaye hydropower projects, Development of Burma's offshore Shwe oil and natural gas fields, India-Myanmar-Thailand Tri-lateral Highway (Moreh-Bagan-Moe Sot) and etc. Unfortunately, disproportionate attention is given to the insurgency problem of the north-eastern India has caused the main focus to shift from *'development-integration-connectivity'* to 'internal security'. Interestingly, it should be noted here that the KMMTT is just one of many infrastructure projects in which India is currently completely involved.

The significance of the 'connectivity' between India and Myanmar has been attested by the visit of the Indian prime minister Manmohan Singh to Myanmar between 27-29 May, 2012. The visit is termed *'historic'* and 'one of its kind', which has happened in the past twenty five years due to the following reasons:

1. The 2012 visit signals the end of India's so called ambiguity between its 'avowed commitment for democracy', and the practice of *realpolitik.*
2. The visit signals the beginning of'new era for Indian diplomacy' in Southeast Asia.
3. Engagement of India with the Myanmar military junta government for ensuring security in the north-east provinces of India.
4. Attest the fact that Myanmar is an essential partner in the Look East Policy of India.
5. Myanmar will be used by India from the perspective of connectivity between India and Southeast Asia.
6. Indian prime minister calling Myanmar 'Natural Partner' to India.

Kaladan Multimodal Transit and Transport Project (KMMT) in Brief as It is till 2013

On 2 April 2008, India and Myanmar signed the agreement on the KMMTT, a cooperative endeavour financed by India at a cost of $120 million. As a part of India's Look East Policy, the aim of the project is to further increase the Indo-Burma economic relationship as well as provide additional opportunities to connect commerce with India's seven sister states in the northeast. Despite being signed in 2008, construction under the agreement only began in 2010.[2]

The project involves development of a trade route between the two countries along the river Kaladan. The river Kaladan is navigable from its confluence point with the Bay of Bengal near Sittwe up to Setpyitpyin (Kaletwa), Myanmar, on its north. Beyond this the river is not navigable owing to shallow water depth and frequent rapids. Therefore, transportation by road is proposed for this stretch. From Sittwe port to Kaletwa, transportation will be by waterway and from Kaletwa to India-Myanmar border transportation will be by road. The objective of the proposal is to provide an access route to the land-locked north-eastern region of India. The project is significant in view of severe pressure on the Siliguri corridor and Bangladesh's continued intransigence in providing transit rights through its territory to the north-east.[3] The route of the project is given in following table:

1.	Kolkata to Sittwe	Sea	539 km.
2.	Sittwe to Setpyitpyin: (Kaletwa) Transport on river Kaladan	Inland Water	225 km.
3.	Setpyitpyin to India-Myanmar border	Road	62 km.

Source: *Ministry of Development of North Eastern Region, Government of India.*

The handling point of the project in India will be Hmawngbu (Mobu) in Mizoram, and the handling point in Myanmar will be Myeikwa. The visual picture of the river is as follows:

The bilateral agreement between India and Myanmar, which was signed in April 2008 for the construction of KMMTT linking the two countries along the river Kolodyne (generally pronounced Kaladan), known as Chhimtuipui river inside Indian border. River Kolodyne emanates from central Mizoram and empties into Bay of Bengal at Sittwe–a port located in the state of Rakhine, Myanmar. This is an important trans-border infrastructure project that will let the land-locked northeastern states gain easy access to the Bay of Bengal through Myanmar. It envisages a multi-modal transport corridor and building of a pipeline that will bring natural gas from Myanmar via north-east to the whole of India. The Kaladan project will link Mizoram with Myanmar. It begins at Sittwe port and moves up along the Kolodyne river that flows through Mizoram and ends at the small port of Paletwa in Myanmar, covering a distance of 222 km. The port will facilitate movement of cargo vessels on inland water routes along Kolodyne river to Sittwe.

This project, once completed, will be of immense help in transforming north-eastern region (NER) from landlocked to land linked and enable the region to leverage the benefits of India's Look East Policy. Movements of goods between NER and mainland India will become easier as it will take twelve hours from Haldia to, and thirty-six hours from Visakhapatnam to, reach Sittwe Port. Myanmar will also benefit from additional revenue by way of transit fee for movements of goods between NER and mainland India as well as between NER and the rest of the world. Thus, the project provides a win-win situation for both India and Myanmar. Besides transit fee, Myanmar will also have a 225 km long navigable waterway in the bargain.

To obtain the optimal benefits out of KMMTT project, there has to be synchronised development of transportation facilities from Sittwe port up to Silchar. A 100 km new alignment road from Indo-Myanmar border to Lawngtalai linking NH-54 has to be constructed. The stretch of NH-54 between Lawngtalai and Aizawl (Silchar-Aizawl-Tuipang) also needs to be improved to take vastly increased load of vehicles and materials. Double laning of 310 km of NH-54 between Lawngtalai and Aizawl is to be done. The construction of Sittwe port along with other supporting infrastructure is expected to be completed by 2013. Although ministry of external affairs, India, conceived the project in 2003, the progress on the ground appears to be very slow.

Briefly speaking, the Kaladan project envisages *connectivity* between the Indian ports on the eastern seaboard and Sittwe port in Myanmar and then through riverine transport and by road to Mizoram. Thus, it is going to provide an *alternate route for transport of goods to northeast India.* From a broader perspective, the KMMTT will also provide connectivity between them, which will lead to the development of trade between India and Myanmar. It will also contribute to the economic development of Mizoram and other northeastern states.

The geographical location of the KMMTT

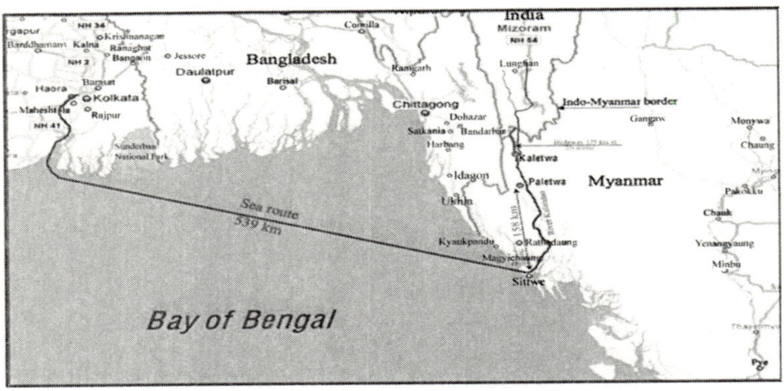

Going by the trade scenario, since 2006, bilateral trade has more than doubled to $1.5 billion, leading many to see the KMMTT as a promoter of future growth. For India, enhanced economic ties are particularly important as lost investment opportunities (e.g., the Lido highway and Tamanthi dam projects) due to other regional competitors (read: China) have presented further challenges in "Looking East"[4]. With Myanmar increasing pro-market oriented reforms, it's not an exaggeration to say that now is the perfect time for India to increase cooperation as prospects for economic growth are on the rise. The KMMTT creates links with West Bengal and India's oldest port of Kolkata.

The impossibility of the other India - Myanmar border connectivity can be understood from the fact that the 1,600-km India-Myanmar border is one of the world's more notional frontiers. It was delineated for the British Raj's convenience in the 1930s. A hill is simply divided by its eastern and western ridges for Myanmar and India. There is no cartographic mapping and it consists of heavily forested hills with a few roads through the less impassable ones. The road-connectivity is no better than as it was in the 1940s when the fourteenth army and the Japanese fought bitterly over the main land routes.

Post-Partition (1947), maintaining connectivity to the northeast got more difficult for India. The Chittagong port and the road-rail-steamer links through what is now Bangladesh, were no longer available. The only land route, thus, remained is the Siliguri Chicken's neck. In 1962, the Chinese could have cut that and grabbed the entire region at will. It is immensely expensive to construct roads and rail tracks in the north-east hills. Efforts are only now being made to put Imphal, Kohima, Aizawl and Itanagar on the railway map. Agartala, the capital of Tripura, was connected by rail in 2008.

Given this scenario, connectivity through KMMTT could have been the most economical and the least time consuming.

Theoretical Framework

The markedly spatial pattern of development, both within and across countries, generally suggests three broad lines of explanation. It could be that areas with high and low levels of development are intrinsically different-ecologically, economically, culturally, sociologically, politically, or historically- in ways that have enhanced/diminished their development potential.

There are many versions of this causal theory, which may rest on the intrinsic properties of a land and its climate[5], population growth in tandem with technological innovation[6], public policies and political institutions[7], cultural properties[8], and historical contingencies.[9]

A second possibility is that development is an essentially zero-sum distributional game in which regions of the world compete. Developed regions are therefore those possessing superior military and geo-political capacities, allowing them to monopolise technology, physical capital, human capital and other factors that contribute to development. The strongest and most systematic version of this theory is associated with the dependency and world systems school of thought.[10] Another possibility is that development is the product of the 'connectivity' of a region. Connectivity, per say, may be understood as a structural feature of the landscape a product of geographic, infrastructural, and demographic features that make it easy or difficult for individuals living in a region to reach those outside the boundaries of that region. (A region may be any size). It is expected that relative ease of movement will facilitate contact and that contact will, in turn, hasten development. To motivate this analysis, the following few may be considered briefly as to why this might be so.

First, connectivity facilitates the diffusion of technology, ideas and norms. Second, connectivity fosters the standardisation of technology, ideas, norms, formal regulations, and language across regions and this by itself (regardless of the quality of these factors) enhances efficiencies and presumably also speeds the ongoing process of diffusion, since ideas travel faster where cultural barriers are less severe. Third, connectivity reduces transaction costs, lowering the price and increasing the variety and availability of consumer goods and the potential markets for producer goods. Fourth, connectivity enhances the mobility of labour and capital, thus reducing inequalities - locally, nationally and internationally (wherever connectivity exists) - according to Ricardian theory. Fifth, connectivity probably strengthens the capacity of governments. It is easier for states to perform basic functions like keeping order, collecting taxes, and surveillance, as well as more complex policy interventions, when the population under its purview is well-connected. Sixth, connectivity enhances the access of non-market, non-governmental actors whose involvement in the project of development is essentially voluntaristic (or at least nominally so). Insofar as missionaries, health workers, educators and other actors rooted in civil society have played a positive role in development, this too may be related to the relative connectivity of different regions.

At the same time, connectivity reduces the power of governments, religions, businesses and other organisations to restrict the flow of ideas and technologies. In this respect, connectivity is inherently anti-monopolistic, fostering a spirit of open competition across jurisdictions that are in contact with one another. Finally, connectivity may nurture a more universalistic set of values and norms, which may in turn play a positive role in the complex and intertwined processes of development. Regions with high connectivity breed cosmopolitan citizens of the world, while regions with low connectivity encourage a parochial outlook on life, love and duty.

Travel-time to various destinations, thus comprises the basic metric by which connectivity may be measured.[11] Destinations of concern are divided into five categories: *transport routes, urbanisation measures, country measures, sub-continental measures* and *global measures.*

Transport routes include, nearness to ocean or navigable river, nearness to trunk road. *Urbanisation measures* include the nearest city, the nearest city in the country, the nearest city in the region and all global cities. Again, it is the travel-time to these destinations that determines the connectivity score. *Country measures* include all country districts. *Sub-continental measures* are identical to country measures except that the territory is defined in purely geographic terms. *Global measures* are similar except that this instance no boundaries are placed upon the analysis. Thus, global measures are devised from all global districts and all global districts weighted by their respective populations. This brings us to the idea that an intuition/population/enterprise that is in a connection to a highly-connectivity district is more valuable than a connection to a low-connectivity district. In this case, the whole area of NER can gain the evitable gains if KMMTT and several other linkage projects are completed between India and Myanmar.

Arguing through the international relations theory of 'functionalism', which rose principally from the experience of European integration. Functionalism is presented as an operative philosophy that would gradually lead to a peaceful, unified and cooperative world. The main concern of the functionalist is to develop piecemeal non-political cooperative organisations, which will not only help establish peace and secure prosperity but also render the practice of war obsolete eventually. Rather than the self-interest that realists sought as a motivating factor, *functionalists focus on common interests shared by states.* The argument evolves around the idea that integration develops its own internal dynamic. As states integrate in limited functional or technical areas, they increasingly find that momentum for further rounds of integration in related areas. This 'invisible hand' of integration phenomenon is termed 'spill-over'. The concept of spillover is similar to that of 'demonstration' effect as used in the discipline of economics. The underlying belief of the spillover concept is that cooperation in one area would open new avenues for similar cooperation in other areas. For instance, successful forging of cooperation in the area of coal and steel production would spill over into other functional areas like transportation, pollution control etc. Such a process of cooperation, the functionalists argue, would eventually lead to political unification of a given region.

Thus, this argument also stands true for the 'linkage projects' between India and Myanmar. Although integration can be resisted, it becomes harder to stop the reach of the integration as it progresses. This usage, and the usage in functionalism in international relations, is the less commonly used meaning of the term functionalism. More commonly, however, functionalism as a term is used to describe an argument, which explains phenomena as functions of a system rather than an actor or actors. *Immanuel Wallerstein* employed a 'functionalist' theory when he argued that the Westphalian international political system arose to secure and protect the developing international capitalist system.[12] His theory is called "functionalist" because it argues that an event was a function of the preferences of a system and not the preferences of an agent. Functionalism is different from structural or realist arguments in that while both look to broader, structural causes, realists (and structuralists more broadly) say that the structure gives incentives to agents, while functionalists attribute causal power to the system itself, bypassing agents entirely. If this argument is implemented then, 'connectivity' can be termed as a variable, as envisaged rightly through various projects, like the KMMTT which will facilitate the integration of the Southeast Asian region.

Kaladan: Connectivity and Integration

Press reporting indicates the project is currently being executed in three stages: (1) dredging and modernising Sittwe port, (2) dredging sections of the Kaladan river for large ship access, and (3) constructing roads from the Paletwa river to the Indian state of Mizoram.[13] The Indian conglomerate the Essar Group was awarded the contract for the initial stage and will reportedly modernise the port on 70,000 sq meters of reclaimed land. The location map of India-Myanmar and Kaladan is as follows:

Underdeveloped infrastructure and unfavourable institutional and business environment seriously limit participation of the economy into regional and global networks. The cross-border connectivity plays a very important role in this scenario. Establishing better connectivity in all means namely, material, institutional and people-to-people connectivity will allow Myanmar, India and then, the other Southeast Asian countries to raise possibilities for collaboration between them and to expand economic synergies for development in the region. Moreover, regional interconnectivity through infrastructure development, trade facilitation and regulatory harmonisation among the respective economies such as India, Myanmar and other ASEAN members can make each economy more dynamic and bring enormous benefits to the entire region.

Myanmar government has endeavoured to develop the socio-economy of the borders by improving infrastructure. Border area development plan was launched in 1989 to fulfill the basic needs of the nationalities, various ethnic groups residing in remote and border areas and social life of the nationals living in those areas. Priority has been given to the development of transport and communications, education, health, electric power and agriculture. The government built many new roads in Sagaing, Kachin and Chin regions, which are being mountainous and endowed with rivers and creeks. They had poor transport in the past. Earth roads have been upgraded into gravel ones and the gravel roads to tarred facilities. Extension of motor road in Sagaing, Kachin and Chin regions increased from 2,581 miles in 1988 to 4,002 miles in 2010, while other modes of transportation also increased at relatively slower rates. Transportation in the border area has specially developed by the government's border area and national races development projects.[14] Simultaneously, the government has targeted to upgrade economies of the Sagaing region, Kachin state and Chin state together with others. As efforts are being made for ensuring development of agriculture as the base and all round development of other sectors of the economy as well there have been good foundations for industrial development in these regions. With a view to bringing development to Kachin state and ensuring development of national races, the government has designated Kachin State Special Region-1 and Kachin State Special Region-2. There are also establishing industrial zones in Sagaing region (e.g., Monywa and Kalay).[15] Similarly, the government is encouraging a particular crop, tea that grows well in Chin state and materialising the concept of 'one state-one product' in Chin state as a major tea growing region.

On the Indian side, the north-eastern regions faced challenges to become an attractive destination for private investment and regional trade due to its geographical remoteness, inherent deficiency in infrastructure and the bad publicity for recurrent ethnic strife and militant activities. Since closer cross-border economic ties have been forged around the world, cross-border trade and tourism have come to be seen as a mean for breaking out from being geographical isolation. While trade with Bangladesh and Bhutan has assumed important in the wake of attempts to forge greater South Asian regional cooperation, trade with Myanmar has acquired added significance in the context of India's proclaimed

'Look East' policy because of Myanmar's geographical proximity to the Southeast Asia.

These developments revealed that there are great possibilities and opportunities to improve economic cooperation with bordering regions/countries like India and Bangladesh, Thailand and China. Linking the states of Myanmar with bordering regions of India and Bangladesh will provide an outlet for their local produce and will stimulate economic activities, bringing in greater investment and prosperity to the border areas of all connecting nations. On the other hand, Myanmar is the sole land bridge between ASEAN and India. The cross-border connectivity plays a very important role in this scenario. Establishing better connectivity in all means namely, infrastructure, institutional and people-to-people connectivity will allow Myanmar and India to raise possibilities for collaboration between them and to expand economic synergies for development in the region. Moreover, regional interconnectivity through infrastructure development, trade facilitation and regulatory harmonisation among the respective economies such as India, China, Bangladesh, Myanmar and other ASEAN members can make each economy more dynamic and bring enormous benefits to the entire region. Some scholars also argue that through this connectivity India and Myanmar are encircling Bangladesh. The following map explains the same.

Conclusion-Thinking Beyond

Myanmar and India have historical, cultural and natural links. Since India shares a land boundary of 1,643 kilometers connecting Arunachal Pradesh, Manipur, Nagaland and Mizoram with mainland Southeast Asia through Myanmar, the border states of Kachin in the north, Sagaing in the middle and Chin in the south of Myanmar are the ones directly linked to the borders of northeast India and Bangladesh. Although the economies of these regions are relatively underperformed by several reasons including poor infrastructure, all three states enjoy considerable endowments for horticulture - vegetables and fruits, bamboo and medicinal plants. In addition, the states of Kachin and Sagaing are also rich in minerals. High potential horticulture and rich mining deposits should be able to finance infrastructure development. Tourism is another economic activity that can be promoted.

India enjoyed friendly relations with Burma from 1948 to 1962. Prime ministers Jawaharlal Nehru and U Nu were instrumental in cementing initial political and diplomatic ties between two countries. India provided Burma with military and economic assistance during this period. India's relations with Burma totally froze after its military takeover in 1962. General Ne Win who seized power, nationalised all private enterprise in Burma and ordered expulsion of the Indians. This created a bad blood in India-Burma relations. India had to arrange ferries and aircrafts to lift its citizens out of Burma. India's war with China in 1962 and military regime siding with the Chinese too had repercussions on India-Burma relations. General Ne Win's idea of cocooning Burma from the rest of the world further distanced India from Burma. During Indira Gandhi's rule, India avoided any contact with Burma and was critical of its suppression of democratic movement and maintaining a poor human rights record. There was no change in India's policy towards Burma during Rajiv Gandhi's regime. Rajiv Gandhi criticised the State Law and Order Restoration Council (SLORC) for assuming power in 1988 and extended moral support to the pro democracy movement in Burma. His government also provided thousands of Burmese citizens with 'refugee status' in India after they fled Myanmar in wake of military repression. The real shift in India-Myanmar relations came when the NDA government assumed power in 1998. Since then a new momentum was infused in the dormant India-Myanmar relations. Fresh diplomatic engagement with Myanmar was made to achieve India's stated objective outlined during Narashima Rao's regime. The high point in Indo-Myanmar relation was the visit by General Than Shwe to New Delhi in October 2004. It was for the first time that the head-of-state of Myanmar had visited India in twenty-four years. Several agreements like setting up cultural exchanges, cooperation in non-traditional security issues, Tamanthi hydroelectric project in Myanmar were signed during his visit. The two sides explored how to expand cooperation in areas like, industry, energy, rail transportation, communications, science and technology and health. India raised the issue of insurgency in its northeast region with bases in Myanmar and the military ruler assured to take necessary steps to oust the rebels from its soil.

Given the above argument, the KMMTT projects, when completed will provide the following benefits:

- The implementation of the project will open up many opportunities for people of diverse background of this region.
- The development of transportation facilities from Sittwe Port, Myanmar, up to Silchar.
- The project, will demand more infrastructures, from water to land to electricity, which will create the input for more business.
- Mizoram is to become the Gateway to Southeast Asia – Mizoram will be the gateway to South-east Asian countries after the construction of the KMTT project in neighbouring Myanmar.
- The building of a pipeline will bring natural gas from Myanmar via north-east to the whole of India.
- The land-locked north-eastern states will gain easy access to the Bay of Bengal through Myanmar.
- The region will officially interact through channels, which will bring transparency.
- Elements of good governance will automatically flow with the enhancement of development.
- Integration process of the population will become easy.
- KMMTT will become an icon for the 'Look East Policy', which is aimed at reaching out to the ASEAN nations.

However, some negative factors shall also be taken into consideration, while talking about KMMTT:

- Rohingya uprising may have a negative impact, because the Sittwe port of Mynamar is within that state.
- The possible deluge of immigrants that the projects will attract, may bring in their culture and tradition, and would even want to practice it, in contrast with the least tolerant Mizo community.
- Perhaps conflicts will arise due to demand. Unless the government is ready with a blueprint to tackle that problem, then this connectivity may prove detrimental. In fact, even more roads and connectivity will be demanded as the intention is to make Mizoram a trade-centre for the whole of the north-east.

- There is a possible negative environmental impact too, as happened in most other development works. A preliminary report released by the Arakan Rivers Network (ARN) argues that a planned transport facility on the Kaladan river in the western Myanmar's Arakan state will wreak environmental devastation on the river, and negatively impact the lives of many of the approximately one million civilians living along it.[16] The ARN report outlines three primary areas of concern for the civilians inhabiting areas around the Kaladan: the environmental impact of such large-scale development on one of the world's few remaining untouched rivers; the human rights implications of a significantly increased military presence along the river; and the devastating effects on individual livelihoods of both environmental degradation and the abuses stemming from militarisation of the area. The environmental concerns centre on the fact that the Kaladan has remained unpolluted and unaffected by development over thousands of years, therefore, its ecosystems may be too fragile to cope with the impacts of dredging, including changes in river flow and turbidity, as well as increased traffic and pollution on the river. The Kaladan and its watershed are also home to numerous rare or endangered species. They argued that the framework of agreement of the KMMTT project makes no mention of environmental impact surveys or standards for the development. In fact, there is only reference to the environment occurs in the article binding the Burmese regime to provide for free any "permissions from the local authorities on account of environment."[17]
- The project, according to ARN report predicts that millions of people may find a sudden and rapid depletion of their food supplies as the coast near Sittwe and the 225 kilometres of the Kaladan river will be dredged of almost 2.5 million cubic metres of material. The river, lined with the homes of approximately one million people, is for many a key source of water, fish and crabs, and is surrounded by paddy fields. Food security is of particular concern now due to a famine affecting Arakan and Chin states, which has steadily worsened since 2007 and has caused many to leave their homes.[18]
- The truckers across India are often cited for the spread of HIV/AIDS across the country and if so, the project will open up the tribal-dominated rural areas, and with the poverty and backwardness, is the government ready to tackle the humanitarian and social problems inevitable with the change.

- The KMMTT, after completion will be handed over under the control of the government of Myanmar as per the MoU. Mizoram has often blamed the Burmese, especially the immigrants from the Chin state, of the drug problems. A trade routes under the direct control of the Myanmar government regime, notorious for its opium plantation which may turn into a freeway for more drugs, and even more supplies for the insurgent groups.
- There will be displacement of millions of tribals, and certainly many lives will be uprooted. Will the government take the onus of rehabilitating its victims?
- When the project will be finalised the implication may not be desirable, especially for the radical section of the YMA and MNF (Manipur National Front). The projected route will pass through the rather neglected Lais, Maras and Chakmas dominated southern Mizoram. This means they can hold Mizoram to ransom by blocking the road and all in all, a more influential and more potent southerner is not in the interest of the rather egoistic Mizo community.
- The Indian strategic thinkers are worrying about the ability of the Indian navy to guard Sittwe port.

Be that what it may, when the KMMTT project will be actualised, certainly it will bring possibilities beyond our imagination. Simply speaking, a container from Kolkata to Imphal via the KMMT will go via a convoluted, cross-border route. First, 550 km on an ocean-going vessel, followed by 225 km on a river barge, and then by truck traversing 140 km of Burmese highways and finally, 100 km from Moreh to Imphal. By road, Imphal-Kolkata involves driving about 1,600 km and Aizawl-Kolkata is about the same. The KMMT is both cheaper and quicker. It also considerably improves the NE's links with ASEAN. Thus, KMMT should trigger massive expansion of local trade. Certainly, the environmental factors along with displacement and conservation of the local rare species of flora and fauna are to be adjusted, as has happened in most development projects. If sustainable development can be implemented with the concerted efforts of the involvement of the countries of the region, then the fruits of the development through this connectivity project will certainly reach the millions of the inhabitants, which will connect them to the greater regional integration. As observed in other parts of the world, development always brings equity in development, thereby ensuring a systematic transformation. Conceptually speaking, policy decisions today, in the context of Southeast Asia, is more driven by the institutional and ideational shifts, which reflect and institutionalise the shift in policy accountability away from its traditional centres, towards a diverse range of policy actors and to the subjects of development and integration. That in itself will prove beneficial in the long run. Understanding the links between environmental sustainability and equity is critical if we are to expand human freedoms for current and future generations.

The remarkable progress in human development over recent decades, which the global *Human Development Reports* have documented, cannot continue without bold global steps to reduce both environmental risks and inequality. Stronger accountability and democratic processes, in part through support for an active civil society and media, can also improve outcomes. Successful approaches rely on community management, inclusive institutions that pay particular attention to disadvantaged groups, and cross-cutting approaches that coordinate budgets and mechanisms across government agencies and development partners.

References

1. The Kaladan river is a river in eastern Mizoram State of India, and in Chin State and Arakan (Rakhine) state of western Myanmar. It forms the international border between India and Burma.
2. Manipur Update, http://manipurupdate.com/?p=31793
3. http://www.mdoner.gov.in/content/introduction-1
4. http://www.defence.pk/forums/indian-defence/187817-india-burma-kaladan-multi-modal-transit-transport-project-sittwe. html#ixzz 2Ed Odqin2
5. Douglas A. Hibbs, Ola Olsson, Jared Diamond, "Geography, Biogeography and Why Some countries are Rich and Others Poor", *Proceedings of the National Academy of Sciences,* Vol. 101, 2004, pp. 3715-3720; David S. Landes, *The Wealth and Poverty of Nations: Why Some Are So Rich and Some So Poor,* New York: W.W. Norton, 1999.
6. Ester Boserup, *The Conditions of Agricultural Growth: The Economics of Agrarian Change under Population Pressure,* Chicago: Aldine, 1965; Oded Galor, David N. Weil, "From Malthusian Stagnation to Modern Growth" *American Economic Review,* Vol. 89, No. 2, May 1999, pp. 154 ; Marvin Goodfriend, John McDermott, "Early Development." *American Economic Review*, Vol. 85, No.1, March 1995, pp. 116-33; Michael Kremer, "Population Growth and Technological Change: One Million B.C. to 1990", *Quarterly Journal of Economics,* Vol. 108, No.3, August 1993, pp. 681-716.
7. Daron Acemoglu, Simon Johnson, James A. Robinson, "Institutions as the Fundamental Cause of Long-Run Growth," *NBER Working Paper*, 2004, p.10481; Edward L Glaeser, Florencio Lopez-de-Silanes, Andrei

Shleifer, "Do Institutions Cause Growth?", *Journal of Economic Growth*, no. 9, 2004, pp. 271-303.

8. Murat Iyigun, "Monotheism (From a Sociopolitical and Economic Perspective), Harvard University- Centre for International Development [CID]: Institute for the study of the labour [IZA], *Working paper*, 2007; David S. Landes, "Why Europe and the West? Why Not China?" *Journal of Economic Perspectives*, Vol. 20, No. 2, Spring 2006, pp. 3-22.
9. Kenneth Pomeranz, *The Great Divergence: Europe, China, and the Making of the Modern World Economy*, Princeton: Princeton University Press, 2000.
10. Lauren Benton, "From the World-Systems Perspective to Institutional World History: Culture and Economy in Global Theory," *Journal of World History*, Vol. 7, No.2, 1996, pp. 261-295; Albert Bergesen (ed.), *Studies of the Modern World-System*, New York: Academic Press, 1980; Raul Prebisch, "The Economic Development of Latin America and Its Principal Problems," *Staff Report for the United Nations*, New York: United Nations, 1950; David Snyder, Edward L. Kick, "Structural Position in the World System and Economic Growth, 1955-1970: A Multiple-Network Analysis of Transnational Interactions", *American Journal of Sociology*, Vol. 84, No. 5, March 1979, pp. 1096-1126; Ronan Van Rossem, "The World System Paradigm as General Theory of Development: A Cross-National Test," *American Sociological Review*, Vol. 61, No. 3, June 1996, pp. 508-27; Immanuel Wallerstein, *The Modern World-System. Capitalist Agriculture and the Origins of the European World Economy in the Sixteenth Century*, New York: Academic Press, 1974.
11. One might also construct a measure of connectedness based on the cost of transport, and this could be further disaggregated into cost as a per cent of GDP in a given country – thus capturing the fact that it is easier for Americans to travel to Kenya than for Kenyans to travel to the US. However, this requires data that are virtually impossible to gather for eras prior to the late twentieth century. Even so, in a purely cross-sectional analysis (focused on 2000) it might be worthwhile.
12. Wallerstein, n.10; Ernst B. Haas, *Beyond the Nation-State: Functionalism and International Organisation*, Stanford: Stanford University Press, 1964; R. O. Keohane and S. Hoffmann, *The New European Community: Decision-making and Institutional Change*, Boulder, Colorado: Westview Press, 1991; D. Mitrany, *The Functional Theory of Politics*, New York: St. Martin's Press, 1976; J. A. Scholte, in J. Baylis and S. Smith (eds), *The Globalisation of World Politics*, New York: Oxford University Press, 2001, pp. 13-34.
13. http://www.mdoner.gov.in/content/introduction-1.

14. Government of Myanmar, 2009, www.iprcc.org/userfiles/Myanmar(2).pdf.
15. *Ibid.*
16. ARN Director Aung Marn Oo spoke at the Kaladan Report Press Conference, which was published on 12 November, 2009.
17. *Ibid.*
18. *Ibid.*

12

Bangladesh-India Relations and Its Future

Imtiaz Ahmed

Ever since the current Awami League regime came to power in 2009 and Bangladesh signed a 50-clause historic Communiqué with India following Bangladesh prime minister Sheikh Hasina's visit to New Delhi in January 2010 there has been great expectation with regard to the development of Bangladesh-India relations. Such expectation, however got slightly marred following the visit of India's prime minister Manmohan Singh to Dhaka in September 2011, particularly when the water sharing agreement over Teesta could not be signed and had it cancelled at the very last minute. Still, very few think that Bangladesh-India relations can go back to pre-2009 period of uncertainty if not 'distant neighbourliness', as one former Indian diplomat once opined.[1] But is that the case? Can we seriously speak of a qualitative change in Bangladesh-India relations? If so, why that is the case? If not, why not? In sum, what can we expect from Bangladesh-India relations in the future is what this Paper will focus is upon.

A precise approach could be identified when it comes to foreign policymaking in this part of the world, particularly with reference to Bangladesh and India. And this could be referred to as the *biriyani* approach. Derived from the Persian word *berya* (n) meaning 'fried' or 'roasted,' the word *biriyani* refers mainly to the gastronomic delight consisting of rice, meat, eggs, potato, even one or two fruits, and then cooked with special care with various spices, certainly by a competent chef. Some say that the travellers and merchants from Iran while others say that the Mughals had introduced it in India in the sixteenth century.[2] There are now variations of it found throughout South Asia, mostly called by the name of the place or the competent chef, like the Hyderabadi biriyani, Bhatkali biriyani, Kacchi biriyani, Lucknowi biriyani, Fakruddin biriyani, Hajji biriyani and many more, and has become integral to what is known as the Indian or South Asian cuisine. In the same vein, the biriyani approach in foreign policy-making refers to the state's use of multiple elements – political, social, economic, historical, security, environment, even culture – all at the same time when negotiating with another state. A good example in this regard would be the Joint Communiqué mentioned above. The Communiqué not only included issues related to the 1974 land boundary agreement, supply of electricity, transit, environmental impact of Tipaimukh dam and counter-terrorism but also overseeing the joint celebrations of the 150th birth anniversary of Rabindranath Tagore! If this sounds comprehensive and inclusive of multiple elements it is also *biriyani*-like and that is where the uniqueness of the approach lies. But bereft of a 'competent chef' the approach is always under stress when it comes to cooking or rather implementing it. The Paper while keeping the *biriyani* approach in mind reflects on five areas pertaining to Bangladesh-India relations.

The Political Dimension

Matters could have been different if it were not for some providential circumstances when both Dhaka and Delhi had political leaders at the very top who were tied up historically. Sheikh Hasina, the daughter of Sheikh Mujibur Rahman, and Sonia Gandhi, the daughter-in-law of Indira Gandhi as head of the ruling Congress party, and indeed, through Manmohan Singh, were certainly in a position to build up on the friendship between the two countries that began at the very birth of Bangladesh in 1971 when Indira Gandhi and Sheikh Mujibur Rahman needed and supported each other. Although it must be quickly noted that Bangladesh-India relations nurtured in 1971 could not be continued without some hitches here and there and by 1974 some of these hitches became too apparent to be ignored.

There was also a second critical factor. Both Indian National Congress and Bangladesh Awami League, the two ruling parties, were blessed by what is referred to as track two diplomacy, with some of the policy-makers of both these countries knowing each other and having had the opportunity of working together at the track two level for a number of years. This allowed both the governments to have almost a ready-made agenda, knowing very well what could be put on the table when leaders of both these countries would meet. And this is precisely the reason why so many items were inserted in the January 2010 Joint Communiqué, indeed, items about which there were a series of dialogues at the track two level prior to Hasina's coming to power.

Both the countries, however, despite having a consensus at the political level to develop and fundamentally transform inter-state relations, are beset with two constraints. Firstly, having a bureaucracy that is relatively conservative when compared to the vision and agenda of the political actors. This, however, is the case more with India than Bangladesh given that the former has a much older bureaucratic tradition and relatively a powerful one compared to the latter. Secondly, domestic compulsions, which in India's case relates to electoral politics and the power of the states in relation to the central government, while in the case of Bangladesh the pro- and anti-Indian sentiments are divided along party lines with the ruling Awami League perceived to be friendlier towards India than the main opposition party, the Bangladesh Nationalist Party. Both of these in combination either slow down the process of transformation or create newer hurdles in the relationship between the two countries.

What has made a difference lately and this has impacted upon the two bureaucracies as well is the rapid change sweeping the world in the name of globalisation and the possibility of both these countries embarking upon a win-win relationship. And this is particularly with reference to the development of northeast India, and there are good reasons for this. In fact, what is worrying for India is the marginalisation and alienation of the northeast and the impact that China's development could have on the region, as one critic pointed out:

> The development of infrastructure by China in its border regions with India' has been so rapid and effective and the Indian response so lackadaisical that the Indian Member of Parliament from Arunachal Pradesh was forced to suggest, in sheer exasperation, that the government should allow Arunachal to get a rail link from China as, even sixty years after independence, India has failed to connect this state to the nation's mainland.[3]

In fact, before work began in September 2010 to extend the world's highest railway line onwards from the Tibetan capital Lhasa west to the second largest city, Xigaze, near the Nepalese border, China had already announced another rail extension east to Nyingchi, less than fifty km from the line of actual control in Arunachal Pradesh.[4] India could respond only by deploying two additional army divisions, heavy tanks and ramping up its air power in the region,[5] a far cry from the kind of development that is required to assuage the sub-nationalist aspirations amongst the people of northeast India. This is where globalisation and the impetus for newer Bangladesh-India relations come.[5]

But if this newer relationship between Bangladesh and India has a direct benefit to India's northeast states,[6] the so-called 'seven sisters,' there is less enthusiasm of it in the Indian state of West Bengal, now under the chief ministership of Mamata Banerjee, something which the policy-makers of both these countries seem to have ignored or thought could be overrided given the sheer importance that the central government has given to the development of the northeast and the newer relationship that is required with Bangladesh to make this effective. But centre-state relationship in India has always been problematic and tension-ridden and more so when the states find the central government nationally weak. Indeed, in the aftermath of the 2G spectrum scam and corruption related to the holding of the Commonwealth games and in the backdrop of all these the Anna Hazare anti-corruption movement did make Manmohan Singh perceptively weak and out of touch with realities. Mamata Banerjee seized this opportunity and thought that this was the time she could best bargain with Delhi and safeguard the interests of West Bengal. In fact, since the time when the Joint Communiqué was signed in January 2010 and when Manmohan Singh decided to visit Dhaka in September 2011 things have changed politically within India. Not only were the Communists in West Bengal with whom Bangladesh had a cordial relationship for over two decades were routed out in the state assembly elections of April-May 2011 but also Manmohan Singh's position got tainted and few even did not mind suggesting names for his possible replacement! Mamata knew she could bargain well with Delhi, which led her not only to decline joining the prime minister's entourage to Dhaka but also stall the signing of the Teesta water sharing agreement with Bangladesh.

Notable in this context is the Uttar Pradesh (UP) state assembly elections in February-March 2012 and the dismal performance of both Congress and the widely believed 'prime minister-in-waiting,' Rahul Gandhi. The ruling party is now less in a position to alienate Mamata Banerjee, requiring her support more than ever for the Congress alliance to remain at the centre, which is likely to strengthen Mamata's position in dealing with the latter, including flagging some of her reservations related to Manmohan-Hasina agreement on Bangladesh-India relations. In fact, Mamata has recently flagged her opposition to the exchange of enclaves and the implementation of the 1974 land boundary agreement, which is now awaiting ratification in the Indian parliament. It may be pointed out that Bangladesh has already ratified the 1974 land boundary agreement in

October 1974 but now that the wording of the agreement with respect to the Teen Bigha Corridor has been changed from the original 'lease in perpetuity' to '24-hour access to Bangladeshis' the question that merits attention is whether Bangladesh has to ratify the agreement afresh? At the national level this could be a source of contention and vex the relationship between the two countries. But that is not all.

Delhi's inability to bring Mamata on board and deliver on the Teesta, coupled with issues like the BSF (Border Security Forces of India) firing in the border area, has created a negative impression about India in the minds of many a Bangladeshi, which the opposition Bangladesh Nationalist Party found convenient to hype up with anti-Indian rhetoric. A regime change is likely to further slowdown, and this time on the part of Bangladesh, the pace of implementing whatever has been agreed upon between these two countries, including transit or transhipment of Indian goods through Bangladesh. It must be quickly pointed out, however, that none of the regimes in Bangladesh since the time of independence has thus far abrogated any international agreements signed bilaterally or multilaterally. A slowdown, particularly in areas not immediately beneficial, cannot be ruled out, however. This warrants a closer exposition of some of the areas critical to Bangladesh-India relations.

Security and Connectivity

With respect to the northeast, India's primary concerns are security and connectivity or rather 'transit,' that is, getting access to the region through Bangladesh. In the minds of India's policy-makers both these issues are central to forging a newer relationship with Bangladesh. And there are good reasons for this. Indeed, on the issue of security, India requires the support from Bangladesh in not only getting hold of the militant insurgents, mainly members of the United Liberation Front of Asom (ULFA) and the National Democratic Front of Bodoland (NDFB), who are allegedly hiding in Bangladesh, but also putting an end to the alleged sheltering of such insurgents within Bangladesh. Knowing well that this alone would not curb the militancy in Assam or elsewhere in the northeast, the central government made economic development a priority in the region and that is where connectivity understood as 'transit' and a helping hand from Bangladesh becomes critical. For Bangladesh, however, security is more of a secondary concern now that India has stopped sheltering its erstwhile dissenters, the Shanti Bahini or members of the non-Bengali Hill people. Rather, for Bangladesh, access to India's market, including that of the northeast region, remains a priority. Added to this is connectivity not in the Indian sense of the word, that is, movement of goods from one side of India to another through Bangladesh, but rather transporting goods to Nepal and Bhutan through India. Attempts were made to combine all four elements – security, India's connectivity, Bangladesh's connectivity, and market – but few would agree on their success at this stage. Let us explain.

When it comes to security, the two countries did make substantial progress and this is well documented in the Joint Communiqué of January 2010. In fact, the first three sub-sections of clause 48 of the Communiqué deal directly with security are: agreement on Mutual Legal Assistance on Criminal Matters; agreement on the Transfer of Sentenced Persons; and agreement on Combating International Terrorism, Organised Crime and Illicit Drug Trafficking.[7]

This issue of security was once again reiterated and even extended when the two prime ministers met in September 2011 in the joint statement:

> The two prime ministers underscored the need to conclude an Extradition Treaty between the two countries expeditiously to complete the legal framework for bilateral security cooperation while expressing satisfaction that the Agreement on Mutual Legal Assistance on Criminal Matters, Agreement on the Transfer of Sentenced Persons and Agreement on Combating International Terrorism, Organised Crime and Illicit Drug Trafficking, signed in January 2010, were now in force following their ratification.[8]

The Extradition Treaty, however, is yet to materialise, although insurgents belonging to India and residing in Bangladesh had been allegedly pushed back and handed over to the Indian authorities, indeed, informally, during 2010-2011. Notable among them were ULFA 'captain' Antu Chaudang, 'second lieutenant' Pradeep Chetia and Saurav, and 'chairman' Arabinda Rajkhowa.[9] Bangladesh also handed over Ranjan Daimary, chief of the outlawed NDBF to India. It may be mentioned that during the caretaker government under Fakhruddin Ahmed (2007-2008) India repatriated over seven Bangladeshi petty criminals out of a total of 400 residing in India.[10] But surprisingly, no criminals got repatriated during the current regime despite the fact that the latter had pushed back and handed over key northeast insurgents to India. Moreover, when the two home ministers met in February 2011 both of them submitted to each other a list of wanted criminals, which in the case of Bangladesh included two convicted killers of Sheikh Mujibur Rahman and a few accused of involvement in a grenade attack on the ruling Awami League in 2004.[11] But India is yet to respond to this. What could be the reason?

One reason could be to bring pressure on Bangladesh to release the most wanted insurgent, the general secretary of ULFA, Anup Chetia. The latter was arrested in Dhaka in December 1997 during the previous tenure of Sheikh Hasina as the prime minister of Bangladesh (1996-2001), mainly on charges of carrying foreign currencies and a satellite phone illegally under the Foreigners Act of 1946 and the Passports Act of 1952. Later he was sentenced to seven years of imprisonment by a Bangladeshi court and is now being held at Kashimpur jail in the outskirts of Dhaka. Bangladesh, however, contends that since there is no Extradition Treaty between the two countries it is difficult for them to handover Anup Chetia to India. And this brings us to the second point.

The signing of the Extradition Treaty itself is a problem. Not only would it sacrifice one of the core values of Bangladesh enshrined in its Constitution in Article 25 para (c): "(The State shall) support oppressed peoples throughout the world waging a just struggle against imperialism, colonialism or racialism," and this more in the light of the fact that much of the struggle in northeast India is emancipatory and just, but would also close the door for many a dissenter taking shelter in India in the future, as was the case with Sheikh Hasina, Kader Siddiqui and many others following the military takeover of the country in August 1975. Put differently, India has a greater stake in having an Extradition Treaty than Bangladesh, unless of course India can convince the Government of Bangladesh that such a treaty would bring back the killers of Sheikh Mujibur Rahman and hundreds of other petty criminals now residing in India, along with a guarantee that political asylum in the future would be beyond the scope of the treaty. But then who can guarantee that political dissenters would not be dubbed as criminals and make the national courts justify it?

The issue of security with India, however, has taken a different turn for Bangladesh in recent times, particularly in the backdrop of BSF firing in the border area. In fact, over the past ten years BSF killed over 1,000 people, mostly Bangladeshis, turning the border area into, as one reporter commented, "a South Asian killing fields."[12] The BSF, however, contends that criminal elements, mainly smugglers, were shot at and killed in the border area, and back this up by providing figures of both Bangladeshis and Indians killed as a result of BSF firing (Table 1).

Table 1: Firing and Death in Indo-Bangladesh Border 2006-2010 (till 31 October)

Year	*Incident of Firing*	*Deaths in Firing*	
		Bangladeshis Killed	*Indians Killed*
2006	688	97	49
2007	791	81	56
2008	572	46	37
2009	598	48	39
2010	210	22	18

Border Guards of Bangladesh (BGB), however, provide a higher death figure of the number of Bangladeshis killed from BSF firing. According to BGB, 1154 Bangladeshi civilians and sixteen BGB personnel were killed by the BSF in the period between 1972 and September 2010. BGB incidentally do not keep a tally of Indians killed as a result of BSF firing. Two things emerge very clearly from the above set of statistics. Firstly, all incidents of firing have taken place on the Indian territory. And secondly, most incidents of firing relate to cattle smuggling. This requires further exposition.

The 1.5 million cows worth $500 million are smuggled from India into Bangladesh each year.[13] The question that merits attention is why smuggle the cows? Why the cows cannot cross over to Bangladesh from India legally? When such questions were raised in Bangladesh-India track two dialogues on 16 July 2011 the Indian delegation maintained that live cattle cannot be exported legally because of religion. Since cow is sacred to the Hindus any attempt to de-smugglise the animal would face resistance from the Hindu fundamentalists, including the main opposition party in India, the Bharatiya Janata Party (BJP). And this, no political party in India, including the publicly proclaimed secular Congress, would be willing to do.

But then how valid is this contention? Frankly, shrouded in a mystery! This is because India does export live bovine animals, including cattle, and Nepal over the years has been the leading market for Indian live animals.[14] *Export policy* of the Government of India, however, mentions that export of live cattle and buffaloes are "restricted," that is, "permitted under license" while export of beef of cows, oxen and calf are "prohibited."[15]

But then Ritambhara Singh in the 2010 *Annual Report on India's Livestock and Products* points out:

> Buffalo cows, particularly those which have completed their lactation cycles, are predominantly used for meat. There are about 3,900 licensed slaughter houses in the country authorised by local bodies. In addition, there are around 26,000 unauthorised slaughter houses. However, there are now 13 export-oriented, modern, integrated abattoirs or meat processing plants registered with the Agricultural and Processed Food Export Development Authority (APEDA). There are also 24 meat processing and packaging units, which receive dressed carcasses from approved municipal slaughter houses for the export of meat. It is likely that other export plants will be developed in the future given India's export focus.[16]

And this despite the fact of having anti-cow slaughter legislation in several Indian states, although West Bengal, from where the bulk of the cattle enter illegally into Bangladesh, is not one of them. Beef, it must be pointed out, is consumed in West Bengal as well. Why the restriction in exporting cattle to Bangladesh then? The most likely reason is that the profit from cattle-smuggling is so hefty that few in the power are in a position to stop it. It may be pointed out that a cow in Jharkhand in India can be bought for $100, but when this cow enters Bangladesh its price can become as high as $350 to 900.[17] Another estimate showed that BSF captured 70,000 Indian cows worth $ 62 million in Bangladesh in 2008.[18] In fact, according to a survey carried out in 2002, forty three per cent of the total value of illegal trade, which now stands to the tune of $ 2.7 billion annually in favour of India, is live cows and buffaloes.[19] And it is this lucrative profit which is making policymakers at the highest level in Delhi unable to stop not only cow smuggling but also BSF firing! The negative impact that the latter is having in the minds of the people in Bangladesh is otherwise putting a lid on to the prospect of a newer relationship between Bangladesh and India, and that includes the issue of transit as well.

The success of transit, however, would require a publicly demonstrable win-win outcome for both. While India's economic gain from the transit is understandable but until the people and business entrepreneurs in Bangladesh find substantial gain in the transit the chances of it taking off is slim. Although reports indicate that when the Indian prime minister Manmohan Singh came to Dhaka in September 2011 and met the leader of the opposition, Khaleda Zia, the latter is reported to have said that 'transit is reality.'[20] This, of course, is a statement of a politician and therefore ought to be judged politically. As indicated earlier, slowing down the process in implementing transit, as understood and prioritised by India, is always an option for Bangladesh, and the recent remark of the finance minister of Bangladesh, AMA Muhith, is a good indicator of this: "...existing infrastructures at home are not enough to support transit....Transit is important but the development of infrastructures is the basic and more important for making the transit effective."[21] There is no doubt that Bangladesh is looking towards the resolution of other issues with India as well, including the extent to which such transit would benefit the country in real terms and open the door for its own goods not only to India but also Bhutan and Nepal. But then the saleability of the issue could get dampened for reasons of electoral politics in Bangladesh. In fact, the Awami League government may desist from implementing it fully before the next general election lest it becomes an election issue and a vote-killer!

Trade, Investment and Employment

Three inter-related points remain pertinent to the issue of formal trade between Bangladesh and India. First is the balance of trade excessively in favour of India. During 2010-2011 Bangladesh's imports from India were $4.586 billion and exports to India were $512.5 million. This is a great jump in five years from 2005-2006, when Bangladesh's imports from India were $1.864 billion and exports to India were merely $241.96 million (Table 2).

Table 2: Trade between India and Bangladesh: 2005-2011[22]

(Figures in $ million)

FY: July to June	*2005-2006*	*2006-2007*	*2007-2008*	*2008-2009*	*2009-2010*	*2010-2011*
India's Exports	1864.70	2268.00	3364.00	2841.06	3202	4586.8
India's Imports	241.96	289.42	358.08	276.58	305	512.5
Total trade	**2106.70**	**2557.40**	**3722.08**	**3117.64**	**3507**	**5099.3**

Source: *Bangladesh Bank/EPB.*

The balance of trade in favour of India remains obvious and has increased over the years. There is an expectation, however, that with the recent agreement between the two countries Bangladesh would be able to reduce the gap and this brings us to the second point. During Manmohan Singh's visit to Bangladesh in September 2011 India agreed to "remove all forty-six textile lines which are of interest to Bangladesh from India's negative list for LDCs under the provisions of SAFTA, thereby reducing the applicable duty rate to zero."[23] But there is a structural limit to Bangladesh expanding its textile market to India, as one critic perceptively pointed out by referring to the World Bank report on India-Bangladesh bilateral trade:

> The [World Bank] study... pointed out why Bangladesh RMG exporter may not be interested in exporting in India. The margin of export would be very thin (due to small difference in retail market price) which is again vulnerable to Rupee-Taka exchange rate (i.e., if Indian rupee is devalued, the profit margin may be wiped off). Instead, if they focus on exporting the same RMG to Europe and USA where Bangladesh enjoy less tariff barriers and healthy profit margins, they can have a sustainable market share.[24]

But then in the age of globalisation a country-to-country calculation of trade imbalance may not be appropriate in understanding the state of economic relationship and the impact such imbalance could have on the economy. This is because the trade gap between India and Bangladesh also includes the import of twenty per cent of Indian cotton which after being utilised in Bangladesh fetches a hefty amount from the export of its textile goods to West Europe and US. It may be pointed out here that Bangladesh has a trade surplus with both west Europe and US to the tune of $5.8 billion and $2.9 billion respectively (2009 figures). This, however, does not discount the fact that the trade imbalance with India is a continuing source of contestation, with Bangladesh pleading to India to open latter's market for former's goods not on the basis of reciprocity but unilaterally. A qualitative transformation in the relationship between the two countries can certainly come about if India, given its regional position and prospective global role, decides to remove all 480 items from the negative list without waiting for Bangladesh to reciprocate.[25] At this stage there is little reason to believe that this would take place and the final point is a good indicator of that.

Despite the signing of various trade agreements between the two countries the entry of Bangladesh goods into the Indian market is marred by what is referred to as non-traditional barriers (NTBs). This could range from SPS-TBT (sanitary and phytosanitary-technical barrier to trade) to tariff quotas, license requirements and anti-dumping countervailing measures.[26] Not only the Indian customs authority asks for the laboratory test for each and every consignment of food products, cosmetics, leather and textile products but also the laboratory report itself takes fifteen to twenty days as the samples are sent by ordinary mails to the laboratories located far from the land customs stations which delays the clearance of consignment and increases the cost of the products.[27] Apart from these, India also from time to time resorts to imposing extra duty on items such as cement or battery imports from Bangladesh or bans exports of key raw materials such as the one it has done very recently, that is, cotton. Both China and Bangladesh, India's biggest customers of cotton, have criticised the move, and see this as India's attempt to curtail their textile production unfairly. Local trade analysts, however, see this "as yet another sign of the Congress-led ruling coalition's indecisiveness, especially after its drubbing in recent state elections."[28] Whatever may be the reason, the NTBs do hamper trade relations to the point that Bangladesh entrepreneurs get disinterested in opening up new ventures with India and thereby stall further economic development between the two countries.

Moreover, the ban on cotton exports to Bangladesh is particularly counter-productive to India in the light of the recent Indian investment in Bangladesh garment sector, as the following blog reports:

> The investment by Indian companies in Bangladesh garment sector is bound to surge as Indian firms try to take advantage of the lower production cost in the neighbouring country. It is estimated that Indian textile and garment companies have already invested Rs 30 billion (US$ 600 million) in Bangladesh during the current fiscal 2011-12, and this investment is likely to rise significantly. Last year, the Indian Government took a decision to permit import of 48 textile and garment items from Bangladesh at zero-duty. This has also contributed to the increase in investment by Indian firms in Bangladesh. Some Indian companies are even or relocating their production base to Bangladesh.[29]

If this is the case the unreliability in getting Indian cotton would only push the Indian companies to look for other sources, which is bound to cut down on their profit margin. Indeed, in the age of globalisation, NTBs could have a negative impact to the country enforcing them, while at the same time creating mistrust externally. Put differently, with Indians and Bangladeshis (the latter at this stage is far fewer than the former) investing and working in each other's country is destined to create a newer dynamics in the economic relationship between the two countries. Already the chief minister of the Left Front government in the Indian State of Tripura has voiced in favour of 'investment from Bangladesh,' while Sheikh Hasina during her visit to Tripura 'expressed her government's readiness to set up joint ventures in India's North East.'[30] And there lies the hope[30]

In fact, when it comes to joint ventures there is already something of that kind in operation, albeit in a modest form. This refers to the border *haats* (common market place) that the two countries had agreed to establish during Hasina's visit to Delhi in January 2010. Initially, two border *haats* are being established, one on the border stretch between Kalaichar in West Garo Hills district of north-eastern Indian state of Meghalaya and Baliamari of Kurigram district in Bangladesh and another one at Lauwaghar in Sunamganj district of Bangladesh and Balat in east Khasi Hills district of Indian state of Meghalaya. Such *haats*, however, are marked by two interesting features, which only show that much work is needed between the two countries if benefits are to be fully accrued from such initiatives. One is the manner in which such *haats* are to operate and the following report is a good indicator of it:

> Market sheds have been constructed to facilitate trade by 25 vendors from each side, who have been identified and trained by both countries to sell their produce. Three hundred people from each side will also be allowed to visit the *'haat'* with passes. The market will work every Wednesday, from 10.00 a.m. to 4.00 p.m. in the summer and 10.00 a.m. to 3.00 p.m. in the winter. Both Indian and Bangladeshi currencies will be accepted by the traders, who will exchange them in banks working in the two border districts.[31]

It is not difficult to see that such restrictions will not take this venture very far. What is required is the establishment of 'border *haat* plus,' that is, along with the market the establishment of cinema halls, schools, hospitals, and the like for the people of both these countries to share jointly while allowing them to mingle joyfully.

Humans, after all, are not only political and economic beings but also cultural and psychological beings. And addressing the former is as important as addressing the latter. Moreover, and this brings us to the second feature, what is being sold is no less critical, as the above report continued by stating that "China's proxy presence in the *'haat'* was evident from the fact that the large carton in which (the buyer) had brought the product carried the 'Made in China' mark."[32] If this is the case then the chances of such ventures really thriving, particularly in Bangladesh-northeast India region, apparently requires the inclusion of China as well. But then the mindset of those in power is yet to catch up what is being practised at the ground level!

Water and Environmental Security

One could argue that Mamata Banerjee had good reasons to stall the agreement over Teesta with Bangladesh. From her standpoint, given the paucity of water and before deciding to share with Bangladesh, she wanted a guarantee from Delhi as to how much water the state of Sikkim, from where the Teesta originates, would be willing to release and share with West Bengal. This is a fair demand. But then critics believe that Mamata also took the opportunity to pressurise Delhi for an economic package for West Bengal in exchange for her consent to the Teesta agreement. Things have proved difficult on both the accounts. Bringing Sikkim into the fold, in addition to West Bangal for negotiating an international agreement would dilute the power of the federal government and that is something Delhi is unwilling to part. As for the economic package from Delhi in exchange for consenting to India's foreign policy initiative vis-à-vis Bangladesh, indeed, a federal matter, amounts to 'blackmailing' the central government over and above the embarrassment that Mamata had caused to prime minister Manmohan Singh by dropping out from his travel entourage to Dhaka at the last minute, and for this Delhi probably is unwilling to deliver the economic package to Mamata so easily.

But lack of progress on Teesta meant three things. Firstly, there is now pressure on the ruling Awami League domestically, with the criticism being mounted by the opposition as well as a sizeable section of non-partisan civil society members that the ruling party 'gave in' to India's demands while getting little in return. And this with respect to the agreement on 'transit' understood, however, more in the Indian sense of the term, as indicated earlier. Secondly, there is now a slight strain in Dhaka-Delhi relationship, with the former privately blaming the latter that the incident has not only irked Hasina personally but also cost the ruling Awami League its face and now it has to salvage the situation almost by taking a less flexible, if not an apathetic, posture against Delhi. And this became clear when Bangladesh, interestingly along with Pakistan, failed to attend a counter-terrorism meeting of the experts from SAARC countries hosted by Delhi in February 2012.[33] Finally, there is now misgiving about Mamata Banerjee whether her opposition to Teesta and exchange of enclaves is more an economic one, catering to the interests of non-Bengali business community in West Bengal who are supposedly less keen on a newer Bangladesh-India relationship, including 'pan-Bengali fondness,' as it would create space for Bangladeshi entrepreneurs and make them a competitor, particularly in the northeast where the non-Bengali business community hold a monopoly when it comes to economic activities there.

But then Teesta is not the sole issue. Sharing of waters on other rivers, particularly Feni as well as Manu, Muhuri, Khowai, Gumti, Dharla and Dudhkumar, all got stalled as a result of India's or rather Mamata's *faux pas* over Teesta. A resolution of the issue before India's next federal election seems very unlikely, but that could make the ruling Awami League further unpopular within Bangladesh! Delhi needs to reflect on this seriously and act accordingly if it wants to consolidate the progress in Bangladesh-India relations made thus far.

When it comes to water the sharing of rivers on an equitable basis is only one aspect of the problem facing Bangladesh-India relations. No less problematic is India's passion to develop dams, and in this respect the proposed Tipaimukh dam has already had its share in marring Bangladesh-India relations. And there are good reasons for this. Indeed, critics, particularly environmentalists and several technical experts, on both sides of the border have questioned the feasibility and safety of the proposed dam. The original consideration for the dam was to contain the flood water in the Cachar plains of Assam but later the emphasis of the dam shifted to the hydroelectric power generation. The dam will have an installation capacity of 1500 MW with only a firm generation of 412 MW, that is, less than thirty per cent of the installed capacity.[34] People residing in the area soon reflected on the impact the construction of the dam would have on their livelihood and began to oppose the project earnestly, as the following report indicates:

> Anti-dam campaigners continue to voice against the construction of Tipaimukh Dam in the State [of Manipur]. United Community Development Platform, Moirang, People's Action for Development-Tiddim, Social Action Committee, Moirang-B Gram Panchayat and Bishnupur District Youth Council joined organised a cycle rally at Moirang today.... Later, the rallyists faxed a memorandum to Prime Minister Dr Manmohan Singh demanding the revocation of memorandums of understanding (MoUs) signed among Manipur Government, National Hydro Electric Power Corporation and Satluj Jal Vidyut Nigam Limited (SJVNL) on April 28, 2010 and October 22, 2011 for the construction of Tipaimukh Dam at the confluence of Tuivai and Barak rivers.
>
> Demanding protection of environment, nature, indigenous life and tradition, the memorandum also stressed on upholding indigenous people's rights and spelling out clearly the purpose

> of construction of the dam. The memorandum also demanded for immediate halt of all the processes of Tipaimukh Dam construction, taking consent from people in this regard and construction of small dams instead of big dams. The representation also reminded the Prime Minister that 7.8 million trees and 24, 822, 22 hectares of forest will be submerged if Tipaimukh Dam is commissioned.[35]

Similar is the opposition to the dam in Bangladesh, indeed, for reasons ranging from environmental degradation, hydrological drought, and unpredictable outcome from possible seismic changes, loss of agricultural production to the massive displacement of people. And it is this alarm that got reflected in January 2010 joint communiqué and later in the September 2011 joint statement issued by Hasina and Manmohan: "The Prime Minister of India reiterated the assurance that India would not take steps on the Tipaimukh project that would adversely impact Bangladesh." But then, India's unwilling to halt the project is not only creating mistrust but also bad feelings in Bangladesh vis-à-vis India, a factor which the ruling Awami League could ill-afford given the risk it had taken to resolve some of the contentious issues that had marred the relationship between the two countries for over three decades.

On the top of this, almost like a bolt from the blue, came the Indian Supreme Court's verdict on 27 February 2012 in favour of 'nationalisation and inter-linking of rivers' of India, which, like Teesta and Tipaimukh, has similar, if not greater, potential of impacting upon Bangladesh-India relations. And there are good reasons for this. In fact, Bangladesh has fifty seven cross-boundary rivers, of which fifty four are shared with India and the remaining three with Myanmar. Any change in the flow of any of the fifty four rivers shared by Bangladesh and India is bound to impact upon Bangladesh economically, socially, environmentally and even politically. Bangladesh being a riverine and a lower riparian country remains sensitive to matters of water, whether inland or maritime. But let us examine the Court verdict and see to what extent Bangladesh needs to be worried about. Let us limit to four areas.

First, let us discuss the river systems. India has three major river systems: the Indus rivers; the Himalayan rivers; and the Peninsular rivers. Insofar as Indus and Peninsular river systems are concerned there is little Bangladesh can do as changes in those river systems do not affect Bangladesh directly. Although much of the content of the court's verdict deal with the Peninsular rivers system there is one reference to the Himalayan rivers system and that is where Bangladesh's worries lies. As the court verdict states:

> Apart from diverting water from rivers which are surplus, to deficit areas, the river linking plan in its ultimate stage of development will also enable flood moderation. It was comprised of two components: Peninsular Rivers Development and Himalayan Rivers Development. The first involved major inter-linking of the river systems and the latter envisaged the construction of storage reservoirs on the principal tributaries of rivers Ganga and Brahmaputra in India, Bhutan and Nepal. This was to help transfer surplus flows of the eastern tributaries of the Ganga to the West, apart from linking the main Brahmaputra and its tributaries with the Ganga and Mahanadi rivers.[36]

Apart from the fact as to why Bhutan and Nepal would be interested to 'storage' surplus water and have them diverted to India there is also the problem of having such storage impacting upon Bangladesh as the rivers of the latter are linked to the Himalayan rivers system, including Brahmaputra and Ganga. The verdict seems to have overlooked the regional and international implications of linking what the Indian court considers 'the rivers of the country.' This indeed may be true with respect to the Peninsular rivers but certainly not for the Himalayan rivers.

Secondly, we discuss the apprehensions and the dissenters. Although the verdict of the Indian court acknowledges that "The Union of India and some states have shown their concerns and their apprehensions about these projects, including questioning the reliability of water supply from distant sources, distribution of water given the existing tribunal awards and the continued availability of existing water surpluses" still it goes on to claim that "these projects are in the national interest, as is the unanimous view of all experts, most state governments and particularly, the central government." At the same time, the verdict mentions that "The Court is not equipped to take such expert decisions and they essentially should be left for the Central Government and the concerned State." And this is followed by a similar statement: "this Court may not be very appropriate forum for planning and implantation of such a programme having wide national dimensions and ramifications." If that is the case then why provide such a 'what is to be done' kind of a verdict with respect to the river-linking project? And given the concern expressed by both national and international environmentalists to the project the Indian court's claim that the project constitutes 'the unanimous view of all experts' remains a suspect. But more importantly, although the court acknowledges that 'some Indian states' are opposed to the project it fails to go beyond the territoriality of India and see notable dissenters beyond the border and in the region, particularly Bangladesh.

Thirdly, we discuss displacement. The court verdict did make reference to 'displaced people' and 'development induced displacement' and as such remains aware of the 'cost of resettlement of displaced people' without, however, knowing or calculating what that 'cost' would actually be. Arundhati Roy once tried to calculate the cost of another development induced displacement, the one resulting from the construction of large dams, in India and her finding remains pertinent to the river-linking project as well:

> According to a detailed study of 54 Large Dams done by the Indian Institute of Public Administration, the *average* number of people displaced by a Large Dam in India is 44,182. Admittedly, 54 dams out of 3,300 is not a big enough sample. But since it's all we have, let's try and do some rough arithmetic. A first draft. To err on the side of caution, let's halve the number of people. Or, let's err on the side of *abundant* caution and take an *average* of just 10,000 people per Large Dam. It's an improbable low figure, I know, but...never mind. Whip out your calculators. 3,300 x 10,000 = 33,000,000. That's what it works out to. 33 *million* people. Displaced by Big Dams alone in the last fifty years. What about those that have been displaced by the thousands of other Development Projects?[37]

Roy's question remains valid now that another development induced displacement is in the offing and this is something the court verdict on the river-linking project failed to address in a meaningful way. What is worrisome for Bangladesh, however, is not the internal displacement of people within India but the displacement of its own people from the ecological imbalance that is bound to result from the construction of storage reservoirs and the linking of the Himalayan rivers. In this context, India needs to be mindful of the fact that any displacement of people within Bangladesh has the potential of creating newer conflict between Bangladesh and India as part of the displaced could end up as environmental refugees across the border!

Finally, let us discuss about rivers rights. If anything that has been thoroughly ignored in the verdict of the Indian Court is the *right of the rivers,* something to which Ashish Nandy, Ajaya Dixit and I had jointly adhered to and advocated some eighteen years ago:

> Right of the rivers must be codified and guaranteed by the state and the people. Such "rights" have already been codified for oceans and seas. Under the United Nations Convention on the Law of the Sea, it is now the "general duty" of all coastal states to protect and preserve the resources and the riches of the oceans

> and seas, not simply for the consumption of future generations but for the reproduction of human life itself. River rights can be enacted with similar goals in mind....
>
> Rivers also have their rights, including the right to be relatively pollution free, to be a safe habitat for riverine forms of life and, within limits, to flow freely....While interference with rivers has contributed to modernisation, bringing electricity and irrigation facilities to a wider section of people, such diversion of water from its natural course has often led to disasters, their magnitude determined by the scale of interference. For example, while large-scale surface irrigation has worsened the problems of water-logging and soil salinity, unregulated withdrawal of water by dams located upstream has dried up downstream beds of several rivers. In places, this has meant an attack on the economic and other life-support systems of the people, in turn leading to the creation of environmental refugees.[38]

The verdict otherwise is bereft of imagination, which, however, is required not only when it comes to managing the environment for future generations but also in channelising newer relationship between India and its riverine neighbours, including Bangladesh. Any extension of the river-linking project beyond the peninsular rivers and into the Himalayan rivers is bound to de-roll whatever 'goodwill' had been achieved so far and this neither India nor Bangladesh can afford.

India, Bangladesh and the Regional Dimension

When it comes to reinventing the region and making use of economic globalisation to everyone's advantage there is some merit in Jairam Ramesh's conceptualisation of *Chindia* (a portmanteau word referring to China and India) and how the two economies with 2.5 billion people or over one-third of the world's population could collectively make a difference to the world. To make sense of this, one must take note of the fact that in the eighteenth century China and (undivided) India were the first and second largest economies of the world respectively.[39] So, what we are witnessing is not just a rise but a *re-rise* of the region provided, of course, both China and India are able to mend all the fissures both within and outside their respective borders. And this is where cooperation becomes critical and a rationale for China, India, Bangladesh and even other neighbours like Nepal, Bhutan and Myanmar to work and prosper together. Let us examine this further.

Hasina and Manmohan both came to the understanding that Nepal and Bhutan ought to be brought in if a newer relationship between

Bangladesh and India is to be materialised. And this got reflected in the January 2010 Joint Communiqué:. "The Prime Ministers agreed that Rohanpur-Singabad broad gauge railway link would be available to transit to Nepal. Bangladesh informed of their intention to convert Radhikapur-Birol railway line into broad gauge and requested for railway transit link to Bhutan as well." Indeed, when Bangladesh refers to 'transit' the road and rail links to Bhutan and Nepal is what gets the priority. Such transit, however, is beset with two sets of problems. Firstly, non-traditional barriers (NTBs), more on the Indian side of the border, such as issuing permission, security clearance, delay at the border, cumbersome visa regime, lengthy process of standard testing and lack of infrastructure could make this unattractive if not dysfunctional. NTBs could also raise the cost of the product and lower down the margin of the profit and thereby limit the business activities that the transit was intended to foster. And secondly, Bangladesh is yet to create infrastructure and amenities, including recreational facilities, in Mongla or Chittagong catered towards Nepal and Bhutan and as such the latter would be unwilling to readily use the Bangladesh route and replace the Kolkata port to which they are used to for almost a century or two. The idea of 'transit' therefore should not be limited to transporting goods only but must include human connectivity and requirements of all kinds, from school to scuba diving, from hotel to hospitals.

Myanmar too could benefit from a newer Bangladesh-India relationship. Moreover, Bangladesh and China plan to construct a road link via Myanmar. In fact, given China's relationship with Myanmar and Bangladesh and India's relationship with Bangladesh and Myanmar and now with the prospect of Chindia it can be said with some certainty that a collective effort on their part would bring prosperity to all and transform the region beyond recognition.[40] An important step in this quest would be to provide both China and Myanmar 'full membership' to the South Asian regional body, SAARC. It may be mentioned that currently both of them, along with Japan, Australia, US, Iran, South Korea, Mauritius and the 25-member European Union, have observer status in the SAARC. The merit for China's full membership of SAARC is even greater given the fact that the largest trading partner of almost all the South Asian countries, including India, is China. In contrast, since its birth in 1985 the intra-regional trade within SAARC moved from 3.2 per cent in the 1980s to just 5.8 per cent in 2009. At the same time, the largest development partner of Pakistan, Nepal and Sri Lanka is also China. The latter is otherwise *economically* a South Asian country and as such having China included in the SAARC process as a full member would not only rejuvenate SAARC as an economic region but would also help SAARC overcome its current limitations resulting from the irreconcilable differences between Pakistan and India.

But then India is yet to reconcile its political differences with China and this despite the fact that the latter is India's largest trading partner and that the India-China bilateral trade had already hit a record $ 73.9 billion in 2011, registering a growth of 23.51 per cent over 2010. The trade deficit in 2011, however, piled up to $ 27.07 billion even though Indian exports to China went up to $ 23.4 billion registering a growth of almost 12.26 per cent compared to the same period in year 2010.[41] But as indicated earlier in the paper, *bilateral* trade deficit makes little sense in the age of globalisation and particularly so when the deficit country (in this case India) is also having an overall growth in its economy. How India then is able to differentiate the trade or the economic from the political and balance the two? India, it seems, is shedding off its *biriyani* approach when it comes to China and, in fact, is following or should we say reciprocating China's *yin and yang* approach. Let us explain.

In line with its conceptualisation in the Chinese philosophy, the *yin and yang* approach refers mainly to the idea of 'balancing' the opposites, albeit devoid of good/bad distinctions and other dichotomous moral judgments. Contradiction otherwise is part of life, and the *yin and yang* by their interaction, as Fung Yu-Lan maintained, "operate to produce all things, and these in their turn produce and reproduce, so that transformation and change continue without end."[42] Interestingly, even on the issue of 'achievements' there is always an attempt on the part of the Chinese to play it down to avoid promoting envy, as Gurcharan Das highlighted:

> The Chinese...cope with envy by appearing to be excessively and hypocritically modest and seek to disparage their achievements. 'O sir, I am your mean and humble servant who just happened to hit upon this idea,' is not an uncommon refrain. If one sets too high a value on one's abilities, it makes one commit the social offence of regarding oneself as better than others. Thus, the well-known Chinese fear of 'losing face' is a ritualised attitude, in part, to avoid envy.[43]

In fact, there are critics who believe that China actually plays down its economic achievements,[44] and this could be for the reason of shelving off possible international envy or hostility. But the contradiction in China's foreign policy making is more explicit when it comes to nurturing relationship with different countries. Take the case of its relationship with

Taiwan, for instance. China considers Taiwan to be its integral part and is hostile to anyone providing political recognition to the island but at the same time it has no problem in maintaining economic relations and inviting Taiwanese investment to the mainland. Similarly, with India, China has serious border disputes in the Arunachal Pradesh and Aksai Chin region and considers them to be a part of China, and then again on the question of Dalai Lama it remains openly hostile to India's position, but at the same time India's largest trading partner is China. It is not difficult to see that China prefers to keep politics and economics apart, making use of the one that works the best. Indeed, if both politics and economics get stalled China probably would settle for *ping-pong diplomacy* with its counterpart![45] And it is this approach that India seems to be nurturing with China, indeed, reutilising what China had been pursuing with India.

But then it cannot be said that India is pursuing the *yin and yang* approach elsewhere, indeed, not even with the US. In fact, India is very much interested to befriend the US and even consider it as an 'Asian power' mainly to offset the rising power of China. But this will not take India very far, as Suhasini Haidar cautions, "Instead of being alarmed at China's growing inroads in the region, India needs to take a harder look at its own role and find new ways to win neighbours and increase influence in the region's growth story."[46] And there lies India's limits, although it must be quickly pointed out that there are other reasons for India to befriend the US, including keeping Pakistan out of Afghanistan's orbit and acquiring the much required nuclear technology to overcome its energy crisis. India's recent voting alongside with the US against human rights abuse in Sri Lanka, and that again, in contradistinction to the voting of some of its immediate neighbours like Bangladesh, Pakistan and China only tells that domestic compulsion aside (the DMK factor in the State of Tamil Nadu), India is willing to go a long way to keep the US in good humour so that the latter remains within its reach both politically and economically. But if this is a policy intended to overcome China and Pakistan phobias then it is bit short sighted. China has already made an inroad into South Asia, as indicated earlier, and this is projected to deepen further. On the other hand, Pakistan-US relationship is much deeper with the civil and military elite of Pakistan completely beholden if not subservient to the wishes of the US and this despite the fact that the military had sheltered Osama bin Laden for years. India cannot afford to be likewise.

Where does all this place Bangladesh and India regionally? Possibilities have emerged for a win-win relationship not only between

Bangladesh and India but also with a host of other countries in the region and beyond, including China and the US. But much of this depends on the extent to which Bangladesh and India can demonstrate to its people and the region the benefits of the newer relationship. That is a tall task by itself but not something beyond the realms of possibility. And there lies the hope!

Referenes

1. Deb Mukharji, "Distant neighbours: India and Bangladesh," in Atish Sinha and Madhup Mohta (eds.), *Indian Foreign Policy: Challenges and Opportunities*, New Delhi: Academic Foundation, 2007, pp. 557-568.
2. Alan Davidson, *The Penguin Companion to Food*, London: Penguin Books, 2002, p. 612.
3. Harsh V. Pant, "China Rising," in Ira Pande, (ed.), *India China: Neighbours Strangers*, Noida: Harper Collins, 2010, p. 98.
4. The International Institute for Strategic Studies, *The Military Balance 2011*, London: IISS, March 2011, p. 212.
5. Pant, n.3, p. 99.
6. This includes the Indian States of Arunachal Pradesh, Assam, Meghalaya, Mizoram, Manipur, Nagaland and Tripura.
7. "Joint Communiqué issued on the occasion of the visit to India of Her Excellency Sheikh Hasina, Prime Minister of Bangladesh," 12 January 2010, http://www.mofa.gov.bd.
8. "Joint Statement by Bangladesh and India," 7 September 2011, http://www.mofa.gov.bd.
9. IDSA Task Force Report, *India-Bangladesh Relations: Towards Convergence*, New Delhi: Institute of Defence Studies and Analyses, September 2011, p. 46.
10. "India hands over two more top criminals," *The Daily Star*, 8 March 2008.
11. IDSA Task Force Report, n.9.
12. Brad Adams, "India's shoot-to-kill policy on the Bangladesh border," *The Guardian*, 23 January 2011.
13. Ashfaqur Rahman, "From India with love," *The Daily Star*, 22 January 2012.
14. "India's Exports of Live Animals," *Science Tech Entrepreneur*, September 2007, http://www.techno-preneur.net/information-desk/sciencetech-magazine/2007/sep07/India_s_exports.pdf.
15. *Extracts from Foreign Trade Policy* (2004-2009), Government of India, http://wccb.gov.in/AR08.pdf; accessed on 13 March 2012.
16. Ritambhara Singh, *India Livestock and Products Annual 2010*, USDA Foreign Agricultural Service, GAIN Report Number: IN1082, 22

September 2010, http://agriexchange.apeda.gov.in/MarketReport/Reports/Indiaper cent20Livestockper cent20 report.pdf.

17. Rahman, n.13, see also Jyoti Thottam, "A Great Divide," *Time*, 5 February 2009, p. 4.
18. *Ibid.*
19. The World Bank, "India-Bangladesh Bilateral Trade and Potential Free Trade Agreement," *Bangladesh Development Series*, Paper no. 13, Dhaka: The World Bank Office, December 2006, p. 60. See also Rahman, n.13.
20. Swadesh Roy, "Sub Regional Economic Cooperation - North East India and Bangladesh," *Times of Assam*, 23 February 2012.
21. Mizan Rahman, "Bangladesh rules out early transit facility," *Gulf Times*, 26 February 2012.
22. Ministry of External Affairs, Government of India, "India-Bangladesh Relations," January 2012. www.mea.gov.in.
23. "Joint Statement by Bangladesh and India," n. 8.
24. The World Bank, n.19; "On India-Bangladesh Trade Imbalances," *The New Horizon*, see http://horizonspeaks. wordpress.com/2010/02/02/on-india-bangladesh-trade-imbalances.
25. Sajjadur Rahman, "Analysts urge India to erase trade barriers to Bangladesh," *The Daily Star*, 11 January 2010.
26. Mustafizur Rahman (et.al), "Bangladesh's Export Opportunities in the Indian Market: Addressing Barriers and Strategies for Future," *Occasional Paper*, n. 90, Dhaka:Centre for Policy Dialogue, July 2010, pp. 20-21.
27. "Trade Gap with India increases to $2.91 b," *The Financial Express*, 22 October 2010.
28. Ratnajyoti Dutta, "India bans fresh cotton exports - for now," *Reuters*, 12 March 2012, http://in.reuters.com/article/2012/03/12/cotton-india-exports-idINDEE 82B05120120312? type=economic News.
29. http://www.aplindialinx.com/latest_high.php?lh=Mjky.
30. Sujit Chakraborty, "Tripura CM welcomes Bangladesh investment," *Express Buzz*, 19 January 2012.
31. Sushanta Talukdar, "India, Bangladesh revive border 'haat'," *The Hindu*, 23 July 2011.
32. *Ibid.*
33. Pallab Bhattacharya, "Saarc experts discuss anti-terror mechanism," *The Daily Star*, 10 February 2012.
34. Mohiuddin Alamgir, "India's Tipaimukh dam: another Farakka for Bangladesh in the offing?", *NewAge Extra*, 12-18 June 2009.
35. "Protest against Tipaimukh Dam Continues in Manipur," *Northeast Today*, 23 February 2012, http://www.northeasttoday.in/our-states/

manipur/protest-against-tipaimukh-dam-continues-in-manipur/; accessed on 26 March 2012.

36. Indian Supreme Court's verdict on 27 February 2012.
37. Arundhati Roy, *The Greater Common Good,* Bombay: India Book Distributors, 1999, pp. 9-10.
38. Imtiaz Ahmed, Ajaya Dixit and Ashis Nandy, *Water, Power and People: A South Asian Manifesto on the Politics and Knowledge of Water,* Colombo: Regional Centre for Strategic Studies, 1997, pp. 9-10.
39. Martin Jacques, *When China Rules the World: The End of the Western World and the Birth of a New Global Order,* New York: The Penguin Press, 2009, p. 80. See also Tan Chung, "Towards a Grand Harmony", in Ira Pande (ed.), *India China: Neighbours Stranger,* Noida: Harper Collins, 2010, pp. 2-18.
40. Thant Myint-U, *Where China Meets India: Burma and the New Crossroad of Asia,* London: Faber and Faber, 2011.
41. "India-China trade hits all time high of $73.9 billion in 2011," *NDTV Profit,* 29 January 2012, http://profit.ndtv.com/News/Article/india-china-trade-hits-all-time-high-of-73-9-billion-in-2011-296742?pfrom=home-otherstories.
42. Fung Yu-Lan, *A Short History of Chinese Philosophy,* New York: The Free Press, 1966, p. 270.
43. Gurcharan Das, *The Difficulty of Being Good: On the Subtle Art of Dharma,* New Delhi: Penguin Books, 2009, p.13.
44. "China as a Global Player," *World Economic Forum,* 28 September 2008, http://www.weforum.org/news/china-global-player. See also Bertel Schmitt, "Gordon G. Chang: China's Car Sales are a Fraud," *The Truth about Cars,* 23 October 2009, http://www.thetruthaboutcars. com/2009/10/gordon-g-chang-chinas-car-sales-are-a-fraud/#more-332953. Also Francis Fukuyama, *The Origins of Political Order: From Prehuman Times to the French Revolution,* London: Profile Books, 2011.
45. This refers to cultural diplomacy but more specifically to the exchange of table tennis players between the United States and China in the 1970s. This later paved the ways for President Richard Nixon to visit China.
46. Suhasini Haidar, "Only our fears can encircle us," *The Hindu,* 27 September 2010.

13

Connectivity and Security Concerns: Issues on India-Nepal Border

Sanjay K Jha

Introduction

The imperatives of greater connectivity and regional integration in South Asia call for creation of a variety of cross-border mechanism for relatively easy movement of people, goods and services. Creation and institutionalisation such mechanism, it is argued, would lead to common understanding on some of the pre-requisites for regional integration at economic, security and at political level. However, paradox for such imperatives is that creation of such mechanism not only facilitates process of regional integration, but also expedites cross-border movement of terrorists, insurgents and other destabilising forces. How then can facilitation of greater connectivity and regional integration be reconciled with the need to ensure security?

The situation is much more complex in the case of South Asia, where a host of domestic instabilities are product of inter-state relations or state itself, in many cases, is seen as facilitator of domestic instability in the neighbouring state. In India, such concerns are reflected in the debates on national security. We find that internal security has become an integral and arguably the dominant component of India's national security management. The discourse on internal security suggests that most of terrorism and internal security related problems in India have cross-border linkage. Apart from domestic factors, the growth and survival of a majority of them have been sustained by dynamics of inter-state relations, politico-security environment in the neighbouring countries and ability of these groups to exploit porous/open borders. Not surprisingly, therefore, border security or border management, as it is generally referred to, has become one of the most crucial elements of India's internal security management.

In this context, while borders with Pakistan and Bangladesh have long been in focus, the India-Nepal border has assumed significance only in last two decades due to internal political instability in Nepal and reports of a range of subversive activities along its open borders with India. Some of the concerns articulated in this regard include emergence of Nepal as a staging ground for Pakistan supported anti-India activities, reported activities of religious fundamentalist organisation and alleged proliferation of religious institutions, spillover of Maoist movement, smuggling of fake Indian currency notes (FICN), small arms, narcotics etc. A careful examination of available evidence on these issues state response suggests that threat perception and the management practices along India-Nepal border have largely remained an under researched and under documented areas. As a result, we find conflicting reports, exaggerated accounts on a number of issues, particularly on the issue of activities of religious fundamentalist groups, alleged proliferation of religious institutions and their linkage with terrorism in India.

It is, therefore, pertinent to examine existing and projected threat perceptions and the entire gamut of management strategy along India-Nepal border. An attempt has been made in this paper to understand some of the issues articulated in the framework of imperatives of internal security in India. The paper proposes to address following themes:

(a) Issues that have contributed to greater connectivity and integration.
(b) Open border and India's security concerns.
(c) Border management policy: Role of security/enforcement agencies and need for an integrated approach.

Evolution of Open Border

(a) Profile of the Border : The 1751 km India-Nepal border runs through twenty districts of five Indian States.[1] Unlike Nepal-China border, which runs mainly through high altitude mountains, most of India-Nepal border runs through plains and along rivers, called *Terai.*[2] The border is open and there is no visa regime for persons for both the countries crossing the border. The passport (Entry into India) Rules 1950, do not apply to Nepali nationals entering India by land or air from Nepal. There are twenty two agreed routes for mutual trade and fifteen land routes for traffic in transit. However, only at six transit points out of them movement was permitted to nationals of third countries who require entry and exit visas to cross the border.[3]

Though we have evidence of movement of people and close interaction between people from both sides since historical times, some of the important issues underlying the open border in terms of demarcation and migration of people can be traced back to the British period. The nature of relationship between the British and Nepalese rulers and their respective interest conditioned the evolution of open border and pattern of cross-border movement of people. The first major attempt to demarcate the border was made after the Anglo-Nepal war and the subsequent Treaty of Sugauli (Segowlee) signed between the two in December 1816. Under this treaty, the *Mahakali* river formed the western boundary, while the Mechi formed the boundary in east along with ridges in the Darjeeling hills and Sikkim.[4] However, no demarcation was made under the treaty for the western part of the *Terai* region, which was ceded to British India in 1816.[5] The reason was that the entire western Terai was almost covered with dense forests and, at the same time, there was no physical basis to discern its northern limits. It was only after 1860 the boundary between the two countries was more or less stabilised when Britain ceded certain parts of the territory between the rivers *Mahakali* and *Rapti* to Nepal as a mark of recognition for the help Nepal had rendered during the revolt of 1857.

There existed a free and an unrestricted movement of people even before the Treaty of Sugauli, and factors such as Bengal famine of 1769-70, frequent floods in Bihar and British repression encouraged Indian migration to Nepal. However, the Indian migrants were neither permitted to purchase land nor entitled to have tenancy rights. It was only after the restoration of far western *Terai* to Nepal in 1860 and formulation of legal code by prime minister Jung Bahadur (1846-1877) made provisions for the allotment of land to Indian nationals through sale and purchase, significant changes took place in the *Terai* landscape. Prime minister Bahadur encouraged Indians to settle in the *Terai* region for agriculture and other economic activities. In course of time, growth of communication network and industrial development of *Terai* also facilitated migration of Indians to Nepal. There has been a significant contribution of the Indian technical manpower and skilled immigrants to the industrialisation of the *Terai*. Employment opportunities generated by industrialisation in the *Terai* also attracted Indian immigrants.

The British government also favoured an open border and encouraged migration from Nepal to India. Nepal government's earlier reluctance to send Gurkhas to join the British East India Army led to the East India Company encouraging Gurkhas to settle in the hills of India. Consequently, Gurkha colonies sprang up in Kangra, Dehradun, Darjeeling, Shillong etc.[6] Moreover, the British wanted to have secure and easy supply of raw materials from Nepal into India, such as, timber, herbs and other forest resources. The British policy to encourage Nepalese to settle in the east and north-east India to provide cheap labour to run tea plantations led to colonies of Nepalese in the region. In certain areas, the Nepalese outnumbered the local population.[7] The other important factor for maintaining open border by the British was trade relations between Nepal and the Indian states of Uttar Pradesh, Bihar and West Bengal. Moreover, Nepal acted as a catalyst in the development of East India Company's trade with Tibet and Central China.[8]

The India-Nepal Peace and Friendship Treaty, signed on 31 July 1950 formalised the open border between India and Nepal. Article VI of the Treaty states that "Each government undertakes, in token of the neighbourly friendship between India and Nepal, to give the nationals of the other, in its territory, national treatment with regard to participation in industrial and economic development of such territory and to the grants of concessions and contracts relating to such development".[9] Article VII of the Treaty agreed to "grant, on a reciprocal basis, to the nationals of one country, in the territories of the other, the same privilege in the matters of residence, ownership of property, participation in trade and commerce, movement and other privilege of similar nature".[10]

The Treaty of 1950 also reflected the economic and political compulsions of both the countries. According to one commentator, "The Treaty is also an expression of Nepal's recognition of India's security concerns and Indian accommodation of Nepal's socio-economic progress and stability".[11] The geo-strategic concern after Chinese military deployment in Tibet and its annexation in 1950 also influenced Indian decision to develop friendly relations with Nepal.

(b) Socio-Cultural Linkages: Since 1950s, there has been a change in the regional distribution of population in Nepal. Population growth in the Terai has shown an increasing trend since 1961. The Terai, only with 23.1 per cent of the total land area of the country, accounted for only 32.5 per cent of the population of Nepal in 1952/54, had 50.21 per cent of the total population of Nepal in 2011.[12] As per 2011 census, hill and mountain constitutes forty-three per cent and 6.73 per cent of total population of Nepal respectively.

The religious and linguistics overlapping and matrimonial links over the years between bordering states in India and people of Terai region made socio-cultural interaction indispensable further accelerated the pace of movement of people from one country to another. Such links also led to a greater flexibility in the attitude of the people in accepting the movement of people from each other's country.The open border has also economically benefited the nationals inhabiting both sides of the border in agriculture, business and transportation sectors.

The demographic profile of the Terai, cross-border linkages and its impact on Nepal's cultural identity as articulated by its successive rulers have shaped the perception of successive Nepali government on the issue of open borders.[13] Attempts to make a mono-cultural ethos over the multi-cultural society were mainly because of suspicion regarding the close interaction and socio-cultural linkages between the Teraians and Indians. The open borders also had an impact on evolution of democracy in Nepal. Right from the beginning, democratic forces in Nepal have enjoyed sympathy in India. The open borders facilitated easy movement of Nepalese political activists into India for mobilising democratic forces in Nepal.

The economic implications of migration have also influenced the discourse on open borders with India in Nepal. The relatively greater industrialisation and development in the Terai region than the adjoining districts of neighbouring Bihar and Uttar Pradesh, with relatively higher density of population and less development, have reinforced the perception on Indian domination in economic sphere.

Open Border and Indian Concerns

***(a) Informal Trade*:** In India, the open border is being increasingly viewed, particularly since 1990s, as a threat to security since the unrestricted movement across the border has facilitated illegal activities including movement of criminals and terrorists. Most of the border areas run through underdeveloped and populous areas where poor governance, inadequate infrastructure, ill-equipped police force and existence of a collaborative arrangement among smugglers, insurgents and corrupt government officials provide a conducive atmosphere for various forces inimical to Indian and Nepalese interests to operate and flourish. A number of reports have indicated the existence of smuggling and criminal syndicates with trans-border linkage on Indo-Nepal border.

As a result, despite the treaty on trade and transit informal trade between the two countries continues to thrive.[14] Open border and free movement of people make transaction costs in the informal channel significantly lower than the costs for the formal channel in both the countries. A study by the Federation of Nepal Chamber of Commerce and Industries states that illicit trade along Indo-Nepal border alone amounts to 38.9 per cent of Nepal's foreign trade. Every year Nepal loses close to Rs 3 billion in royalty because of the black market.[15] From Nepal, we find a large scale diversion of foreign made electronic gadgets and other contraband goods for sale in the Indian grey market.[16] According to a study, goods traded from India to Nepal are procured by and large from the Indian states of Bihar, Uttar Pradesh, and West Bengal, bordering Nepal. On the other hand, goods traded informally from Nepal to India are by and large goods originating in third countries like China, Japan, Thailand, Hong Kong and Singapore.[17]

The arrangements and networks developed as a result of informal trade also facilitated the growth of organised smuggling rackets. For instance, there is a high volume of illicit trade in forest products and wildlife. In the absence of proper documentation, such illegal trade is by and large unaccounted for. Reports also indicate illegal trading of fur coats, tiger bones and other wildlife product presumably from India to Tibet and China.

***(b) Drug Trafficking*:** The nature of border and absence of a comprehensive law enforcement mechanism have also contributed to drug smuggling. Available evidence suggests that both India and Nepal have emerged as a transit point for traffickers to ship drugs to international market. There exists a two-way smuggling of narcotics and drug through India-Nepal border. Cannabis (primarily *Hashish* and Marijuana (*Ganja*) are routinely smuggled from Nepal to India. On the other hand, opium and its derivatives (both brown sugar and white heroine) and banned pharmaceutical products are smuggled from India to Nepal. Government of India figure for 2009 says that half of the Hashish captured in India had been smuggled out of Nepal. Illicit consignment of Hashish from Nepal are transported overland to India and China and then by cargo couriers from India to Bangladesh and then to Europe and North America.[18] At the same time, much of the heroine available in Nepal is sourced from India.[19] A 2005 report of the International Narcotics Control Strategy Report reveals that the production of cannabis was growing in the southern areas of Nepal and in recent times and more number of people are now involved in trafficking.[20]

According to an IDSA report, smuggling of narcotics takes place mainly through Bihar and Uttar Pradesh border through following routes:[21] (a) Birganj-Raxaul-Motihari-Patna; (b) Nepalganj-Rupaaidiha-Baharaich-Barabanki-Lucknow; (c) Bhairahawa-Nautanwa-Gorakhpur; (d) Lumbini-Shohratgarh-Siddharthnagar.

In the past, when Maoists were involved in armed insurgency in Nepal, a number of reports indicated that Nepal's Maoist insurgents are involved in smuggling of drugs to India to raise money to buy arms.[22] However, a report prepared by International Crisis Group, discounted large scale involvement of Maoists in narco-terrorism.[23] Maoist groups operating in India are also believed to be involved in narcotics business. In August 2012, minister of state for home, Jitendra Singh, told in the Rajya Sabha that Maoists are raising funds by encouraging opium/ganja cultivation.[24] Reports also indicate an increase in opium production in certain Naxal affected areas. Police, on a number of occasions seized large contrabands of Marijuana that was being brought from states and specifically areas which are Naxal affected.[25] These drugs are peddled by Naxal-linked middlemen in large quantities.[26]

***(c) Fake Currency*:** The increased frequency of the detection of modules smuggling FICN from Nepal also point to a network operating in border areas. Media reports on the subject suggest that smuggling network, allegedly supported by Pakistan have set up a large and resourceful network of agents from Kathmandu to Birganj and all along border to push FICN to India.[27] In Jan 2013, the Reserve Bank of India (RBI) alerted all the branches of Banks in north Bihar adjoining India-Nepal border to take serious precaution in transaction of currencies at their counters.[28] Earlier on 23 November 2010, in a written reply to a question in Lok Sabha the then minister of state for home, Ajay Makan confirmed that India-Nepal border areas have become vulnerable to smuggling of FICN with border districts being used as transit and storage points. Biranj, one of the biggest towns in Nepal's Terai region has become a major transit point for almost all the fake currency entering India. Even Nepal government admitted to the existence of racket. Nepal government has already banned exchange of Indian currency notes of 500 and 1000 denominations. On a number of occasions the role of Pakistan embassy officials came to light in this connection. On several occasions, the Neaplese police seized fake Indian currency from ISI agents, Pakistan embassy officials and underworld operatives.[29]

***(d) Terrorist Incursions*:** The government of India, on a number of occasions, highlighted the fact that Nepal is increasingly becoming the preferred route for terrorist incursions into various parts of the country. With strict vigil on Line of Control (LoC) and International Border with Pakistan militant groups operating in Jammu and Kashmir and Northeast use Nepal's porous border to take shelter and push their cadres into India. Activities of groups such Lashkar-e-Toiba (LeT), Jaish-e-Mohammad (JeM) and Hizbul Mujahideen (HM) have been reported in this connection.

A study conducted by the International Peace Research Institute (PRIO), Oslo, in 2009 said that "a tight-knit network of informal (or black market) traders is exploiting a vacuum of governance and law enforcement in southern Nepal and India-Nepal border area to generate operating capital of LeT. The traders mostly of Pakistani and Kashmiri origin operate out of cities along the Nepal side of India-Nepal border taking advantage of the larger population base that they provide, legal loopholes, lack of infrastructure and corruption".[30]

If we analyse government pronouncements and writings on the subject, including media reports, it emerges that the ISI began cultivating Nepal's political establishment in the mid 1980s as part of its strategic policy of proxy war against India. According to one commentator, "the ISI members have extensively cultivated Nepalese police, intelligence personnel and bureaucrats; all these in the face of a large Indian intelligence set up in Kathmandu".[31] This is evident by the close involvement of Mirza Dilshad Beg, a very influential former Nepali minister with Dawood Ibrahim.[32]

The issue of use of Nepalese territory by terrorist groups came to limelight, once again, in 1999 when Indian Airlines Flight IC-814 was hijacked en-route from Kathmandu to Delhi and diverted to Kandahar. In 2000, a report believed to have been prepared by one of the intelligence agencies was leaked to the weekly news magazine *India Today*. The report titled "The Nepal Gameplan" accused ISI and Pakistan-based intelligence group of planning and executing the hijack. It accused the ISI and LeT, of jointly coordinating twenty six criminal organisations operating in the Terai with sixty six ISI-funded, LeT-run madrassas along the Indo-Nepal border. The then prime minister, GP Koirala called the report a "despicable attempt at casting aspersions on the friendly relations between India and Nepal".[33] The report claimed that ISI agents were using locations in Nepal as safe havens to prepare for attacks in India.[34] The role of Pakistani embassy also came to the fore during the hijacking of the Indian Airlines in December 1999. One of the embassy staff, Mohammed Arshad Cheema, is alleged to have passed on a bag to the five hijackers of the flight before they boarded the aircraft.[35] This was not the first time Cheema's hand had been seen in subversive activities. In November 1998, Sikh militant Lakhbir Singh, who was arrested from the Valley View Hotel in Kathmandu with 19 kg of RDX, revealed during interrogation that it was Cheema who supplied him the explosives.[36]

The India-Nepal border is also used by former J&K militants to reach J&K to avail the government's rehabilitation scheme for former militants despite designating four specific routes for their return. However, from these four routes militants can return only with Pakistani permission.[37] Reports also suggested that there were credible inputs about militant outfits such as Hizb-ul-Mujahideen trying to push subversive elements in the guise of former militants via Nepal.[38]

(e) Proliferation of Religious Institutions: Another area which generated serious debate within security community in India is religious extremist consolidation in border areas and alleged proliferation of religious institutions. There has been little effort to document and properly analyse this aspect and as a result we find a number of conflicting report on the issue. The Government of India, on a number of occasions, brought to the notice of Nepal the issue of proliferation of Islamic learning centres in border areas of Nepal. Though the recommendations of the task force on border management regarding *madrassas* were not published, certain media reports said the task force had asked the union government to mount greater surveillance not only on mosques and *madrassas* on the country's border, but also on the activities of teachers, visitors and inmates of Islamic institutions.[39]

It has been alleged that not only these madrassas provided shelters to the ISI and indoctrination centres for future *jehadis,* they were also trying to bring about a demographic change in Indian border districts. According to one commentator, "The Muslim pockets of the *Terai,* especially Bardia, Rupandehi, Banke and Parsa-Morang belt have seen increasing 'tablighi' activities, and construction of mosques and *madrassas* with financial flows from Pakistan-often directly from the embassy at Kathmandu-from Saudi Arabia and from a range of pan-Islamist organisations".[40] Activities of groups such as Jamaat-e-Millat-e-Islamia; the Nepal Islamic Yuba Sangh; the Nepal Muslim League; the Nepal Muslim Ektasangh; and the Democratic Muslim Welfare Association have been reported in the region. Some of them are believed to be getting support from Pakistan.[41]

Majority of Muslim population (approximately ninety-seven per cent) live in Terai region. As per 2011 census Muslims constitute 4.27 per cent of total 26.6 million population of Nepal.[42] In 1954, they constituted

2.54 per cent of the total population.[43] However, according to some estimates exact figure of Muslim population in Nepal is much higher than shown in the census figures and they constitute not less than six per cent of total population.[44] There are also reports of large scale migration of Bihari Muslim refugees from Bangladesh in Terai region after 1971. However, we do not have adequate data to confirm such reports.

Is there a link between attempted Islamist consolidation, growth of religious institutions along the border and India's internal security? It has been argued that the identity assertion of Muslim population in Nepal is also linked to installation of multi-party democracy in Nepal in 1990, which paved the way for pluralism and group politics. Assertion of religious identity was not possible during monarchy period.[45] Therefore, any shift in the nature of mobilisation need to be analysed in terms of group politics within multi-cultural society. It is important that any co-relation between increase in the number of religious institutions and their potential threat to India must be examined in the light of empirical evidence. According to a study conducted by Delhi-based Indian Social Institute, no conclusive proof has yet been offered for such assertions. In fact, the study brands such accusation as an attempt by the Indian right wing political forces to malign the Muslim community.[46] Empirically also, it is very difficult to relate growth of religious institutions along border areas with terrorism and anti-India activities.[47]

Maoist Incursions

Another important factor that conditioned securitisation of India-Nepal border since 1990 was linkage between Maoist groups operating in Nepal and India and their cross-border movement. Though situation is different since Maoists in Nepal joined mainstream politics, which impacted their relationship with Maoist groups operating in India, apprehensions are still there about their possible linkage. In November 2010, the then Indian ambassador to Nepal, Rakesh Sood wrote a letter to deputy prime minister and foreign minister, Sujata Koirala, accusing Nepali Maoists of providing military and ideological training to hundreds of Indian Maoists also called Naxalites inside Nepali territory.[48]

What is the exact nature of relationship between UCPN (Maoists) and CPI-Maoist? Government assessment of linkage particularly after 2006 when Maoist joined mainstream politics suggests that both the groups are linked at ideological level only. On 7 March 2007, minister of state for home, Sriprakash Jaiswal, said in the Rajya Sabha that government is aware of ideological/fraternal links between the Maoists of Nepal and Indian Naxalites. There is no evidence of any material relationship.[49] The then union home secretary, VK Duggal reiterated the same view while speaking in Hyderabad on 4 July 2006, "There is no physical link between Maoists in Nepal and India. However, there is an ideological link."[50]

However, before 2006, the Government of India, on a number of occasions, had attested to the existence, particularly during Maoist insurgency in Nepal of such linkage.[51] During the period when Maoists in Nepal were involved in armed conflict, a number of reports suggested that they have been working for their larger strategy to carve out a Compact Revolutionary Zone (CRZ), 'Revolutionary Corridor' spreading from Nepal through Bihar and the Dandkaranya region to Andhra Pradesh.[52] However, the feasibility of the exact nature of CRZ across Nepal, nature of Nepalese Maoist linkage with Indian Naxalite groups, particularly after they came to power and their attitude towards India have been subject of debate. During the period of insurgency, the relationship between Maoists and Naxalites remained confined to ideological and to some extent, logistical coordination. At the ideological level, the success of Maoists in Nepal gave a certain boost to left wing extremism in India. It is evident both from expansion in the area of influence of Naxalite groups, their unification and greater ideological coherence provided by activities of several front organisations in the last few years.[53] The most significant manifestation of this ideological synergy was the merger of the Maoist Communist Centre of India (MCCI) and the Communist Party of India, Marxist-Leninist (People's War) in the united formation, the CPI-Maoist, in September 2004. Available evidence suggests that Nepalese Maoist leader, Prachanda played a role in bringing these groups together.

Nepalese Maoists benefitted more in material terms from this association. This is evident from a number of reports about their use of open India-Nepal border for shelter, training and medical treatment. Reports also suggested that Maoists were using certain Indian cities as transit route for hideout, mobilisation of cadres and supply of arms. Certain media reports also suggested their joint training camps in bordering districts of Bihar particularly in the dense forests of Bagha and Balmikinagar in west Champaran district.[54]

Apart from Naxalite groups, the Maoists also developed relationship with other Indian insurgent groups. Their linkage with United Liberation Front of Asom (ULFA), the National Democratic Front of Bodoland (NDFB) and the Kamtapur Liberation Organisation (KLO) were frequently reported in the media. It was suspected that the ULFA played a role of major conduits for supply of weapons to the Nepali and the Indian Maoist or groups based in Bangladesh at double the price, good enough to pay for their own acquisition.[55]

The open border also facilitated Maoist attempts to establish networks in certain areas with substantial Nepali population such as Darjeeling and Siliguri in north Bengal. A number of Maoists, including some senior leaders were arrested from this area.[56] In addition, Maoists are active, through several front organisations, in Nepali dominated areas to mobilise and arrange financial aid. The government banned the *Akhil Bhartiya Nepali Ekta Samaj* (ABNES) under the Prevention of Terrorism Act (POTA) on 1 July 2002, for its linkages with the Maoists in Nepal.

Given Nepalese Maoists staunch anti-India position, there was a general apprehension that the open border regime would pose serious problems if Maoists came to power in Nepal. They argue that successive monarchs and Nepal's political leadership have compromised Nepal's national interest vis-à-vis India. The fear of Indian expansionism and India's 'hegemonic' image figured prominently in speeches by Maoist leaders. They have demanded restructuring of India-Nepal relations through revision or abrogation of some of the important bilateral treaties like the Treaty of Peace and Friendship of 1950 and the Mahakali Treaty of 1996. They project India as an exploitative and hegemonic power in South Asia.[57]

However, the Maoist threat along Nepal border need to be assessed in the light of a careful analysis of the trajectory of Maoist movement in Nepal, their growth in Nepal's politics, their attitude towards India and nature of their linkage with various Indian insurgent groups.[58] Despite their external linkages, Maoism both in Nepal and India have largely remained indigenous movement and their growth have been shaped by a host of internal factors. Their linkage remained largely at ideological level. After Nepalese Maoists joined mainstream politics, their relationship with Indian Naxalites underwent a sea change. Their attitude towards India was also conditioned by a host of other factors such as compulsion of domestic politics and internal and regional politico-security environment.

Border Management: Policy Initiatives

Earlier, various state governments in India had their own arrangements such as the constitution of Special Task Force or Special Police Force to guard the border. As the open border became increasingly associated with internal security problems, the government started serious deliberation on the issue. The group of ministers (GoM) on national security took a comprehensive view of the entire gamut of border security.[59] It remarked, "The term border management must be interpreted in its widest sense and should imply coordination and concerted action by political leadership and administrative, diplomatic, security, intelligence, legal, regulatory and economic agencies of the country to secure our frontiers and subserve the best interests of the country."[60] Some of the measures suggested by the GOM to improve security along India-Nepal border included:[61]

(a) deployment of the Indo-Tibetan Border Police (ITBP) along the border;

(b) upgradation and strengthening of police stations in border areas with sufficient number of trained personnel for crime investigation and intensive village surveillance;

(c) need for sufficient trained personnel in border district police headquarters for adequate intelligence work and for assistance to directorate of revenue intelligence (DRI)/customs in organising anti-smuggling raids/ambushes. Integration of preventive activities of the customs with DRI;

(d) increase in the number of immigration check posts (ICPs) to cover all transit points and their integration with land customs stations (LCS), cargo profiling and computer link to Kolkata customs to ensure effective recording of all movement of material and personnel, including those from third countries;

(e) mandatory pass clearance for vehicles of Nepal registration entering India; and

(f) unified/joint command for co-ordination of intelligence as well as operational activities.

Force Structure

The report of the GOM on national security clearly visualised that for any effective border management regime, there must be a credible force structure, better coordination and creation of skill, knowledge, attitude and infrastructure in various government agencies involved in the task. The most visible change in the government policy in this regard came when it declared SSB as a border guarding force and lead intelligence agency (LIA) for India-Nepal border in January 2001 and India-Bhutan border in March 2004.[62] It is not clear whether the selection of the SSB was part of a concerted policy to utilise its previous experience in intelligence related operations. The SSB is expected to function on the patterns of the other border forces like the ITBP and the Border Security Force (BSF) and like these forces has been brought under the home ministry. In 2007, the parliament passed SSB Act[63]. (a) To promote sense of security among the people living in the border area, (b) To Prevent trans-border crimes and unauthorised entries into or exit from the territory of India and (c) To prevent smuggling and other illegal activities.

Currently, the SSB has strength of fifty four battalions (total strength 47079) with five frontiers and eleven sector headquarters.[64] As of December 2012, at total of 619 BOPs have been established out of which 479 are on India-Nepal border and 140 on India-Bhutan border, Persons crossing the border are subject to checking and frisking. Besides, special *nakas* and patrolling are conducted on the border. Though the Government of India claims that the security situation along India-Nepal border has improved after deployment of SSB, the nature of the border, terrain and free movement of people requires a comprehensive approach beyond deployment of central paramilitary force and augmenting its strength.

Regulation of Movement

Would the situation improve if a mechanism to regulate the movement of people across the border is put in place? As discussed above, the free movement of people has created much deeper concerns in Nepal than in India. Almost all major political parties in Nepal have favoured some kind of the regulation on free movement of people across the border. Therefore, right from the beginning, the successive rulers have adopted measures to curtail migration from India. In 1957, the Government of Nepal made necessary possession of citizenship certificate mandatory for Indians working as teachers in Nepal. In 1958, restrictions were imposed on foreigners including Indians, on buying immovable property in Nepal. Strict citizenship laws were adopted that made reading and writing of Nepali compulsory to apply for citizenship in 1962. Later, a number of regulations were introduced to regulate the migration of Indians to Nepal.

To discourage migration through the open border, the Nepali government, in 1983, appointed a commission to study the impact of internal and international migration in Nepali. Most of its recommendations were related to the regulation of India-Nepal border. It recommended three stages for the regulation of human traffic across the border. In the first stage, people crossing the border should be made to register their name at specific border points. In the second stage, to be introduced a year after the first stage, was the entry permit system and people residing within 10 kms of the border would be provided with multi-entry permit system to be renewed each year and others would be issued only entry permit system. In the third stage, to be implemented at an appropriate time, regular passport system would be introduced between both the countries.[65] The Commission also criticised the 1950 Indo-Nepal Treaty on the ground that "the treatment which Indians are successfully getting in Nepal has been far from bilateral."[66] However, the report was not implemented. The argument of transforming the open border into a regulated one-regulating the entry of Indian nationals is stronger in Nepal. In Nepal, a survey, commissioned by a private agency in 2000, found that a resounding majority of Nepalese want traditional open border with India to be regulated, with 42.9 per cent calling for outright introduction of passport system between the two countries.[67] According to a Nepali commentator, "There has always been an influential school of thought in Kathmandu that recommends that the open border should be sealed off, or at least regulated, to check an increasing number of Indian workers from entering Nepal."[68] In India also, the need for some sort of regulation on movement of people across the border is gaining ground. In October 2000, India and Nepal agreed to introduce a rule requiring air travellers to carry either a passport or photo identification. Therefore, keeping in view security and economic parameters, some mechanism may be evolved to check and regulate the free as well as illegal movement of people and goods across the open border within the overall framework of India-Nepal relations.

Intelligence Sharing and Inter-Agency Coordination

One of the main instruments to identify criminal and anti-national elements along the border is setting up of an effective and well-coordinated intelligence mechanism. The SSB, as a LIA, has created an intelligence mechanism on the India-Nepal border for sharing of intelligence input among the various concerned agencies. However, the question remains can merely the presence of a well-equipped force suffice to instill a sense of security among the people? Clearly, an integrated approach towards the border population has an important role to play in this regard. Consequently, there is a need for a more comprehensive institutional arrangement between the SSB, state governments of India and other agencies to secure this common goal.

Similarly, prevention of trans-border crime will remain a daunting task without proper coordination and cooperation with the civil police in border districts, custom officials, and the officials of the Narcotics Control Bureau and DRI. Since local police officers are better acquainted with the area and have a steady flow of intelligence regarding movements of criminal elements, it is viable to involve local security agencies in scrutinising such problems. Regrettably, certain practical problems limit the degree to which state and local police authorities have been involved in combating the problem. First, since the responsibility of border management comes under the union government's jurisdiction, the state police more often are not clear regarding the extent of their authority concerning such violations. Also, lacking common data bases and an efficient interface with agencies directly involved in border security, the local police lack timely access to specific information regarding criminals who they could, otherwise, detect, detain or interdict. Further, there are problems relating to skill, attitude and resources. Moreover, the problems like overlapping of jurisdiction due to the presence of various agencies affect the operational efficiency.

Another significant aspect to the creation of an effective intelligence network is the interface with local population. Border policing can be improved significantly if the assistance of local people could be factored into the task of the security agencies. The limitation of any force in terms of knowledge regarding the terrain, people, language and local sensitivities could be overcome if such an arrangement is in place. In this context, the achievements of the Border Area Development Programme (BADP) need to be assessed properly and, if need be, re-prioritised. The BADP is a 100 per cent centrally-sponsored programme under which funds are provided to the states as special central assistance for execution of approved schemes on a 100 per cent grant basis.

Conclusion

Border management is undoubtedly a vital component of internal security management and the role of border guarding forces needs to be located within this broad framework. A comprehensive border management policy calls for an integrated approach to realise its prime objectives. Elements of a comprehensive border management policy should include setting of an effective mechanism to keep an eye on subversive element without hampering the trans-border movement of people, effective surveillance, a comprehensive and coordinated intelligence apparatus, involvement of local population, a greater role of local administration and law enforcement agencies, better governance and better coordination with enforcement agencies on the other side of the border.

There is a need for establishing a permanent and credible threat assessment mechanism by creating comprehensive database at suitable places, preferably at district headquarters. It is essential to have a more institutionalised mechanism for sharing of data, information, experience and resources at the local level. These are all critical inputs for effective border security planning and management. Also, there is a need to evolve an effective strategy for the development of border areas and revival/ strengthening of institutions of civil governance and law enforcement agencies in those areas.

References

1. Uttaranchal-263 kms, Uttara Pradesh-560 kms, Bihar-729 kms, West Bengal-100 kms and Sikkim-99 kms.
2. The Terai belt starts from the foothills of Siwalik range of the Himalayas and stretches upto the Gangetic plain of Bihar and UP in India. The *Teraiplain* is low in elevation, flat, and fertile, being a northern extension of the Gangetic Plain and is some 26 to 32 km wide in the southern part of Nepal. The area is also called '*Madhesh*', derived from Sanskrit word '*Madhyadesh*'. People living in this region are also called as 'Madheshi'. For details see Hari Bansh Jha: *The Terai Community and National Integration in Nepal*, Kathmandu: Centre for Economic and Technical Studies in cooperation with Friedrich Ebert Stiftung, 1993.
3. Indo-Nepal Treaty of Trade, Ministry of Commerce and Industry, Government of India, 5 March 2002, commerce.nic.in/nepal.doc
4. According to Article 3 of the Treaty of Segowlee, "the ruler of Nepal ceded to the East India Company in perpetuity the whole of low lands between the River Kali and Rapti, the whole of low lands (with the exception of Bootwul Khass) lying between the Rapti and the Gunduck, the whole of low lands between the Gunduck and Coosah, in which the authority of the British government has been introduced, or is in actual course of introduction, all the low lands between the Rivers Mitchee and the Teestah and all the territories within the hills eastward of the river Mitchee including the fort and lands of Nagree and the Pass of Nagarcote leading from Morung into the hills, together with the territory lying between that Pass and Nagree". See The Treaty of Segowlee, http://www.nepalicongress.org.np/contents/nepal/treaties/2.php
5. Vidya Bir Singh Kansakar, "Nepal-India Open Border: Prospects, Problems and Challenges", http://www.nepaldemocracy.org/documents/treaties_agreements/nep_india_open_border.htm
6. Leo E Rose, *Nepal:Strategy for Survival*, Berkeley: University of California Press, 1971, p. 140.
7. RL Sarkar, "Some Ecological Considerations for Tea Growing in the Eastern Himalayas", in SK Chaube (ed), *The Himalayas: Profiles of Modernisation and Adaptation*, New Delhi: Sterling Publishers, 1985, p. 52.

8. SangeetaThapliyal, *Mutual Security: The Case of India-Nepal,* New Delhi: IDSA and Lancer Publishers, 1998, p. 15.
9. Treaty of "Peace and Friendship" between the Government of India and the Government of Nepal, 1950, http://www.insof.org/treaty/31071950_Treaty_ of_Peace_ and_ Friendship 1950.htm
10. *Ibid.*
11. SangeetaThapliyal, "Movement of Population Between India and Nepal: Emerging Challenges", *Strategic Analysis,* Vol. 23, No. 5, August 1999.
12. Central Bureau of Statistics, National Planning Commission Secretariat, Government of Nepal, http://cbs.gov.np/wp-content/uploads/2012/11/Major-Finding.pdf.
13. Smruti S. Pattanaik, "Indo-Nepal Open Border: Implications for Bilateral Relations and Security", *Strategic Analysis,* Vol. 22, No. 3, June 1998.
14. The term informal trade has been used to denote economic activities not regulated by the government. It can be trade in daily use items to trafficking in drug and arms.
15. Upendra Pokharel, "The other side of trade, Nepal", *Nepali Times,* 612, 6-12 July 2012, http://nepalitimes.com/news.php? id=19447#.UQzESx04t_U.
16. Mahendra P. Lama, *India-Nepal Relations: Challenges Ahead,* New Delhi: Rupa and ORF, 2004, p. 280.
17. NishaTaneja and Sanjib Pohit, *Characteristics of India's Informal and Formal Trading with Nepal: A Comparative Analysis,* New Delhi: Indian Council for Research on International Economic Relations, 2001, http://www.gdnet.org/fulltext/taneja.pdf
18. Report of the International Narcotics Control Board for 2011, http://www.incb.org/documents/Publications/AnnualReports/AR2011/AR_2011_E_Chapter_III_Asia.pdf
19. http://www.unodc.org/pdf/india/publications/south_Asia_Regional_Profile_Sept_2005/1 2_nepal.pdf
20. "International Narcotics Control Strategy Report -2005", http://www.state.gov/g/inl/rls/nrcrpt/2005/vol1/html/42366.htm
21. Pushpita Das, "Drug Trafficking in India: A Case for Border Security", *IDSA Occasional Paper,* No. 24, Institute for Defence Studies and Analyses, New Delhi, May 2012.
22. "Maoists smuggling drugs to India for arms: official", *Deccan Herald,* 16 May 2005.
23. Nepal's Maoists: Their Aims, Structure and Strategy, Asia Report N°104 - 27 October 2005, Kathmandu/Brussels:International Crisis group, 27 October 2005, http://www.crisisgroup.org/~/media/Files/asia/south-asia/nepal/104_ nepal_ s_maoists_ their_aims_ structure_and_strategy.pdf

24. Maoist organisations backing Maruti agitation: Centre, *The Hindu*, 23 August 2012.
25. "Drug menace: Narcotics Control Bureau tightens screw," *Daily News and Analysis*, 6 April 2011.
26. "Ganja trail leads to Naxal belt," *The Hindu*, 24 August 2010.
27. *Ibid.*
28. RBI alerts banks on Bihar-Nepal border on fake note circulation, *Times of India*, New Delhi, 16 January 2013.
29. *Times of India*, 10 January 2000.
30. Jason Miklian, "Illicit Trading in Nepal: Fuelling South Asian Terrorism", South Asia Briefing Paper, No.3, Oslo: International Peace Research Institute, 2009.
31. Major General Ashok K Mehta (retd), "The Hijack and the Kathmandu Connection".
http://www.rediff.com/news/2000/jan/25jos.htm
32. Mirza Dilshad Beg was assassinated in 1998 allegedly by the *Chhota Rajan gang.*
33. Farzand Ahmad, "Wake-up Call", *India Today*, 12 June 2000.
34. Harinder Baweja, "The Kathmandu Nexus", *India Today*, 12 June 2000.
35. Cheema was expelled from Nepal in 2001 after authorities in that country found 16 kg of plastic explosive in his home. He was spotted at Kathmandu's Tribhuvan airport on the morning of the hijacking. See "The Playground of the Spies", *Frontline*, Vol. 18, No. 9, 28 April- 11 May 2001.
36. Josy Joseph, "Diplomatic Intrigue", http://www.rediff.co.in/news/2000/jan/17jos2.htm
37. In 2010, the J&K government launched a 'return and rehabilitation scheme" for former Kashmiri militants who crossed over to PoK for undergoing terror training at the peak of insurgency in late 1980s and early 1990s. More than 200 militants returned to the valley, but mostly via Nepal. DeeptimanTiwary, "India asks Nepal to prevent terror groups from using its soil for infiltration," see http://articles.timesofindia.indiatimes.com/2012-12-07/india/35669829_1_militants-terror-groups-terror- camps.
38. *Ibid.*
39. Chandan Nandy, "Border vigil blueprint singles out mosques", *The Telegraph*, 17 December 2000.
40. Ajai Sahni, "South Asia: Extremist Islamist Terror and Subversion", in KPS Gill and Ajai Sahni (eds), *The Global Threat of Terror: Ideological, Material and Political Linkages*, New Delhi: Bulwark Books and Institute for Conflict Management, 2002, p. 236.
41. Pranava K. Chaudhary, "ISI uses Nepali Muslims for anti-India campaign", *The Times of India*, 22 July 1997.

42. *Nepal Population Report*, 2011, Population Division, Ministry of Health and Population, Government of Nepal, Kathmandu.
43. Sudhindra Sharma, "Muslim Population in the Terai: Security Perspective", in *India-Nepal Relations: Challenges Ahead*, New Delhi : Rupa and Co. in association with Observer Research Foundation, 2004, p. 105.
44. Among the Terai caste/ethnic groups, Muslim constitutes the third largest group after Tharu and Yadav. They constitute the single largest group in the districts of Parsa, Rautahat, Kapilvastu and Banke. See Mollica Dastider, "Muslims of Nepal's Terai", *Economic and Political Weekly*, Vol. 35, No. 10, 4-10 March 2000, pp.766-769.
45. Dastider, *ibid.*
46. *Muslim Institutions in the Indo-Nepal Border Districts*, New Delhi: Indian Social Institute, 2004, p. 60.
47. S. Ubaidur Rahman, "Nepal-border madrasas : No iota of 'terrorism' or 'ISI' activity", http://www.milligazette.com/Archives/15072001/06.htm
48. Nepal Probing Maoist Arms Training to Indian Naxalites, http://news.outlookindia.com/items.aspx?artid=700965.
49. Links between Nepal Maoists and Indian Naxals, Rajya Sabha release ID 25508, 7 March 2007, http://pib.nic.in/newsite/erelease.aspx?relid=25508.
50. *Ibid.*
51. P. V. Ramana, Linkages between Indian and Nepalese Maoists, http://www.idsa.in/idsacomments/LinkagesbetweenIndianandNepaleseMaoists_pvramana_091110.
52. In an extraordinary meeting on left-wing extremism held in Delhi on 4 April 2000, the then Home Minister, LK Advani, drew particular attention of the States towards availability of intelligence inputs suggesting a possible growth of a compact revolutionary zone in the near future stretching an area from Indo-Nepal border to Andhra Pradesh through the Dandkaranya region. See "Meeting of Union Home Minister with Chief Ministers on Left Wing Extremism", http://mha.nic.in/pr0400.htm. Also see Annual Report, Ministry of Home Affairs, Government of India, http://www.mha.nic.in/AR2004-2005/AR04-05Eng.pdf
53. Prominent among such organisations which have been active are: the Coordination Committee of Maoist Parties and Organisations of South Asia (CCOMPOSA), the Revolutionary Internationalist Movement (RIM), the World People's Resistance Movement, South Asia (WPRM South Asia), the *Krantikari Jansangarsh Ekjutta Samiti* and outfits involved in the Mumbai Resistance 2004. For example, Maoists in South Asia formed the Coordination Committee of Maoist Parties and Organisations of South Asia (CCOMPOSA) in 2001. The objective of this Maoist front is to 'share experience' and to help in spreading the Maoist campaign to various parts of the region. Apart from the CCOMPOSA, the Revolutionary Internationalist Movement (RIM),

which came into existence in 1984, has also been trying to coordinate the activities of Maoist parties in South Asia.

54. "Naxals expanding base in north Bihar: Police", *The Times of India*, 24 September 2002.
55. Subir Bhaumik, "Guns, drugs and rebels", http://www.india-seminar.com/2005/550/550per cent20subirper cent20bhaumik.htm
56. Most prominently, Mohan KiranVaidya, a senior Maoist politburo member was arrested near Siliguri in West Bengal in March 2004. Subsequent investigations not only confirmed Maoist linkage with KLO but larger Maoist design to consolidate its base in North Bengal.
57. S.D. Muni, *"Maoist Insurgency in Nepal: The Challenges and the Response*, New Delhi: Rupa, 2004, p. 63.
58. *Ibid.*
59. The Group of Ministers (GoM) on 'Reforming the National Security System' was constituted on 17 April 2000, to review the national security system in its entirety and, in particular, to consider the recommendations of the Kargil Review Committee (KRC) and formulate specific proposals for implementation. The GOM under the Chairmanship of Shri L.K. Advani also included the Defence Minister, External Affairs Minister and Finance Minister. See http://pib.nic.in/archieve/lreleng/lyr2001/rmay2001/23052001/r2305200110.html
60. *Ibid*, Report of the GoM on National Security, 2001. See http://www.vifindia.org/sites/default/files/GoMper cent20Reportper cent 20onper cent20Nationalper cent20Security.pdf
61. *Ibid.*
62. Its earlier name was the Special Security Bureau (SSB). It was set up in early 1963 in the wake of the 1962 Indo-China conflict to build people's morale and inculcate a spirit of resistance in the border population against threats of subversion, infiltration and sabotage from across the border. Its activities were confined to then NEFA, North Assam, North Bengal, hills of Uttar Pradesh, Himachal Pradesh, and Ladakh. The scheme was later extended to Manipur, Tripura, Jammu (1965), Meghalaya (1975), Sikkim (1976), border areas of Rajasthan and Gujarat (1989), Manipur, Mizoram and some more areas of Rajasthan and Gujarat (1988), South Bengal, Nagaland (1989) and Nubra Valley, Rajouri and Poonch district of Jammu and Kashmir (1991). See "Special Security Bureau", Annual Report 2002-03, Ministry of Home Affairs, Government of India. The SSB has been assigned the task of guarding the 1751 kms long Indo-Nepal border along the states of Uttaranchal, (275 kms.-Distts. 03), Uttar Pradesh (551 kms. - Distts. 07), Bihar (726 kms.-Distts.-07), West Bengal (100 kms.-Distt-01) and Sikkim (99 kms-Distts-02).

    See http://www.ssb.nic.in/index.asp?linkid=59&sublinkid=32.
63. The Sashastra Seema Bal Act, 2007, No. 53 of 2007, http://www.ssb.nic.in/shared/linkimages/658.pdf

64. Two Bns, one Ops and one Reserve are in Delhi/NCR and one Reserve Bn at Madgaon (Goa), http://www.ssb.nic.in/index.asp? linkid= 59&sublinkid=34.
65. Nepal His Majesty's Government, Population Commission on Internal and International Migration, Summary and Recommendation (Unofficial Translation), 1984.
66. *Ibid.*
67. Krishna Shrestha, "Should Open Border Between Nepal And India Be Regulated?" http://www.newslookmag.com/archives/exclusives/ msi_poll2.html
68. Nischal Nath Pandey, *Nepal's Maoist Movement and Implications for India and China,* New Delhi: Manohar Publisher, 2005, p. 132.

14

India-Pakistan Initiative for Conflict Resolution: The Challenges Ahead

Rajpal Budania

Introduction

India-Pakistan relations have been blemished by unending conflict. Neither diplomacy nor war has succeeded so far in resolving the key conflict. But atmosphere is changing and there is optimism for peaceful management and even resolution of the India-Pakistan conflict. India-Pakistan relations have witnessed considerable improvement since peace process between them gained momentum with the beginning of the composite dialogue. There have been unprecedented initiatives, both bilateral and unilateral, raising new hopes for resolution of the conflict. These initiatives have generated pressures on both the governments to address the key issues in the conflict. The initiatives also indicate the emerging flexibility between the two countries on the main contentions. The two governments have held dialogue on all the contentious issues and developed institutional mechanisms to resolve them. All the major powers have welcomed India-Pakistan peace process and their bilateral efforts for resolving disputes. Interests of the extra-regional powers in South Asia are changing and that is having an impact on the prospects for conflict resolution in the region.

State-sponsored terrorism has been the most acrimonious issue between India and Pakistan. Both the countries have been locked in terrorism and counter-terrorism impasse. Terrorism has been used by Pakistan to weaken India and settle the Kashmir issue according to its desire. Today, encouraging signs are being witnessed between them on tackling terrorism. Both the countries have changed their approaches on the issue. At the same time they have evolved bilateral structures to address the problem. Success of India-Pakistan cooperation on terrorism, Kashmir and other issues depends on several national, bilateral, regional and global factors.

The peace process is not without impediments. Internal developments in Pakistan, increasing regional rivalry in Afghanistan, the fate of the Kashmir issue, and threats to secularisation in Kashmir and elsewhere are among the main challenges to the peace process. This Paper highlights the optimism building around the increasing institutional mechanisms and realisation in both India and Pakistan that the trend of cooperation on tackling contentious issues must be taken to its logical conclusion. The focus of this Paper is on India and Pakistan peace process and the consequent development of structures for management and resolution of the bilateral conflict. Furthermore, the Paper also seeks to analyse the challenges and limitations facing the peace process.

Peace Initiatives

Negotiations and bilateral agreements are the most viable means of settling the core issues of state-sponsored terrorism and Kashmir. Such an approach is also bound to have a positive impact on other outstanding issues between India and Pakistan. Despite the ever lurking trust deficit, India and Pakistan have taken a number of initiatives for management and resolution of the bilateral issues and disputes. A novel beginning in this regard was made with the initiation of the composite dialogue in the year 1997. The composite dialogue covers all the issues of contention between India and Pakistan. Several rounds of talks have taken place on the various issues under the composite dialogue mechanism. The composite dialogue has certainly contributed to confidence building and changed mindsets to resolve the contentious issues between the two countries.

The Vajpayee visit to Pakistan in February 1999 was a path-breaking one in the sense that it took place after both India and Pakistan overtly went nuclear. The Lahore declaration and Memorandum of Understanding (MoU) were important milestones in building trust and common desire to address the security issues through mutual understanding and cooperation. But the hopes of better relations were belied by the Kargil conflict in 1999 after the Indian prime minister's visit to Pakistan. However, in late 1999, General Musharraf staged a coup and usurped power in Pakistan. Pervez Musharraf wanted to transform Pakistan society and polity. He took a number of initiatives to improve relations with India.

To his credit, it must be said that he took bold steps to improve relations with India. After the September 2001 terrorist attacks on the US, his government came under tremendous international pressure on the issue of state-sponsored terrorism from the soil of Pakistan. Pakistan became a partner in the US' war on terror in Afghanistan. Immediately after the 9/11 attacks on the US, there were terrorist attacks on India too, first on the Jammu and Kashmir assembly building in October 2001 and thereafter, on Indian parliament in December 2001. Musharraf unequivocally condemned both the incidents. The condemnation was unlike the reluctance reflected in the past by the Pakistan government whenever the terrorists struck in India. However, the attack on Indian parliament derailed India-Pakistan relations. Yet the leadership of the two countries showed maturity and took sensible steps to restore normalcy of relations. In April 2003, Atal Behari Vajpayee while on a visit to Kashmir took a peace initiative by which restoration of normal relations between the two countries was envisaged. At the same time India also showed willingness for resumption of the composite dialogue and of rail, bus and air services between the two countries. In November 2003, Musharraf took a constructive step by declaring ceasefire along the Indo-Pak border. India reciprocated the move.

It would not be wrong to say that after 9/11 Pakistan's position on terrorism became untenable. The terrorist outfits were banned and their financial supply lines were disrupted. The US policies changed on the issue of terrorism. All these developments started to have positive impact on management of terrorism bilaterally and regionally in South Asia. Pakistan had no option but to cooperate with India on the issue. Both India and Pakistan became party to the global regime on combating terrorism. In this regard a mention must be made of the United Nations Security Council resolution 1373 (September 2001) and resolution 1540 (April 2004) which specifically deal with nuclear terrorism.

India and Pakistan took further steps to institutionalise counter-terrorism in their policy pronouncements. On 6 January 2004, on the sidelines of the SAARC (South Asian Association for Regional Cooperation) summit at Islamabad, Indian prime minister Vajpayee and Pakistan president Musharraf signed a joint statement pledging that Pakistan will not allow its territory for terrorist activities directed against any country. The joint statement read:

> "Prime Minister Vajpayee said that in order to take forward and sustain the dialogue process, violence, hostility and terrorism must be prevented. President Musharraf reassured Prime Minister Vajpayee that he will not permit any territory under Pakistan's

> control to be used to support terrorism in any manner. President Musharraf emphasised that a sustained and productive dialogue addressing all issues would lead to positive results".[1]

Thus, it was recognised that normalisation of their bilateral relations is dependent on containment of terrorism. Moreover, terrorism became the core and the foremost issue to be addressed. It was a significant departure by Pakistan from its past policy of using terrorism as a state policy against India.

President Musharraf visited India from 16 to 18 April 2005 with much fanfare. Prime minister Manmohan Singh and president Musharraf reviewed the progress in India-Pakistan relations and expressed satisfaction. In their joint statement the two leaders reaffirmed:

> [t]he commitments made in the Joint Press Statement of January 6, 2004 and the Joint Statement issued after their meeting in New York on September 24, 2004 and expressed satisfaction on the progress in the peace process and the improvement of relations between the two countries that has since been realised. Conscious of the historic opportunity created by the improved environment in relations and the overwhelming desire of the peoples of the two countries for durable peace and recognising their responsibility to continue to move forward towards that objective, the two leaders had substantive talks on all issues. They determined that the peace process was now irreversible.[2]

It was recognised that the environment was favourable to carry forward the peace process and address the contentious issues between the two countries. Pakistan was under tremendous international pressure to improve relations with India and that was possible only when Pakistan sincerely stopped giving any kind of support to terrorist outfits operating from its soil against India.

The cooperative spirit and momentum between the two countries was further reinforced during the Non-aligned Movement (NAM) summit in Havana, Cuba, in September 2006, when prime minister Manmohan Singh and president Musharraf resolved to consolidate peace process by deciding to have an India-Pakistan Joint Anti-terrorism Mechanism (JATM). The idea behind having this structure was to spot and put into operation counter-terrorism measures. The JATM is specifically meant for intelligence sharing for forestalling designs of the terrorists. There was lot of scepticism expressed in India about this mechanism. Critics in India wondered how one could share sensitive information with those who are sponsors of terrorism. It was called a Pakistani trap. Indian counter-terrorism expert, B. Raman cautioned India against any Pakistani design to involve India in projection of cross-border terrorism in Baluchistan.[3] Similarly, in Pakistan the JATM was termed as an Indian tool to manipulate the dialogue process and make terrorism the core issue and sidetrack the other bilateral issues such as Kashmir, Siachen, Sir Creek, etc. Pakistan's former foreign secretary Shamshad Ahmad stated, "The peace process that we are following now is no longer about resolving our disputes with India or redressing our grievances over India's transgressions in Siachen and Sir Creek. This peace process is now all about "terrorism" which has become our bête noire and which we have undertaken to fight, first on behalf of the US and now on India's behalf."[4] Undoubtedly, despite criticism, the JATM is an innovative and fresh idea to deal with the problem in a collective manner. This also amounts to recognition by both the countries that the menace of terrorism is common threat and it has to be fought at all fronts - national, bilateral and multilateral. For bridging the trust deficit between two countries such bold steps would be needed despite their inherent deficiencies, doubts and divergent interpretations.

Pakistan has come up with several proposals on Kashmir. In December 2006, Musharraf made a statement to an Indian television channel that Pakistan would give up its claim on Kashmir if India showed similar flexibility.[5] In December 2006, he made a four-point proposal for settling the Kashmir issue. The four-point formula included: making borders irrelevant, demilitarisation, self-governance and joint management.[6] He also said that Pakistan would give up its claim on the state if India too did the same for resolving the issue.[7] India said that it was not ready to joint management of J&K as proposed by Pakistan.[8] It also did not agree to the Pakistani concept of self-governance in the state. India believes that the state already enjoys it by having a popular government. India, however, is supportive of the idea of softening of LoC, particularly to allow trade relations.

President Musharraf, while addressing the foreign affairs committee of the Spanish Congress in Madrid on 25 April 2007, observed that military solution was not an answer to resolve the Kashmir issue as the option of using force to settle bilateral disputes between India and Pakistan never worked in the past.[9] He rather optimistically said, "The world may see the resolution of the Kashmir dispute earlier than expected. A reasonable progress on this count (Kashmir issue) has already been achieved."[10]

The Government of India and political parties in the state of J&K, particularly Peoples' Democratic Front, National Conference, Jammu and Kashmir Liberation Front, believe in being open to all new ideas on

Kashmir. In that context, important ideas in Musharraf's proposals could be discussed. But most of Musharraf's pronouncements were aimed at his own political survival rather than resolution of the issue. The first task for Pakistan should be to help India in restoring peace and tranquility in J&K. In this regard, his proposals would become meaningful only when Pakistan showed a change of policy and ability to end terror acts against India. Moreover, a resolution of the Kashmir issue has to be incremental. A hurried resolution would neither be wise nor workable.

India has made it clear to Pakistan and the international community that there is no religious or territorial solution to the Kashmir problem and the boundaries between India and Pakistan cannot be redrawn. It was prime minister Vajpayee who while delivering the independence day address on 15 August 2000 said that borders could not be redrawn "either in the name of religion or on the strength of the sword ... that it [Pakistan] would not be able to get its way through the undeclared war that it has been waging against India".[11] Similarly, prime minister Manmohan Singh, while inaugurating bus service between Amritsar and Nankana Sahib in Pakistan in March 2006, echoed similar approach to Kashmir issue. He said: "I have often said that borders cannot be redrawn but we can work towards making them irrelevant - towards making them just lines on a map."[12] He reiterated India's position on border settlement in November 2009. He emphasised the point that borders in Kashmir cannot be redrawn. He maintained: "I have publicly stated that there can be no redrawing of borders (in Jammu and Kashmir)... but our two countries can work together to ensure that these are borders of peace, that people-to-people contacts grow in a manner in which people do not even worry whether they are located on this side of the border or that side."[13] This did not go well with the Pakistani side. Pakistan foreign office spokesman Abdul Basit reacted by saying that Jammu and Kashmir was a disputed territory awaiting settlement in accordance with the relevant UN resolutions and aspirations of the people of Jammu and Kashmir.[14]

It was at the NAM summit at Sharm El Sheikh, Egypt, on 16 July 2009 that the Indian prime minister Manmohan Singh and the Pakistan, prime minister Yusuf Raza Gilani signed a joint statement which specifically dealt with the problem of terrorism in both the countries. By now it was well-established that terrorism was undermining peace and stability not only between India and Pakistan but in the entire region and even beyond. Once again the centrality of terrorism to national securities of both the countries was highlighted in the joint statement:

> Both leaders agreed that terrorism is the main threat to both countries. Both leaders affirmed their resolve to fight terrorism and to co-operate with each other to this end. Prime Minister Singh reiterated the need to bring the perpetrators of the Mumbai attacks to justice... Prime Minister Gilani assured that Pakistan will do everything in its power in this regard. Both leaders agreed that the two countries will share real-time credible and actionable information on any future terrorist threats. Prime Minister Gilani mentioned that Pakistan has some information on threats in Balochistan and other areas. Both prime ministers recognised that dialogue is the only way forward. Action on terrorism should not be linked to the Composite Dialogue process and these should not be bracketed.[15]

The main features of the joint statement are: (a) terrorism is a serious threat to both the countries and the same requires cooperation for its eradication; (b) bring the perpetrators of Mumbai attacks to speedy justice; (c) dialogue is the only sensible way forward and it should not be linked to action on terrorism; (d) there is a need for effective regional cooperation for combating terrorism; (e) India recognised the terrorist problem being faced by Pakistan in Baluchistan. This joint statement clearly marks a significant departure from the past policy pronouncements by India and Pakistan. India now is of the view that Pakistan has become a victim of terrorism and that requires new policy nuances. It lays a lot of thrust on the efficacy of dialogue for managing terrorism even in the most adverse circumstances.

But this stance of having dialogue under any conditions has been put to severe test because of the lack of sincerity on the part of Pakistani establishment in controlling extremists and terrorists in Pakistan, who are freely indulging in anti-India activities. Activities of Lashkar-e-Taiba have not been controlled by Pakistan. The incident of beheading of two Indian soldiers by the Pakistani forces along the Line of Control (LoC) on 8 January 2013 suddenly escalated the tensions between the two countries. This turned out to be the worst violent incident along the LoC since the ceasefire was agreed upon in November 2002. There was such a huge outcry in India against the inhuman treatment that the Indian army chief General Bikram Singh had to address the Indian public, expressing the need for a strong and befitting reply to the Pakistani dastardly act. In the press conference on 14 January 2013, General Bikram Singh talked unusually tough saying that 'the beheading was "unacceptable" and "most unpardonable" and the troops would respond immediately, aggressively and offensively if provoked… India reserves the right to retaliate at the "time and place" of its choosing.'[16] There was so much public angst against the incident that the Indian prime minister had to state that there cannot be business as usual with Pakistan in the aftermath of the "barbaric act" of beheading of Indian soldiers.[17] But the incident was not allowed to escalate into a major crisis. The management of this incident by both the countries was made possible due to the existing structures of cooperation which had made the peace process workable, if not irreversible. Diplomatic and political statements from both sides were measures and made with a view not to escalate the crisis. Since the fault lied with Pakistan, statements from that side were more constructive and made with a view to defusing the tensions. The Pakistan foreign minister Hina Rabbani Khar showed great magnanimity and even proposed to meet her Indian counterpart for restoring normalcy of the bilateral relations.

India has consistently maintained that normalisation of relations between the two countries is greatly dependent on Pakistan completely discarding its policy of using terrorism as a state policy against India in all of its manifestations. Vajpayee government, however, had adopted a harder approach on the issue when it insisted that there could not be any dialogue with Pakistan until it completely stopped sponsored terrorism against India. Now there is a nuanced departure from that approach and India is insisting that terrorism is the main stumbling block and dialogue will not bear the desired fruit until Pakistan puts in a sincere effort to terminate terrorism. Prime minister Manmohan Singh elaborates India's approach thus: "People-to-people contacts have gone up, trade relations have shown improvement... but there cannot be normalisation of relations between our two countries unless and until terror machine which is still active in Pakistan is brought under control. This has been our policy during the nine years we have been in office. It is the same approach which can guide us in dealing with Pakistan in years to come."[18]

The Challenges Ahead

(a) Internal Developments in Pakistan

India-Pakistan peace process gets key dynamism from complex internal variables. In the case of conflict resolution, domestic factors in both the countries have contributed negatively and constrained bold decision-making. This is particularly true of Pakistani domestic politics where the fundamentalist forces along with the security forces have always acted against normalisation of relations with India. For instance, progress on issues like terrorism, Kashmir and economic cooperation has been influenced by Pakistan's domestic constituencies.

Some believe that resolution of India-Pakistan conflict has become even more difficult to resolve due to the rise of religious radicalism in the domestic politics of both India and Pakistan.[19] Religious radicalism in both the countries has witnessed alarming growth. Secularisation of society and polity has faced reversal, particularly in Pakistan. Islamic radicalism has survived in Pakistan due to the support of the army. In fact, Islamic fundamentalism has been used by Pakistan against India. But after 9/11 events, counter-India justification for Islamic fundamentalism has come under tremendous pressure, and as a result the army is finding it hard to support religious extremism. Religious parties and groups have opposed any move to secularise Pakistan's political institutions and streamline educational system, particularly the *madrassa* system.

The combination of politics and religion in Pakistan has worked as a strong motivation for international terrorism which continues to plague South Asian states. According to one study, the number of religious seminaries *(Madrassas)* rapidly increased after Zia-ul-Haq came to power in Pakistan. Moreover, since 1979 these seminaries also started giving military training, obviously for Jihad against the Soviet forces in Afghanistan and India, particularly in the Kashmir valley.[20] This study shows that in 1975 there were 868 seminaries in Pakistan. By 1988 this figure went up to 3289 and by the year 2000, it stood at 6000. Out of these, about eight to nine per cent of the seminaries have been providing military training.[21]

Over the years, Pakistan, as a state, has weakened a lot. It has been described as a failed or failing state. Yet others have called it a dysfunctional state. Pakistan has faced a serious problem from religious extremism. Religious extremism in Pakistan has been exploited by the military-bureaucracy combine. Stephen Cohen has noted that "the problem is not that most Pakistanis are Muslims and adhere to deep religious beliefs; it is that those beliefs have been exploited by state bureaucracy - notably the army."[22] There have been question marks over the state capacities to deal with these issues. There is growing pessimism round the belief that Saudi-style Wahabism is making inroads into critical institutions of Pakistan and it is visualised that radical Islamic forces might seize control of the country's nuclear weapons. Hasan Askari Rizvi has rightly warned that if the government does not ensure good governance and take bold steps, the country might well crash along several fault lines, such as ethnic, regional, and religious sectarianism.[23] It is believed that strengthening of parliamentary democracy in Pakistan will be fundamental to taking it out of the present impasse.

In recent years, India and Pakistan have re-assessed their respective threat perceptions. Now both countries have realised that the greatest threat to their national security lies within their countries. Indian prime minister, home minister and finance minister had gone on record saying that the greatest challenge or threat to India's national security comes from within the country from the naxalite movement. Indian prime minister Manmohan Singh observed, "I have been saying for the last three years that Naxalism remains the biggest internal security challenge facing our country."[24] Further, Indian finance minister Pranab Mukherjee called naxalism as the biggest threat to India's peace and security.[25] The latest intelligence reports suggest that "armed Naxalites have a presence in 170 districts in 15 states of India as of now, and spreading wide and far." [26]

Similarly, a recent Pakistan army doctrine document has accepted that the main threat to Pakistan comes from within the state from the Taliban and other non-state actors against whom the Pakistan security forces are fighting a grim battle at a great loss of man and material. Thus, changing its operational priorities, the Pakistan army has perceived internal threats such as anti-state terrorist groups as the biggest danger to Pakistan's national security.[27]

One heartening internal development has taken place in Pakistan. The democratically elected PPP-led government in Pakistan in 2008 completed its full term in 2013 before the elections were held to the fourteenth national assembly. After the elections, immediately after winning the elections, Nawaz Sharif expressed a strong desire to impart a momentum to India-Pakistan relations. He even wished to invite prime minister Manmohan Singh to the swearing-in-ceremony of his government.[28] In response to this, India considered sending special envoy Satinder Lamba to meet the prime minister-designate Nawaz Sharif. Reacting to positive atmospherics, Pakistan high commission in India opined that the two neighbours have a historic opportunity to bring about a qualitative improvement in relations.[29] The Pakistan high commission spokesperson Mazoor Ali Memon said that statements emanating from both sides have contributed to improving the atmospherics.[30] He also stated that improvement of ties with India was a foreign policy priority and there was reason for optimism.[31] He also stated that all issues needed to be solved through peaceful means.[32] He also added that it was time for India to acknowledge societal changes in Pakistan and there was a need for shunning stereotypes.[33] Immediately after winning elections in May 2013, Sharif had this to say: "We must become good friends and hold each other's hands ... let us make a new beginning, let us sit down together and let us resolve that we will from now onwards resolve all our outstanding issues peacefully and in a very friendly atmosphere."[34] This clearly establishes one thing that Pakistan now can no more afford a military solution to the issues with India. Nor can it continue the proxy war through terrorism. Dialogue and diplomacy are the only viable means to resolving disputes.

(b) The Kashmir Stalemate

Pakistan has wanted to sustain the Kashmir movement at minimal cost and to force a settlement on its own terms by causing disaffection and alienation among Kashmiris using the religious card, non-performance of elected government and alleged excesses by security forces.[35] Moreover, Pakistan wants to diversify the area of militancy by bringing hitherto unaffected areas, particularly of Jammu region, into its vortex.[36] Diversification of militancy also includes attacks on military and para-military forces and religious minorities such as Hindus and Sikhs.[37] Religious fundamentalism is being promoted and propagated in subtle ways to encourage separatism and communal divide, putting serious challenge to India's democratic and secular values on which the Indian state's survival is staked. Pakistan sponsored terrorism in Kashmir has gone a long way in alienating Kashmiri people from the Indian national mainstream.

The most obstructive feature of terrorism in South Asia has been Pakistan's state-sponsored terrorism in Kashmir. Pakistan-sponsored terrorism has posed a major threat to the core value of unity and integrity in India's concept of national security. Pakistan evolved the strategy of low-intensity conflict as it did not have the capabilities to wage a successful conventional war against India and achieve its objective of wrenching Kashmir from India. The issue of Pakistani support to separatist and terrorist activities in India has entered the phase of psychological warfare in which both sides attempt to win the hearts and minds of the target group. India, to safeguard its national security against the external threats in the form of Pakistan's support to secessionist and terrorist activities, has followed mainly a two-pronged counter-terrorism strategy: waging a limited military operation to eliminate the terrorists, and allowing and encouraging those who resort to terrorism accept the Indian constitution and have a place of honour in the political system provided they give up violence. India's democratic polity has provided peaceful alternatives to state terrorism of one kind or another for resolving such conflicts within the system through negotiations. Moreover, winning the hearts and minds of the people of Kashmir through political and developmental initiatives forms an important component of India's long-term counter-terrorism strategy.

Rise of religious extremism either in Kashmir or the rest of India will obstruct the resolution of the conflict. Since the late 1980s, the state of Jammu and Kashmir has witnessed an alarming rise in the trend of communalisation of the society. The Muslim youth of the valley is radicalised and *Kashmiriyat* or the secular fabric of society in the state has been drastically undermined. This radicalisation of society is having repercussions not only within the state but outside in the rest of India as well. According to one argument, the Muslim communalism or separatism in the valley is fuelling Hindu rivalism. This has suited Pakistan's strategy of communalisation of the Jammu and Kashmir society and promoting *jihadi* terrorism against India. Therefore, curbing communalisation of society and polity within Jammu and Kashmir and outside in the rest of India is fundamental to managing the Kashmir issue internally and externally as well.

(c) The Afghanistan Situation

After the 9/11, the Af-Pak region has become the epicentre of terrorism in South Asia. On 7 October 2001, the US-led international alliance against terrorism intervened in Afghanistan and started operations against the Taliban and al-Qaeda networks. This operation has been named as "Operation Enduring Freedom" and it still remains inconclusive. The US-led coalition forces, with the assistance of Northern Alliance, took control of Kabul in November 2001. In January 2002, UN-mandated International Security and Assistance Force (ISAF) arrived in Afghanistan. The North Atlantic Treaty Organisation (NATO) took control of ISAF in August 2003.

One sensitive part of the US-Afghan strategy deals with developments in Pakistan. It is rightly observed that "like it or not, the leaders, commanders, recruiters, financiers, and families of those running the Afghan insurgency are predominantly based in Pakistan, away from the war zone."[38] Pakistan has been a major stumbling block in containing terrorism in Afghanistan. Afghanistan government has often accused

Pakistan of harbouring terrorist groups, particularly the Taliban, in Afghanistan and creating instability with a view to furthering Pakistan's strategic interests. President Hamid Karzai once remarked, "Afghanistan's Taliban are killing Afghans and making a mockery of their claim to be fighting foreign invaders... It's clear that the fight is not against foreigners, it's for foreigners."[39] The hint was towards Pakistan's sinister role in Afghanistan. In such a situation it is of paramount importance that the international community, particularly the US, puts pressure on Pakistan to mend its ways for dealing with terrorism in Afghanistan or elsewhere. The US-Afghan-Pakistani relations need to be recalibrated keeping in view the objective that Pakistan does not nullify the gains against the terrorist and extremist groups in the entire Af-Pak region. The US is deeply concerned about its limitations in containing terrorism in Afghanistan. It would not be wrong to say that "Washington is on the lookout for ideas about how Pakistan could do more to support progress in Afghanistan."[40]

The US has played a key role in combating terrorism in South Asia in the post-9/11 period. Its direct action against the terrorists in Afghanistan and also in Pakistan has been an enabling factor in bolstering the state capacities to fighting terrorism in the Af-Pak region. Moreover, the US counter-terrorism policies and strategies have played a key role in diminishing the Maoists in Nepal and the LTTE in Sri Lanka.

Both Pakistan and Afghanistan are examples of states lacking capacities to combat terrorism. These two states also have lacked in political will to terminate terrorist groups. Pakistani state has shown lack of will in dealing with terrorists and terrorist outfits which have targeted India. For instance, Hafeez Saeed and the outfit Jammat-ud Dawah (JuD) have been allowed to carry out their anti-India activities. The JuD – a pseudo name for the banned terrorist outfit, Lashkar-e-Taiba - has got active government support. Immediately after the PML (N) came to power both at the national level and in the Punjab province in May 2013 elections, the Punjab province government announced a grant-in-aid of 61.35 million rupees for the administration of the JuD's centre known as Markaz-e-Taiba.[41] The perpetrators of Mumbai attacks of 26 November 2008 have also not been pursued and punished by Pakistan.

It is argued that the Afghan conflict and the conflict in Kashmir must be resolved for durable peace and stability in South Asia.[42] Pakistan has been a key destabilising factor both in Afghanistan and Kashmir. Pakistan wants to resolve these two conflicts according to its ideology of extremism and religious fundamentalism. It is a theocratic state. Theocracy inherently promotes hatred and intolerance. It is the anti-thesis of secularism, liberalism and democracy. Therefore, in South Asia it is essential that fundamentalism and extremism do not become a basis for resolution of the problems in Afghanistan and Kashmir. Solutions to these problems have to be found within secular, democratic and liberal values and strategies.

International Support for Peace Process

Almost all major powers have welcomed the peace process between India and Pakistan. Most of them have appreciated India's perception of the conflict, based on bilateralism and peaceful resolution of contentious issues and stopping all kinds of support to terrorism. In the post-colonial period, the US, Soviet Union/ Russia and China have affected the security environment of South Asia in a critical manner. Their policies were instrumental in abating the conflictual relations between India and Pakistan. After end of the cold war, role of these extra-regional powers is being redefined. Today, their policies and roles are becoming a crucial motivation for Indo-Pakistan rapprochement.

The US is considered as the most important extra-regional player in the South Asian regional security. In fact, the US considers that both India and the US can work together for promoting peace and democracy in the region. Both believe that evolution of Pakistan as a moderate Islamic state will help in maintaining peace and stability in the region.

There has been a view in India that the US policy of regional balance or equating India with Pakistan has emboldened Pakistan to be aggressive against India and create an atmosphere of hostility in the region. However, in recent years, the Indo-US strategic partnership is indicative of the US willingness to no more treat India and Pakistan on parity. With the beginning of the twenty first century, more so after 9/11 events, the Indo-US relationship has acquired a new positive momentum. The US now considers India as a victim of terrorism, supported mainly by Pakistan. The US has, in fact, put pressure on Pakistan to ensure that its soil is not used for terrorist activities against India.

The US is likely to get tougher on Pakistan for its failure to effectively fighting terrorists and Islamists. If the new approach takes concrete shape then that would go a long way in changing Pakistan's perceptions of Jihad and state-sponsored terrorism. That will have a positive impact on the peace process and resolving conflicts between India and Pakistan. Rather India would be more interested if the US could put more pressure on the Pakistani army and the Inter-Services Intelligence (ISI) to make a concerted fight against terrorism and Islamic radicalism. Both India and the US are interested in emergence of a new political set-up in Pakistan that is capable of waging a long-term fight against extremism. The US is playing a constructive role in promoting peace and stability in South Asia. Its global alliance against terrorism has brought about positive results for the management of India-Pakistan conflict.

Russia too has welcomed the peace process between India and Pakistan. The Russian president Vladimir Putin has believed that the peace process would add to the development of the region and resolution of the bilateral problems.[43] Russia has been supportive of India's stand on Kashmir and its resolution according to the Shimla agreement. Both India and Russia have similarity of perceptions on transnational security threats like international terrorism and religious extremism. The convergence of interests between India and other major powers on these issues will put pressure on Pakistan for mending its policies on Kashmir and transnational terrorism.

China's ever growing strategic relationship with Pakistan puts a severe constraint on its claims of promoting peace and stability in South Asia. Lasting peace in South Asia is possible only when China resolves its problems with India and does not cooperate with Pakistan on anti- or counter-India basis.

China has supported the resolution of bilateral disputes between India and Pakistan through negotiations. It has adopted a careful stand on the Kashmir issue. When the Chinese president Jiang Zemin paid a state visit to India in 1996, he suggested that both India and Pakistan put the Kashmir issue on the backburner and devote more time to cooperating in other areas.[44] It is believed that India and China together can sustain peace and stability in the region. Both also share the perception that terrorism is a threat to both of them, and they need to have a regular dialogue and develop anti-terror mechanism.[45]

In the twenty first century world order, the nature of interests of major powers vis-à-vis South Asia is not the same as it was during the cold war. Changes in the major powers' economic and geo-political considerations towards the region will certainly have an impact on the management and resolution of conflicts in the region.

Conclusion

The twenty first century has witnessed several measures being evolved between India and Pakistan for management and even resolution of their contentious bilateral issues and disputes. These initiatives have generated positive atmospherics resulting into flexibility between the two countries on the main contentions. The two governments have held talks on all the contentious issues and even managed crises now and then in a mature and reasonable manner.

Both domestic and international developments have shaped the prospects for conflict resolution between India and Pakistan. The international environment is becoming more suitable for conflict management and resolution in the region. The domestic factors have also undergone change for conflict resolution. However, there are serious problems within Pakistan. The rise of religious extremism there is a worrisome factor. In the absence of a secular society and polity, without a strong and truly democratic government, and serious law and order problems, Pakistan is being described as a failed state. It is doubtful whether a weak Pakistan will be ready for a reasonable settlement of the Kashmir issue without redrawing borders. Resolution of the Kashmir issue is possible only through long-term transformation of internal variables in Kashmir, India and Pakistan. In this process of transformation, Pakistan needs to democratise and secularise its India and Kashmir policies.

Both India and Pakistan have suffered immensely due to their unending conflict. Today, things have drastically changed and Pakistan finds itself in the category of failing states and among the most critically insecure states. There is tremendous international pressure on Pakistan to mend its ways on the issue of terrorism. As a result Pakistan has changed its stance on state-sponsored terrorism. That reflects in its engagement and cooperation with the international community, India and Afghanistan on combating terrorism. There are huge expectations from Pakistan. But we must understand its vulnerable position also.

Both India and Pakistan have engaged on the issue of terrorism and evolved several bilateral intuitions and understanding to deal with the problem in a structured manner. The evolution of several bilateral structures between India and Pakistan also vindicates the argument that terrorism is the core issue in each other's threat perception. Both countries have rightly adopted a new approach on tackling terrorism through cooperative mechanisms and not do anything which would embolden terrorists. A good illustration of this can be found in the fact that India has not deployed its forces on Indo-Pak border beyond operational requirements taking into consideration the exigency of Pakistan army's continuing operations against the Taliban and al-Qaeda terrorists on Pakistan-Afghanistan border.

The policies and role of extra-regional powers have become less intrusive today compared to the cold war period. During the cold war, the US helped Pakistan with a view to counter India. This approach perpetuated the Indo-Pakistan conflict. Now the US has adopted a new approach towards India and Pakistan, and their bilateral relations. The US is no longer helping Pakistan with a view to countering India. As a result, the conflict has become manageable through peaceful means, providing hopes for actually settling or resolving disputes over the longer period.

Internal developments in Pakistan are not altogether negative. A democratically elected government in the year 2008 has completed its full term in the history of Pakistan. Elections for a new government have been successfully held in May 2013. Nawaz Sharif is the new prime minister of Pakistan. After winning the elections, he spoke of taking further the peace process, which was promoted by himself in 1999. Also in the run-up to the elections, anti-India slogans were missing from the election campaigns. Pakistan seems to be strengthening as a democracy and that augurs well for India-Pakistan relations and there is a reason to be optimistic that the bilateral mechanisms will bear the desired fruit.

References

1. "India-Pakistan Joint Press Statement, Islamabad, January 6, 2004." South Asia Terrorism Portal, http://www.satp.org/satporgtp/countries/india/document/papers/indo_pak-6jan04.htm
2. "Text of the Joint Statement signed between the Prime Minister of India and the President of Pakistan in Delhi, 18 April 2005", http://news.bbc.co.uk/2/hi/south_asia/4455545.stm
3. B. Raman, "Reading Musharraf between the lines," *International Terrorism Monitor*, South Asia Analysis Group, 22 September 2006.
4. Shamshad Ahmad, "Unending Peace Pretentions," *Dawn,* 6 March 2007.
5. "Pakistan says it never claimed Kashmir as its territory," *The Hindustan Times,* 12 December 2006.
6. "Musharraf faces criticism for Kashmir proposal," *The Hindu,* 7 December 2006.
7. *Ibid.*
8. "India not ready for joint management of Kashmir," *The Hindustan Times,* 12 January 2007.
9. "Kashmir issue will be resolved soon: Pervez," *The Hindustan Times,* 27 April 2007.
10. *Ibid.*
11. "Borders cannot be redrawn on religious basis: PM," *The Hindu,* 16 August 2000.

12. "Borders cannot be redrawn but we can work towards making them irrelevant" *The Indian Express,* 25 March 2006, http://www.indianexpress.com/news/-borders-cannot-be-redrawn-but-we-can-work-towards-making-them-irrelevant-/1073/0.
13. "PM says borders in Kashmir cannot be redrawn, Pak protests," *The Hindustan Times,* 23 November 2009, http://www.hindustantimes.com/News-Feed/India/PM-says-borders-in-Kashmir-cannot-be-redrawn-Pak-protests/Article1-479297.aspx.
14. *Ibid.*
15. India-Pakistan Joint Statement, Sharm El Sheikh, 16 July 2009, http://news.bbc.co.uk/2/hi/8154282.stm
16. *Ibid.*
17. "PM talks tough, says no business as usual with Pakistan," *The Times of India,* 16 January 2013.
18. "Normal ties with Pak after terror machine shut: PM," *The Times of India,* 9 March 2013.
19. For details see Rafiq Dossani and Henry S. Rower (eds.), *Prospects for Peace in South Asia,* Hyderabad: Orient Longman, 2006.
20. Shaukat Qadir, "The Concept of International Terrorism: An Interim Study of South Asia," *The Round Table,* Vol. 360, 2001, p. 335.
21. *Ibid*, pp. 335-336.
22. Stephen P. Cohen (*et al.*), *The Future of Pakistan,* New Delhi: Oxford University Press, 2012, p. 25.
23. *Ibid,* p. 190.
24. "Naxalism biggest threat to internal security: Manmohan," *The Hindu,* 24 May 2010.
25. "Pranab says Naxalism biggest threat to country," *The Indian Express,* 28 December 2010, http://www.indianexpress.com/news/pranab-says-naxalism-biggest-threat-to-country/730349/
26. "Naxalism: biggest threat to India," *The Times of India,* 10 May 2005, http://articles.timesofindia.indiatimes.com/2005-05-10/india/27843636_1_naxalism-biggest-threat-people-s-war-group.
27. "Internal threats greatest risk: Pak Army," *The News International,* 2 January 2013, http://www.thenews.com.pk/article-82167-Internal-threats-pose-greatest-risk-to-integrityper cent3A-Pak-Army.
28. "Come and visit, Mian Saheb tells Manmohan," *The Hindu,* 14 May 2013.
29. "Pak grabs PMs olive branch, for better ties," *The Times of India,* 3 June 2013.
30. *Ibid.*
31. *Ibid.*
32. *Ibid.*
33. *Ibid.*

34. "We have a lot of love for India (An interview with Karan Thapar)," *The Hindu,* 14 May 21013.
35. Inder Sawhney, "Militants trained by US helping ISI in Kashmir - Proposed white paper lays bare Pakistan's designs," *The Times of India,* 30 October 1998.
36. *Ibid.*
37. As a part of its strategy to create communal and sectarian divide and attract international mediation, Pakistan was blamed to have mastermind the massacre of thirty Six-Sikhs militants in Chittisinghpora village in Jammu district on 21 March 2000. It happened at the time of Bill Clinton's visit to India. See "36 massacred in South Kashmir," *The Hindustan Times,* 22 March 2000.
38. Fotini Christia and Michael Semple, "Flipping the Taliban: How to Win in Afghanistan," *Foreign Affairs,* Vol. 88, No. 4, July-August 2009, p. 44.
39. "Afghan Prez. denounces Taliban for killing countrymen," *The Times of India,* 31 May 2013.
40. *Ibid.*
41. "Pak's Punjab govt grants Rs 61m aid for JuD centre," *The Times of India,* 19 June 2013.
42. Barnett R. Rubin and Ahmed Rashid, "From Great Game to Grand Bargain: Ending Chaos in Afghanistan and Pakistan," *Foreign Affairs,* Vol. 87, No. 6, November-December 2008, pp. 30-44.
43. "Dangers to construct world on unipolar principles: Putin," *The Hindu,* 4 December 2006.
44. John Cherian, "Zhu Rongji in India," *Frontline,* 15 February 2002, pp. 122-123.
45. China is facing a separatist threat in its Xinjiang province from the Uighur militants, who have close connections with the al-Qaeda and the Taliban terrorist outfits operating from Pakistan and Afghanistan.

15

Normalisation of India-Pakistan Relations and Prospects of Economic Development in South Asia

Riaz Ahmed Shaikh

Despite ruling by different families and dynasties, India and Pakistan remained a single territorial identity for at least thousand years. Starting from Sultanate period (1100 AD) to the end of colonial Raj (1947), except very small patches when different states in Southeast and West India, ruled independently and semi-independently from the Delhi's rule. Excellent inter-communal understanding was maintained, Bhagati movement further strengthen the relation between different communities especially Hindus and Muslims. Sufis and Bhagats played very constructive role in bringing communal groups closed to each other. No doubt ruling elites and religious clergies tried to exploit religion and even sectarian factors for their convenience and continued their agenda whenever they found focused it fit for their notorious purposes but it subsided soon as at common men's level such as differences could not sustain for a longer time. All the communal groups had strong dependence on each other, hence differences for a longer time could not be sustained. Forcible conversions were not visible otherwise despite eight hundred years rule of Muslim hardly one fifth (twenty per cent of population) of India converted to Islam. Akbar's religious tolerance policy promoted secularism in the Medieval India and even inter-communal marriages could be seen a very insignificant or at a very symbolic level. Along with this certain phases of intolerance could also be observed. But these must be seen in a broader view where ruling classes interests became more entrenched with the promotion of religious intolerance. But even these could not survive for a long time and we see that during Tipu Sultan and Siraj-ud-Dulla's resistance to British occupations, a joint resistance was put up without any communal differences and the last attempt to stop British from occupying India in 1857 was collectively fought by Hindus and Muslims together.

But the changes introduced by the British during .colonial rule promoted sectarian and communal conflicts. Deliberate attempts were made to discover history with communal perspectives and promoted religious hatred against each other.[1] The 1857 incidents changed the whole scenario of sub-continent. Last Mughal monarch was sent in exile. Muslim elite had to surrender their parks and pilferages. British established its formal writ on India. Former Muslim ruling classes were not willing to accept the new realities. After the British arrival three Muslim classes were directly affected due to this change including (i) Muslim Salariat Class (ii) Ulemas (iii) Feudals.[2] Whereas the rising nationalist trend in Hindus demanded majority rule. System of local government and other democratic reforms introduced by British would have followed the principles of democracy i.e., adult franchise which means majority rule. Even people like Syed Ahmed would not find soft corner for democratic progress as it could be beneficent for a specific communal group by default due to its majority. But this was according to the established principle of democracy, however, certain safeguard could be demanded and may be extended to different communal groups including Muslims. But Muslim minority became scare of majority rule, but they had never felt any danger when they were ruling India for about 800 years despite being in minority.

Muslim Salariat classes of Muslim minority provinces (especially Uttara Pradesh, Central Provinces (CP is now divided into present day Provinces of Madhya Pardesh, Maharashtara, Chhattis Garh and Bihar) became the flag barriers of the Muslim identity and demanded for separate Muslim home land. Muslim majority provinces except Bengal hardly find any attraction in this slogan and remained attached to secular and anti-communal politics till the very end. Muslim League failed to show any impressive performance in Muslim majority provinces in the election of 1937. The election result of 1946 are quoted as a barometer of change in Muslim majority provinces and it is considered as a favourable vote for the creation of Pakistan but this development should be seen from the developing fear of Muslim feudal who became terrified from the congress open socialist agenda and land holding open claim for land reforms where as Muslim league decided to pursue with the same status quo despite its claim for the end of exploitative system.[3] After partition Muslim League pursued the land reform agenda but with a very limited scope and only in East Bengal with a clear communal outlook.

Demand of Muslims of minority provinces for a separate homeland by Muslim League had never envisioned that partition would invite worst time of communal riots and bring such a permanent damage to the communal harmony of the people of both countries especially among the migrant communities. This hate psyche with the fear of occupation by the giant India and desire to hold the flag of Muslim rule again at Red Fort persuaded the politics of conflict. Unresolved disputes including distribution of assets, indigenous states and award of boundary commission founded the seeds of new hatred legacy which continued till now. Kashmir became the issue of life and death for both states. Pakistan was well aware that it can not get Kashmir liberated through conventional military means hence promoted asymmetric wars.[4]

Despite these differences and initial military conflict in Kashmir in October 1947, relations were not damaged. Karachi declaration signed by prime ministers Nehru and Liaquat provided footings for the future ideal relations between both neighbouring states and mechanism to resolve all standing disputes. But major distrust developed in early 1950s, when Pakistan in order to balance its defence capabilities against India, decided to get into the US -sponsored alliances. Although capitalist block offered membership to Pakistan in SEAATO and, CENTO alliance to counter communist threat but Pakistan had its own parallel agenda as well. No doubt animosity with Afghanistan on western boarder and USSR's location not far away from country's north-west and especially Afghanistan's refusal to accept British decision of 1893 Durand line as an international border demarcated then between British India and Afghanistan and now international border between Pakistan and Afghanistan. Refugees who arrived in Pakistan brought their prejudices and biases against India. Pakistan's establishment especially the civil bureaucracy further propagated against India. Army made best use of the situation. Within army first major failed revolt by Major General Akbar crooked up due to "Pakistan's not handling" the Kashmir conflict with full force against India. Rest of the provinces especially East Pakistan, Sindh, NWFP (Now Khybar Pakhtoonkhawa) and Baluchistan hardly endorsed Pakistan's foreign policy on the principle of conflict with India and Afghanistan Because these provinces had no representation either in country's most powerful civil and military bureaucracy except marginal presentation of Pushtun in army. Loyalties of various nationalists especially Sindhis, Pushtuns, Balochs and Bengalis were by and large doubted due to their friendly approach towards India.[5] Despite this, relations between Pakistan and India had remained normal for quite sometimes. But major deterioration erupted in their relations in 1965.

Under the SEATO and CENTO agreements Pakistan received sufficient military aid and 1962 war with China resulted in military debacle for India. Pakistan considered by early 1965 to create an environment where an uprising may take place in Kashmir so that a war may be initiated for the separation of Kashmir from India. This seventeen days war (September 6-23) 1965 disturbed the existing relations. Trade activities came to near halt. Visa sanctioning procedure became more complex. Police verification and agencies clearance made travelling very painful. Train, air and other means of communication were cut off. Worst affected by this situation were the divided families. Situation a bit improved with the signing of Taskhant declaration with the involvement of Soviet in February 1966. Soon, Pakistan blamed India of indulging in conspiracy against the separation of East Pakistan by facilitating the meeting of leadership of Awami League at the border town of Agartala. Pakistan placed Shaikh Mujeeb-ur-Rehman and several Awami League's leaders behind the bars.[6]

The relations between the two countries reached to the lowest ebb during the crisis of East Pakistan (March-December 1971). Pakistan accused India of interfering in its internal affairs and supporting Awami League's militant wing-Mukti Bhani. India demanded Pakistan to stop military operation and to normalise the situation in its Eastern part so that East Bengalis should not cross-border and enter into West Bengal. This refugee influx was becoming a big problem for India to handle. Indian forces entered into East Pakistan on 6 December 1971 and after ten days war eventually Pakistan army surrendered and 90,000 prisoners of war (POW) were taken into custody by India. This brought a great humiliation for the armed forces of Pakistan. Thousands of miles of West Pakistan were also captured by India. It was on international pressure that further Indian advance in West Pakistan was stopped, otherwise it was not difficult for them to capture West Pakistan like its Eastern wing.[7]

New Pakistan and Change of Direction

Pakistan has always faced the identity crisis. Conservative and right wing of the country has always denied its links and roots with South Asia. They have always tried to discover their roots either from Middle East or Central Asia. The separation of East Pakistan brought an end to the remaining link Pakistan had with South Asia. Bengali language written in

Devnagari script always remained under criticism from the centralist and they wanted to change it with Arabic one. But separation of East Pakistan closed this attempt.[8] At one stage it was being demanded that Arabic should be declared as the national language of Pakistan to abolish the concept of regional languages.[9]

Zulfikar Ali Bhutto formed government in West Pakistan in December 1971 after the surrender of East Pakistan. The immediate task before him was how to get 90,000 soldiers released from the Indian prisons taken as POW and to retrieve Pakistani land from Indian occupation during ten days war. Bhutto promoted the popular politics. He came under the pressure of religious conservatives and introduced few reforms which further radicalised Pakistani society and placed seeds of religious extremism and hatredness in the country. One important action was the declaration of Ahmedi sects of Muslims as non-Muslim. There is no such precedent in the recent and modern world history where state interferes in the religious personal of its citizens and expels them from their religion. This naturally opened the door of fanaticism in Pakistan. He further banned the consumption and sale purchase of liquor and closed bars. Declared Friday as a weekly off instead of Sunday, and established ministry of religious affairs. On foreign policy issue he moved closer to China, promoted anti-government radicals in Afghanistan by opposing Sardar Dawood's government. Developed relations with Islamic block and convened second conference of heads of state of Muslim countries at Lahore in 1974. These actions were in fact towards discovery of Pakistan's new identity by moving closer to Middle East. He decided to go for nuclear tests after Indian nuclear explosions in 1974.[10]

The most crucial development of period i.e., 1973-77 was further strengthening of Pakistan's relations with the conservative and extremist Wahabi Islam of Middle East, especially Saudi Arabia. Prior to this there was hardly any influential impact of ultra conservative Wahabis on Pakistani society and it was Sufi Islam which was widely practiced in Indian subcontinent including India, Pakistan and Bangladesh. But this new relation changed the existing socio-economic structure. The immediate agent of change became those labour immigrants who went to oil rich countries of Middle East, whose economics got boost after the 1973 Ramazam war and oil embargo imposed by Muslim oil producing countries for several months. This resulted in boosting the oil prices. The newly rich Middle countries provided Pakistanis especially unskilled labour from north and north-west of the country the jobs in the construction and other sectors. This played a very important role in designing new relations and reshaping Pakistani society. These workers got exposed to extremist and conservative Wahabi Islam in the Middle East. On their return they further promoted Wahabi Islam in Pakistan. They gave charity for the establishment of new mosques in the country. A concept of born again Muslim became a popular phenomena.[11]

This conservative face of Islam got further boost during Afghan conflict after the USSR forces entered into Afghanistan in December 1979 General Zia-ul-Haq got a golden opportunity to perpetuate his illegitimate military rule by promoting the slogan that communism is rapidly approaching warm waters by first occupying Afghanistan and next target would be Pakistan. General Zia with the support of CIA and Saudi Arabia converted the small Afghan resistance into a full fledged Islami Jihad. Billions of dollars were provided by US and Saudi Arabia for the Afghan *jihad* and Pakistan's contact which was established in the 1970s with Afghan during Bhutto regime was further strengthened by General Zia during Afghan jihad.[12] Thousands of madrassas were established throughout Pakistan but initially two bordering provinces of Balochistan and Khyber Pushtunkhwa became the ideal places for such networks, as these were close to Afghan border and lot of Afghan camps were already established there. This environment provided suitable ground for the *jihadi* culture in Afghan-Pak region. Soon Jihadis from Middle East started arriving in Pakistan unchecked. Rather they were welcomed and were taken as state guests. Jihadi network gripped Pakistani society.[13]

While General Zia benefitted from his *jihadi* support policy on western border, Khalistan movement in Punjab was also not ignored. Sikhs were encouraged in their resistance movement in East Punjab. On several occasions after receiving protest from India and under war threat he adopted reconciliation to defuse the real time war threat. But this had already wider the concept of *jihad* from western border to eastern border as well.[14]

The Islamic Revolution of Iran resulted in generating new conflict in the region on manifolds: US-Iran rivalry in hostage of US embassy staff members; Iran-Saudi Arabia conflict for hegemony in the Middle East and Persian Gulf and discovery of new Shia identity in the region. Saudi Arabia played a key role in these developments. This situation promoted sectarian conflict in the region and especially Pakistan. In Pakistan, Zia's several Islamisation steps including imposition of mandatory Zakat deduction from bank accounts of all Muslims (without any sectarian differences) was strongly opposed by Shia Muslims of Pakistan. They seized Federal Capital-Islamabad for couple of days until General Zia exempted Shias from this mandatory deduction.[15] But he realised the real power of Shia Muslims who constituted about twenty to twenty-five per cent of country's total population. This further promoted few sectarian identity in Pakistan as well. To counter the Shia influence in Pakistan, Saudi Arabia provided generous financial support and *jihad* mindset of people like General Zia and General Akhtar Abdul Rehman and General Fazal-e-Haq promoted Sunni extremism in Pakistan. Now Punjab emerged as the hot bed of sectarian conflict in Pakistan.[16]

Kashmir–New War Theatre

As the Afghan jihad was approaching to its natural end due to the withdrawal of USSR forces and successfully handling of Sikh separatist movement by India (although prime minister Indira Gandhi lost her life during this conflict) a new theatre was promoted in Kashmir. Due to disputes on elections results and the allegations of rigging in the state elections, unrest of smaller group periodical protest in Indian Kashmir, Pakistan's army tried to take advantage of this fragile situation and opened a new chapter of jihad in Kashmir. Afghan conflict in Kashmir further promoted conflict in the region. Mistrust between India and Pakistan increased because of support to the Kashmiris by certain elements in Pakistani establishment.

In this atmosphere, nuclear tests conducted by India in May 1998, revived the issue of nuclear armament in the region which had first emerged in debate in 1974 after Pokhan's nuclear tests by India. In response to India, nuclear tests in 1974, Zulfikar Ali Bhutto said that Pakistan would eat grass but make nuclear bomb. There was a demand and pressure on prime minister Nawaz Sharif to response in equal terms by detonating nuclear bomb. He did so on 27 May 1998. Although global community condemned the nuclear tests conducted and placed sanctions by the US and other major countries on both the countries. As compare to India, Pakistan felt more serious about economic sanctions and country's economy was jolted to the core by the sanctions.

A New Chapter of Friendship and Lahore Declaration

Despite the nuclear tests, a renewed process of dialogue and friendship emerged between India and Pakistan with the visit of prime minister Atal Bihari Vajpai to Lahore in early 1999. This tour of Vajpai was very significant from various perspectives. First time an Indian prime minister belonging to conservative right wing party–BJP had a dialogue with another central right party's leader Mian Nawaz Sharif. It is the province of Punjab where antagonistic approach has been maintained against India and Punjab's extremists groups and sectarian organisations having links with Kashmir *jihadis* have traditionally never liked any attempt to normalise relations between India and Pakistan. Religious parties including Jamiat-i-Islam and Hafiz Saeed's Jamat-ud-Dawa strongly opposed this visit. Another significance of the tour was Vajpai's visit to the Minar-e-Pakistan- a monument erected to commemorate the passing of 1940 resolution of All India Muslim for the establishment of Pakistan. It was a very graceful gesture from an Indian prime minister to visit this place to undo the impression that India has never accepted Pakistan's establishment.[17]

This visit created a very conducive environment for further dialogue and confidence building measures (CBMs) between both the states. Bus service between Lahore-Delhi and increase in number of flights was also approved. There was considerable opinion that these initiatives would have a long lasting impacts on the lives of both countries. But this wish was still dream and soon Kargil episode rolled back all developments made in this regard. Jihadis, with the support of Pakistan military, occupied the hills vacated by Indian soldiers during extreme winters. In fact Kargil incident ruined the dialogue process between both the states. With the dismissal of Nawaz Sharif government in October 1999 and later tookover by General Pervez Musharaf (considered as the architect of the Kargil episode) chances of any further dialogue became far remote. Three major activities including high jacking of an Indian plane from Khartoum to Lahore and then to Kabul and release of several notorious terrorists from Indian jails in exchange of the hostage passengers, terrorist attack on India parliament and in Srinagar further deteriorated relations between the countries; Forces of both the countries started arriving on borders and it looked like the war was looming on the horizon. Even foreign nationals started leaving and diplomatic staff was evacuated by their missions. But the US, intervened ease the tension between India and Pakistan. It was the same time after 9/11, Pakistan had provided huge intelligence support and air bases by the US for its military operation in Afghanistan.[18]

The US not only successfully handled the war crisis situation but also forced both countries to sit again on the negotiating table in Agra summit. But this summit between Vajpai and Musharaf failed to culminate on any positive outcome. But devastating earthquake of 2005 in Kashmir and Pakistan's northern areas, in which more than 80,000 people lost their lives again brought the agenda of peace in line lime. After several rounds of dialogues, Kashmiris were given certain concessions after more than four decades. New border-crossings were approved first time after 1965 war. Trade on local basis among Kashmiris and free travelling for the divided Kashmiri families on permits (without visa restrictions) were introduced. These were the significant concessions agreed upon by both the countries at least for Kashmiris.

26/11 and Nightmare for India-Pakistan Relations

India-Pakistan relations which have been the victim of historical animosity faced some hiccups. No one can guarantee when the relations will be deteriorated once again even on a petty incidence. After 2005 dialogue of gas pipelines from Central Asian states and Iran to India via Pakistan were being considered and Mani Shankar Aiyar, being the minister for natural resources, took very serious interest to materialise such projects. These projects could be of very significance and could bring huge change in the socio-economic lives of the people of the region. Pakistan would have been the best beneficiary of the pipelines. Not only Islamabad could get royalty for providing facility but this lines could promote cordial relationships between the two countries.[19]

While the negotiations were progressing on relatively slow phase, change of regime took place in Pakistan. General Musharraf had to quit the presidency and Pakistan Peoples Party (PPP) led by Asif Ali Zardari established, new government in 2008. Zardari immediately after elected as president announced that India was not Pakistan's enemy rather extremists operating in Afghanistan and Pakistan were the real enemy of Pakistan and they were causing more damage to Pakistan.[20] India also reciprocated this gesture positively. A new hope of normalisation of relations set in future dialogue, but another disaster was awaited to again roll back the peace initiatives when on 26 November 2008 Pakistan-based extremists did one of the worst terrorist activity in Indian commercial hub-Mumbai.[21] In this unfortunate incident in which more than thirteen dozen innocent people lost their lives including few foreigners, set a sense of sympathy for India in tone and a general impression emerged to target terrorist groups operating from Pakistani soil. Again war like situation emerged between India and Pakistan. India demanded visible action against terrorist groups and jihadis. Due to serious clashing signals emerging from India and Pakistan's response in equal terms, even diplomatic missions of both the countries could not continue their functions.

India conditioned the future restoration of dialogue process with Pakistan subject to the action taken against these militant groups.[22]

After a gap of two years, when a meeting between Indian and Pakistani prime ministers at Sharm al Sheikh, Egypt, opened a new chapter of dialogue between both the states. India, which was initially not willing to consider the option of dialogue without pursuing the culprits of 26/11 agreed for negotion with Pakistan for negotiation. Due to this process, significant development was noted in the normalisation of relations between the two states. Although this time process was a bit slow and cautious, especially in case of India but significant development including new categories of visas for the nationals of both countries, on arrival visa for senior citizen, multiple visa sanctioning for businessmen, liberal grant of visa for patient travelling for medical treatment and even tourist visas were also included for the first time in the sixty seven years of history. On the financial front, investors were allowed to make investment in selective sectors, trading in stock markets and opening of bank branches of national banks in each other countries to facilitate the approval of financial transactions. Pakistan has agreed to declare MFN status to India. India had already granted same status to Pakistan much earlier in 1997. But due to opposition of certain lobbies, interest groups and most significantly religious clerics especially Hafiz Saeed's Jamiat-ul-Dawa, Pakistan postponed the formal sanctioning of MFN status to India.[23]

Nawaz Sharif's Takeover and a New Ray of Hope

For the last one and half decade Punjab's business classes and bourgeoisie have realised the actual benefits of restoring the normal relations between India and Pakistan. Previously they had been opposing the voices of other provinces, demand for the restoration of relations between India and Pakistan to bring peace in the region. Sindh is the province where still a significant population of Hindus live and divided families of Muslim refugees who migrated to Pakistan after partition have also demanded for the restoration of channel of communication. But previously such voices from the small provinces have just not only been ignored but also questioned their patriotism. Even the loyalties of two Sindhi prime mnisters Zulfikar Ali Bhutto and his daughter Benazir Bhutto and political leadership belonging to Baloch and Pashtuns have been condemned and malicious propaganda had been launched to malign them for being closer to India. But now leadership from Punjab is supporting dialogue process between India and Pakistan. Nawaz Sharif, immediately after he became the prime minister announced that he wanted to continue relations with India the way he continued earlier in 1999.

He has said that there is an extreme need to restore normal relations between two states as it will be in the mutual interest and benefit for both. From his gestures it looks that he is very keen to resume the dialogue process immediately, but restrain and cautiousness showed by India and advices received from bureaucracy and military establishment, now seems that things will proceed on normal track instead of accelerated speed but still we should hope that normal course may be more sustainable and durable.

Pakistan is suffering from severe energy crisis and Punjab is worst effected from the shortage of electricity. India can provide more than 1000 MW of electricity to Punjab within months, if any accord is signed in this regard. This may provide immediate relief to Nawaz Sharif's government, because during election campaign he promised to provide electricity to Pakistan and especially to his home province Punjab. Another reason for Punjab's leadership is to explore the huge Indian market. Being a landlocked province it is heavily dependent on Sindh's port. Freight charges increase the cost of any product manifold for Punjab's in doing their trade with rest of the world via Karachi port. Trade through Wagah border may provide Punjab a very cheap and reliable trading route. Pakistani Punjab may provide lot of construction material including cement, steel, tiles and other items desperately needed for the booming Indian market. Even Pakistani textile may find good market in India and being a cotton producing area, Punjab has a good potential to get benefit from the textile trade. Along with this perishable items including vegetables and fruits may also be traded. Most important benefits for Punjab's industries will be the availability of cheap machinery from India. Right now, Pakistani industrialist has to import machinery on very soaring rates from Europe, Japan and other developed countries. But machinery of about same standards from India can significantly cut the manufacturing cost. Pakistani industrialists may sale their furnish goods across the Wagha border with minimum freight charges due to proximity whereas the export of same material to other parts of the world may involved additional cost of transportation and shipments and extra time to reach its destination. The current volume of trade between India and Pakistan is around two billion dollars. This level is again achieved due to the recent initiatives, otherwise traditionally it was very low and had not reached to even one billion dollars. But looking to the existing circumstances there are chances that after the lifting of restrictions and removal of all barriers this quantum may reach to six to eight billion dollars within two years and if Pakistan agrees to provide trade corridors for India to Central Asia, Middle East and Iran then this figure may cross several times high. But for this purpose a lot of investment would be required to upgrade the existing infrastructure of Pakistan. Roads and highways in Pakistan have suffered due to poor maintenance and especially due to consecutive floods during 2010-12. Bridges at certain spots were swept away, but not reconstructed due to financial constraints. Unrepaired roads are other major impediments. The most depressing situation is of Pakistan railways. British rulers constructed excellent railways network in the sub-continent. Pakistan inherited excellent railways network which was forty per cent of the total railways network of United India.[24] Railways were and are one of the cheapest and safest means of travelling of goods transportation. But due to corruption, mismanagement, criminal and negligence, Pakistan railways fleet has nearly came to halt. Especially during General Zia military rule, military establishment developed its own transportation department–National Logistics Cell (NLC). All the military and government transportation were done through NLC instead of railways, which damaged railway's financial health and incurred loss in billions. Now Pakistan railway has become a white elephant incurring losses of billion of rupees annually. Even it has no money to pay for the salary and pension of its staff. India previously offered Pakistan to provide railway engines to meet its requirements. It also offered the repairing of the non-functional engines on very economical rates but bureaucratic red tapism and conventional mistrust have stopped any concrete development. But if a progress is made in this regard, then economy of Pakistan may get a good boost.

Conclusion

Pakistan and India despite being twins have very painful history. Wounds of partition continued its legacy for a long time, due to which both countries remained disconnected for a longer period of time. Despite shameful events of 1947 working relations were maintained by two neighbours till war of 1965. East Pakistan crisis of 1971 revived the memories of past and Pakistan changed whatsoever it had policy of look east and south. It changed its direction to look Middle East and discover its Muslim identity and disconnectivity with South Asia further increased. Currently Pakistan's connectivity with South Asia more specifically with India is through three points: Wagah - Attari (Punjab); Monabao - Khokrapar (Sindh - Rajastan) and Poonch - Rawalakot (Kashmir)

Monabao-Khokrapar route is only used for passenger railway services, whereas Kashmir border permits the movement of divided Kashmiri families and very limited trade. No non-Kashmiri Pakistani and Indian citizen are allowed to use this route. Only Wagah - Attari is a major route used for human travel (bus and train) and trade. Around ninety five per cent of trade is being conducted through this single route. This very limited connectivity has very less trade. Trade between India and Pakistan in 2013 was $ 2.4 billion.

On the basis of above facts it may be said that virtually at the moment Pakistan is hardly connected with South Asia. Because of Pakistan's deliberate ignorance for its connectivity with South Asia.

There is an urgent need for Pakistan to restore its lost links with South Asia. For restoring its link to South Asia, Pakistan has two types of options: restore routes which were previously in vogue but currently not in use and open new routes emerged because of post-partition developments.

Existing relations between India and Pakistan will be much better if this connectivity is restored. The 2910 km long border between Pakistan and India has several possibilities for road crossing and train services. It is very important to note that connectivity between India and Pakistan is quite different from the rest of connectivity among the other nations of the South Asia. Mostly other connectivity will is end in itself but Pakistan - India connectivity will be more than that. Pakistan may act as the trade corridor between South Asia and Central Asia and West Asia. Previously there used to be opposition to any proposal to restore normal relations with India from three sides: Muslim Refugees of minority provinces who had still reflexes of painful memories of 1947 in their minds; Punjab due to its division and worst kind of communal riots and human tragedy and military establishment.

Now refugees have overcome their paradoxes and within Punjab, at least Punjabi political leadership and business community are in favour of cordial relation but military still has reservations. There is shift in the mindset of Pakistani establishment and common Pakistani.

Pakistan Land Port Authority (PLPA), following India and Bangladesh's foot prints, and Integrated Check Post (ICP) at borders are being established. India has already established its ICP at Wagah border. The MNF status for India, relaxation in visa system, opening of bank branches are in progress.

Although Pakistan and India attempted several times in the past to restore normal relations but due to lack of trust and incidents like killings of soldiers in Kashmir in January 2013 stopped trade between both the countries for three weeks and restored later on 29 January 2013. Sharm al Sheikh meeting between India and Pakistan prime ministers in 2009 set new track of negotiations. There is a significance of this phase because: there is a people's support for this process; Pakistan facing threat from internal terrorism; Pakistan's economy lost significantly (dollars 90 billion) in last decade due to terrorist activities by Tahreek-e-Taliban (TTP) and other extremist groups; country's economic growth has nearly stagnant and Pakistan is facing worst kind of electricity shortage and India can help to overcome this problem.

Due to its financial constrains, Pakistan is in favour of connectivity i.e., culture to sports, trade to joint collaborations, student exchange to medical tourism and more.

References

1. R.Thapar, *Somanatha-The many voices of a history.* New Delhi: Penguin Books, 2004.
2. H. Alavi, "Misreading Partition and State Formation", in R. Shaikh (ed), *Back from the Brink- India-Pakistan Ties Revisited,* Karachi: Ushba Publishing International, 2012, pp. 3-37.
3. *Ibid.*
4. A. Jamal, Shadow: *The untold story of jihad in Kashmir,* New York: Melville House, 2009.
5. S. M. A. Shah, *The Foreign Policy of Pakistan: Ethnic Impacts on Diplomacy 1971-1994,* London: I.B Tauris & Co. Ltd., 1997.
6. M.Waseem, *Politics and the State in Pakistan,* Islamabad: NICHR,1994.
7. R. Johnson, *A Region in turmoil. South Asian conflicts since 1947,* London: Raektion Books, 2005.
8. B. Umar, *The Emergence of Bangladesh,* Karachi: Oxford University Press, 2006.
9. H. Haqqani, *Pakistan-Between Mosque and Military*, Lahore: Vanguard, 2005.
10. S. J. Burki, *State and Society in Pakistan in 1971-77*, London: Mcmillan Press Ltd., 1980.
11. N. J. D. Bas, *Wahabi Islam: From Revival and Reform in Global Jihad*, New York: Oxford University Press, 2004.
12. S. Coll, *Ghost wars,* New York: Penguin Press, 2005.
13. R. G. Wirsing, *Pakistan's Security Under Zia,* 1977-1988, London: Macmillan, 1991.
14. A. Jalal, *Partisans of Allah: Jihad in South Asia,* Lahore: Sang-e-Meel Publications, 2008.
15. R. A. Shaikh, "Afghan war- Global Jihad and Sectarian Conflict in Pakistan- Internal and External links", in M. Chatterji (ed), *Conflict Management, Peace Economics and Development,* UK: Emerald, 2011, pp. 243-261.

16. D. Hiro, *War without End: The Rise of Islamist Terrorism and Global Response*, New Delhi: Routledge, 2003.
17. A. Mir, *Talibanisation of Pakistan*, Delhi: Pentagon Press, 2012.
18. J. Willson, *The general and jihad: Pakistan under Musharaf*, New Delhi: Pentagon Press, 2007.
19. M. S. Aiyar, "India-Pakistan: Retrospect and Prospect. Historiography of India and Pakistan", in Shaikh, (ed), n.2, pp.127-154.
20. *The Telegraph*, "Pakistan: India is not the enemy", 24 June 2013, http://blogs.telegraph.co.uk/news/adrianmichaels/100C008E2/pakistan-india-is-not-the-enemy/
21. R. Rodrigues, *Kasab: The face of 26/11*, Delhi: Penguin Books, 2010.
22. R. A. Shaikh, "Ideology and the Changing Shape of Conflict in South Asia: An Analysis of the Mumbai Attacks", in Chatterji (ed.) n.15, pp. 19-34.
23. M. Mujahid, *Punjabi Taliban*. Lahore: Sanjh Publications, 2011.
24. N. Mansur, "Democracy and Muslim Societies", *Daily Express*, 11 July 2013, p. 12.

Index